BRITAIN
against
NAPOLEON

CAROLA OMAN

BRITAIN
against
NAPOLEON

London 1943
READERS' UNION LIMITED
by arrangement with
FABER & FABER LIMITED

This volume is produced in 1943
Its paper and binding conform to the Economy Agreement of the Publishers' Association. It has been printed by Purnell & Sons, Limited, Paulton, Somerset, and bound by Webb, Son & Co., Ltd., London

This is one of the books produced for sale to its members only by Readers' Union Ltd., of 10–13 *Bedford Street, Strand, London and of Letchworth, Hertfordshire. Particulars of R.U. are obtainable from either of these addresses*

Contents

Chapter 1

Declaration of War,
February 1793

❦

A country correspondent wrote from the south of England that filberts were in bloom, and under a sheltered bank he had found primroses, though ragged and beaten by the weather. The throstle had sung a little at different times.

In the streets and gardens of Aberdeen no bird sang, and black figures moved fast against a white background. For some days past, amidst flurries of snow, passers-by had been halting to snatch from the stiffened fingers of their vendors, handbills damp from the press, bearing a startling heading. The unfortunate King of France could by no means be transformed into a romantic figure. He had been notoriously corpulent, obstinate, and quite stupid. But he had shone as a husband and father, and had evidently made a good end. Although nearly all the information as yet available came from the Paris authorities who had guillotined him, no hint existed that Louis Capet had acted on the scaffold with less than royal dignity.

The story eagerly read in the freezing Aberdeen streets was baldly told. On the morning of Capet's death he had asked that his servant Cléry might henceforward be appointed valet to the Queen. Capet had corrected himself when saying this, and added, 'as valet to my wife'. When those who were to escort him to his death arrived, he said, '*Marchons*', and walked briskly through two courtyards to the carriage awaiting him. His drive of three miles was performed in perfect silence. He had arrived at his destination at ten minutes past ten, and taken three minutes to leave the carriage. The delay had been occasioned by Capet's desire to be allowed to make a speech. His costume on the scaffold had been noticed by watchers from windows in the Ministry of Marine to include a white under-waistcoat; he had worn his hair rolled up, as Abbés wear it. 'His Head was severed from his Body. The Citizens dipped their pikes and handkerchiefs in his blood.' A sympathetic English note added that His Most Christian Majesty had spent two and a half hours on the previous day saying farewell to his wife, sister and children. Fears were felt for the reason of the Queen, and for the princess, her only daughter, who was at a critical age.

The leaflet circulated in Aberdeen urged that all citizens who disapproved of the System which had led the people of France to murder their ruler should announce their sentiments by assuming voluntary mourning. The result had been remarkable, even in a part of the world addicted to funeral panoply. Aberdeen, to a man, in the first week of February 1793, mourned the deposed and blameless Louis. All ranks, from the occupants of chariots, with coachmen and footmen in mourning liveries on the box, to the roughest link-boy with a wisp of crape round his hat, displayed their horror at regicide. The attendance had been numerous and respectable at a Mourning Concert given by the Governor and Directors of the City Musical Society, to which any lady and gentleman in black might obtain admittance without a ticket.

A short, stout lady, seated to an unappetizing meal with a pale child, in lodgings close to the Marischal College, had no need to invest in fresh black. Mrs. John Byron, whose temper was the terror of her landlady, already wore weeds. The handsome rascal who had won the heart of an Aberdeenshire heiress in a Bath ballroom and proceeded to break it in London, Paris and other strange places, had died, possibly by his own hand, in the city of Valenciennes, eighteen months past. If Britain was to go to war with France because the demoniac monsters of Paris had murdered their king, it could not greatly affect Mrs. Byron, whose memories of that country were not happy, and whose link with it was severed.

Her sole interest nowadays was her son, and foremost in her efforts for his advancement, the congenial business of keeping out of debt. Although her appearance and manners were preposterous, and indeed nothing about her suggested the gentlewoman, she had been of good birth and not ill-educated. She had a taste for books. George Gordon, the child seated opposite her in a by-street of the Granite City on this gloomy winter's afternoon, had been so christened in memory of his maternal grandfather, a descendant of the poet king, James I of Scotland. He was five, an age at which most children are seldom still. He had inherited his disgraceful father's delicate features and curly dark hair. His eyes were grey, but when the pupil swelled in them, under stress of emotion, they appeared almost black, and his mother had an uncomfortable feeling that the child seemed to be regarding not his parent, his only friend in the world, but some reptile. While he sat, with his legs under the dinner table, it was not possible to understand why the widowed Mrs. Byron's only child was so unnaturally sedate. His right leg and foot were contracted by infantile paralysis. When his furious mother chased him round the room, screaming promises of chastisement, George Gordon could mock her, but could not ultimately escape her.

The light of the short winter's day faded outside the lodgings in Queen Street, where black-robed figures moved against a background becoming a clear blue with dusk. If Mr. Pitt was to declare in the House of Commons on Tuesday that Britain was at war with France, it could not much hurt Mrs. Byron, whose country seat had been sold and fortune squandered years ago. Her husband was dead, and even if the war was to go on for years, her only son could never go to a war, because he was a cripple.

II

The newspapers on the Englishman's breakfast table on the morning of February 12th had provided much intelligence of an unalarming nature. A hurricane had done prodigious mischief in Havannah, and the caterpillar amongst the cotton trees of Jamaica. M. Blanchard, the celebrated French aeronaut, had arrived safely in Philadelphia, where, since the ballooning mania was now almost as strong as it had been in the Old World some years past, many leading citizens had paid a round sum for the privilege of witnessing the expert inflate his machine.

Nearer home, a widowed peeress and her niece had escaped unhurt from the dreadful fire which had broken out at 4 a.m. in their mansion in Hill Street, Berkeley Square. Westminster School Old Boys annual dinner would take place on Friday, and entries for Bath Races must be made to Messrs. Wetherby on, or before, March 1st. Since the season was Lent, play-house prices would be charged at the next Covent Garden concert, where the programme included ' Arm, arm, ye brave! ' and ' Britons strike home! ' but those two items were embedded amongst many others severely classical. Some disorderly persons of Cambridge had sung ' *Ça ira* ' in a neighbouring village, and discharged a gun into the house of a clergyman. The reverend gentleman, however, had pursued them on his horse and taken them into custody. They had proved to be persons of no consideration, an attorney and a farrier. In Cornwall the miners had marched upon various towns in search of hidden corn, which, they insisted, was about to be smuggled to France, but part of the First Regiment of Dragoons had gone to assist the Magistrates to restore peace in that quarter.

The advertisements reflected little popular tension. A manufacturer of Portable Soups recommended the novelty highly to the Army, Navy and Public in General.

Cures for coughs, colds, asthma and inflamed eyes abounded, and the Magic Lantern was suggested as an agreeable fireside entertainment for the domestic circle after dinner. The truth was that since to-day's British Parliamentary Intelligence included His Majesty's announcement to his Lords and Commons that the Assembly now exercising powers of government in France had quite unjustifiably declared war against him, to-morrow's must contain the heading 'War with France'.

In London the execution of Louis XVI was no longer news. An Exact Reproduction of *La Guillotine*, together with a harrowing account of the Massacre of Louis XVI, had been on sale, price 3d., a week past. 'Dreadful indeed was the moment in which the King tore himself from his family. The Queen, delirious and convulsed, embracing his knees, Madame Elizabeth and the Dauphin extended on the ground at his feet, uttering the most violent screams, Madame Royale senseless on her bed. . . .'

In London the day was one of fine weather after snow, some hailstorms and inordinate rain. People said that unless next winter surpassed what they had already endured, that of 1792-3 would be remembered as The Wet Year. Country gentlemen were troubled by the lateness of the bean-setting, and the roads leading to the capital were still swimming. A brisk west wind drove up the ruffled river, and sun penetrated fitfully between grey and white clouds behind the towers of Westminster. It seemed probable that with dusk the cold gusts would cease, and rain would begin again.

Inside the House of Commons candles were already

lit in the massive brass chandelier, surmounted by a crown, pendant from the centre of the ceiling, and in the brackets of the panelled gallery. The long formal chamber was further illuminated by three tall windows with semi-circular heads, through which could be seen riding clouds and some bare branches twisting and turning. The mingled day and candlelight caught reflections from the gold paint of the gallery columns, and the posturing lion and unicorn surmounting the canopy of the Speaker's chair, from the buttons on many single and double-breasted tail coats and knee breeches, from some shoe buckles and pairs of spectacles. The only brilliant colour in the scene centred in a few uniforms and epaulettes, and the draped folds of a tablecloth loaded with despatch boxes. A full house had assembled to hear a great peace Premier lead his country into war, and many of the countenances visible were familiar in caricature. The dress of those present showed little variety, and powdered queues were general. Some members with withered features affected wigs with pomatumed sausage side-curls, and all-black costumes, and wore or carried the collapsible black silk *chapeau bras*, but the days when court dress with sword had been indispensable had already been passing when Mr. Fox had shocked the House by arriving in top boots and a greatcoat with watchman's capes.

To-day's business began quietly with the second reading of the Militia Bill. Members had leisure to reflect, according to their temperaments, on the personal possibilities of war with France. For the gentleman who had been accustomed to send his son abroad, accompanied by a tutor, Paris had for some time been struck out of the itinerary. The dangers of gaming debts, duels and undesirable romances had thus been averted, but at the probable cost of having a bore or a boor at one's table for the rest of one's life. Daughters had already suffered. Pentemont Abbey, the most fashionable finishing school for the English miss, had closed. The Revolutionaries were turning the building into a barracks. It would still be possible, since Britannia ruled the waves, to send a boy or girl to Germany or Italy, but the risks of capture by a privateer were too great. War with France must definitely sound the knell of the Grand Tour for the English family.

As far as learning the language of diplomacy went, there were almost too many opportunities at home. England was crowded with French refugees—a difficult problem. The best of them had founded little colonies in obscure villages, or taken a country house, where they lived in dignified dejection, alternated by bursts of high spirits and violent quarrelling. They might, so long as their funds held out, be regarded as an asset to a dullish neighbourhood. But families of famous name, suddenly transplanted, revealed to the light of day unedifying ramifications, and a great many English gentlemen soberly considered that the French aristocracy had been ripe for chastisement. It was never safe to ask one French refugee to meet another. Very few of them spoke English or seemed likely to learn any. Some, having reached England after heroic adventures, slipped back to France and went to *La Guillotine*. In view of war with France, to possess under one's roof, or in a keeper's cottage, a French lady or gentleman of too resplendent birth, totally penniless, and breathing fumes of home-sickness, was, to the English host, a solemn thought.

The worst of the refugees were not aristos at all, or even honest folk. They were Revolutionary agents, sent over here to stir up trouble. The House had heard some fine verbal fireworks on this subject lately. The country was enjoying one of its periodic bursts of Spy mania. A few weeks ago, during the debate on the Aliens Bill, Mr. Burke had cast upon the floor of the chamber, heralded by the mystic words ' made in Birmingham', a gleaming dagger, one of three thousand, manufactured there, according to him, for the revolutionaries of England. The cartoonists had ridiculed Mr. Burke's dagger scene, but even the coldly correct Prime Minister, who must see statistics unavailable to the general public, admitted that he ' believed in the existence of Revolutionaries in London'. People who had at its beginning looked upon the French Revolution with interest and even approbation, were now disgusted by its manifestations, and decidedly against anything of that kind over here. An authoress, well known as ' the Swan of Lichfield', had spoken for many when she wrote in the current number of the *Gentleman's Magazine*, ' O, that the French had possessed the wisdom of knowing Where To Stop'. Miss Seward, however, had no fear of English Revolutionaries. ' Never do I remember such a universal Glow of Loyalty, such a grateful and fervent sense of our balanced Government, as now seem to prevail in all orders of British Society.' The more level-headed of the members present to-day agreed with her, the Member for Bere Alston, for instance, who had lent the favourite picture of his collection to a handsome young miller with a taste for painting, who happened to live near the home of Sir George's widowed mother. Sir George Beaumont liked to encourage promising beginners with such kindly scraps of advice as, ' a good picture, like a good fiddle, should be brown', and 'always put one brown tree in every landscape'. Besides, he was confident that Mr. Constable, who was a very superior sort of young fellow, would take good care of his Claude.

It was deeply regretted by his party that the bachelor Prime Minister was not a better mixer. The Party had no social rallying ground to compare with the drawing-rooms of the great Whig hostesses. Mr. Secretary Dundas had a broad Scots accent and no literary tastes. Everyone liked Mr. Wilberforce, but he was totally unworldly: he lodged happily in Battersea. Nobody would have gone to an entertainment at the house of Lord Grenville without an inward groan, for Lord Grenville was the least genial of hosts. A privileged few knew that Mr. Pitt offered and accepted invitations to small dinner parties at which he was delightful company; but he seldom entered White's. There were rumours that his financial affairs were embarrassed. It seemed absurd to imagine that the man who had become a masterly Chancellor of the Exchequer at the age of twenty-three, who had from infancy shown a taste for mathematics, was unable to control his household expenses. His servants must plunder him. He was no dandy, but complained of his tailor's bills. A kind friend had pointed out the lamentable fact that at his modest country house in Kent, the Prime Minister's annual account for farmyard manure had been sent in

18

and paid twice. Mr. Pitt was attached to Holwood,
where he was master of a remarkable view and an interesting Roman camp, partly overgrown by fine trees.
But visitors who penetrated there reported no endear
ing tales of the great man at his ease. The general public received the impression that Mr. Pitt never unbent.
He had only once been seen in the House in liquor, or
to be exact, the worse for an entertainment at Lord
Buckingham's house, which he had attended the night
before. Unfortunately the occasion had been rather an
important one. Shading his sicklied brow from the
sunny smiles of the Opposition, and particularly the
eye of Mr. Fox, the Prime Minister had been obliged
to announce in the most invalidish of accents, that he
desired to postpone his answer to this question. In
appearance he was an easy prey for the caricaturists—
a spare figure with a pursed mouth, and brows drawn
together in a slight perpetual frown. The cartoonists
always put a dab of crimson on the tip of his nose. It
was not an aristocratic nose, no Roman hook; it was
obviously of an enquiring nature, and it did Mr. Pitt
great injustice, for he was not an inquisitive man, and
although he admitted to a fondness for Port, there was
reason to believe that he had acquired the taste by
doctor's orders.

Mr. Fox, too, had a country house, at which he re-
galed visitors of all sorts. People who did not object to
the unexplained presence of a lady to whom the more
charitable asserted that their host was secretly married,
or to a cross-eyed young female, reputed a natural
daughter, found St. Anne's Hill the most agreeable
place in the world. ' How pleasant,' reflected a poet

guest, ' it would be to lie here on the grass all day, with a book in one's hand.' ' Yes,' agreed Mr. Fox gently, ' Yes—but why a book?'

Mr. Fox must fight a rearguard action to-day, and he was ready for the fray, seated in a characteristic attitude with his large hat pushed up on his large brow, and his heavy blue chins sunk on his heavy stick. At four and forty he was an arresting spectacle and, according to the sentiments of the beholder, a Noble Ruin, a Colossus, a Fright, an Awful Warning.

The House had disposed of the Accounts of the Commissioners of the National Debt, of some Canal Bills and the Scotch Militia Bill. In the three windows behind the Speaker's chair vivid blue had darkened and the flames of candles within were reflected. At last, amidst an expectant silence, the Prime Minister rose, and a voice full of melody and force, perfectly controlled, began to fill the hushed chamber.

' Whatever differences of opinion may formerly have existed . . .' His least temperamental supporters felt anxiety for their leader to-day. Exactly a year ago he had assured them, 'there never was a time when from the situation of Europe we might more reasonably expect fifteen years of peace'. Accordingly, he had dealt severely with the Army Estimates. Only the astute realized that for the past four years Mr. Pitt had been silently laying aside cherished schemes of reform. Up to the last possible moment he had attempted to represent the affairs of France as something from which England might stand aloof. And the truth was now, that although the King and Mr. Burke wished to fight France on behalf of Monarchy, Mr. Pitt's aim was Security, and France's threat to Holland and the Belgic provinces, not the execution of Louis XVI, had decided Mr. Pitt for War. He had been a highly successful peace Premier. It remained to be seen whether to-day marked a turn for the better or the worse in his career.

' War has been declared on us,' continued the accomplished voice. ' The event is no longer in our option, for War has not only been declared, it is at our very door, War that aims at the total ruin of the freedom and independence of Great Britain.' The events of the past weeks were carefully explained—the dismissal of the slippery French representative, M. Chauvelin, who had been given eight days in which to explain himself and had gone off without a word. France's complaints of England were detailed. She objected to England's increase in naval armaments, to the fact that the English court had gone into mourning for Louis XVI—'an obvious attempt to accuse our King and separate him from his People and Ministers. . . . Thus it appears that war is to be made upon us, firstly because we love our country, secondly because we detest French proceedings, lastly because we presume to grieve over murder . . . It now remains to be seen whether, under Providence, the efforts of a free, brave, loyal and happy people, aided by their allies, will not be successful in checking the progress of a system, the principles of which, if not opposed, threaten the most fatal consequences to the tranquillity of this country, the security of its allies, the good order of every European government and the happiness of the whole human race.'

The House rose at two a.m. To-morrow's newspaper would report a long speech by Mr. Pitt, Mr. Fox attacked by Mr. Burke, and Mr. Sheridan for the defence, all in their best style. The night had turned extremely wet, and during the delay while carriages were called, members had opportunity to exchange snuff and opinions. Except to those who had sons in the services, or were themselves officers of Militia, the prospect of War with France need cause no immediate anxiety. A financial crisis was in any case threatening, owing to the over-trading encouraged by so many years of peace and plenty and the amount of capital locked up in the new canals and factories. Some country banks must fail now. But there were rumours of an issue of Exchequer bonds to the amount of five millions. English gentlemen would continue to add bow windows to the south fronts of comfortable homes, overlooking a familiar pattern of broad lawns, shrubbery, church spire and umbrageous fields where New Leicesters and Durham shorthorns grazed contentedly. The knock of the cricket ball would still be heard from the village green, and the non-resident rector who kept a curate at eighty pounds a year to fulfil his duties, would still ride to hounds. Persons of limited means would still spend enjoyable sea-side holidays in newly erected small dwellings, termed 'villa-kins'. War with France would, of course, mean a great increase in the Fair Trade. In his mind's eye, as he absently watched the rain descending upon a black and sleeping Westminster, many a member saw strings of shaggy ponies shifting on a lonely stretch of beach, and lanterns bobbing in green sea-dusk. It was useless to tell the English gentleman that Port, Sherry, Madeira, Whisky and Beer still remained to him, when what he needed was a glass of Champagne or

Chambertin. Ladies too must have their laces and silks and flowers made by French fingers. The unctuous descriptions of gowns worn at Her Majesty's last Drawing-room contained continual mentions of *crêpe* petticoats, *frivolité* trimmings, and trains of *tigre* and *coquelicot*.

Mr. Pitt had confided to intimates that he hoped for a short war. There was absolutely no organization in France; her financial collapse was imminent. Mr. Burke, sounding solemn, had disagreed, ' No, sir. It will be a long war, and a dangerous war, but it must be undertaken'.

Carriages drew up and drove off into the pelting rain. Gentlemen jogging home to the sleep-inducing sound of jangling bit and purring wheel, had leisure to wonder drowsily if the gutters of Paris were sobbing as wildly this wet night, and if the widowed Queen of France heard them in the Temple prison. She had ceased to touch the clavichord, it was said, and even to perform mechanically on scraps of canvas, the same little tree pattern again and again. The name of the Queen of France did not enjoy great prestige in the British home. Visiting English, who had seen a royal lady seated at a card table with companions whose chief recommendation seemed to be that they would play high, who had watched her treading away as light as air, her arm slipped through that of a favourite companion, male or female, had hardly known what to think. Now, however, she was nothing but an object of pity. ' Whatever have been her errors and her crimes, such have been her sufferings, so great has been her humiliating fall, etc.'

Declaration of War

A Scottish gentleman, bound for a visit to the Governor of Gibraltar, heard next morning on Plymouth Hoe that his country was at War with France. Nevertheless he sailed. Mr. Graham of Balgowan well remembered the Queen of France, who had lent him and his bride a box from which to witness the Play at Trianon. Mr. Graham cherished feelings of undying animosity against the Revolutionaries of France, who had, on his last nightmarish journey through that country, torn open the coffin of his wife, one of the most exquisite ladies ever painted by Gainsborough. He hoped, at Gibraltar, to find opportunity to volunteer to fight against the French.

III

From an early hour on a morning less than a fortnight later, large crowds were gathered on the riverside and London road in the neighbourhood of Greenwich. Four battalions of the Guards were about to embark for foreign service. The King's second son, the Duke of York, was to command the Expeditionary Force: there were well-founded hopes that many members of the Royal Family would be present on an occasion of military pageantry.

The first stir took place about eight o'clock, when a carriage bringing two ladies from London drew up at the Governor's House. The Prime Minister's sister-in-law, Lady Chatham, and her mother, Lady Sydney, dismounted, and a long pause followed before listeners heard the sound of marching feet.

The Guards began to arrive in the Hospital Square at nine-thirty. The background of the scene well

expressed national strength and solidity. In the centre
of the square, formed by four enormous classical buildings and a river terrace 860 feet long, stood a statue
of his present Majesty's grand-father, sculptured from a
single block of marble seized from the French by Admiral
Rooke. Behind the two domed south buildings, which
contained the famous Painted Hall and Chapel of the
Hospital for Disabled Seamen, arose the wooded heights
of Greenwich Park. Not a glint of sun struck metal,
scarlet or pipe-clay as the troops took up their positions
in the stately square. The morning was cold and dark.
Rain had fallen all night, and a keen south-west wind
was doing no more than chase black clouds above the
sombre masonry and raise puffs of powder from pigtails fretting high collars.

At ten o'clock a burst of cheering announced that
royal liveries had been sighted on the London road.
The first coaches to arrive contained Her Majesty
Queen Charlotte and her daughters. Since all six princesses had undertaken the expedition, this detachment
of the Royal Family fully occupied two large vehicles.
The princesses, who ranged in age from six-and-twenty
to nine, conveyed a great impression of good natural
complexions under heavily plumed hats. The two
youngest, still in the schoolroom, displayed a profusion of glittering fair hair. The next coach brought His
Majesty's brother, Field-Marshal the Duke of Gloucester, with his lumpish son and daughter. The Duke of
Clarence, the King's third son, driving alone in a coach
and six, received no particular ovation. Prince William's
frank manner was celebrated. At the last bitterly cold
entertainment offered by his frugal mother, His Royal

Highness had loudly asked the Duchess of Gordon whether she did not wish herself back in the midwinter Highlands. Several such anecdotes had reached the newspapers. ' I keep sober for Mary,' declared the sailor prince at his loveliest sister's coming-out ball, but he had noticeably failed to keep sober for Mary. At a date when a taste for champagne and actresses, on the part of a bachelor prince, were not generally regarded unsympathetically, Prince William was surprisingly disliked. At the theatre, the Pit booed his mistress. Club cynics declared that his papers at the Admiralty bore, in his royal father's handwriting, the words, ' Never to be employed afloat again'.

Punctually at eleven o'clock a word of command rang out, the intermittent cheering rose to a higher note and became continuous, and a band struck up the National Anthem. The King, attended by the Prince of Wales and Duke of York, wearing the uniforms of their respective regiments, rode into the square, holding his cocked hat at arm's length. There had been widespread fears amongst loyal subjects lest a declaration of War might be just the thing to provoke a return of His Majesty's mental malady, but a single glance at that familiar rosy countenance of protuberant features surrounded by a white military wig, showed that the effect had been exactly the reverse. The King, upright and smiling, very trim in his blue and white uniform, happy on his favourite ' Pegasus', a cream charger with a long crimped mane and tail, had never looked better. For the last four years his popularity had been steadily increasing at the expense of that of his sons. The Prince of Wales, a much larger man, fair, florid, mounted on a coal-black charger which formed an admirable foil to 'Pegasus', was obviously handsome, but at one-and-thirty already thickening, notoriously in debt and still without a Princess. The Duke of York, suitably married but childless, rivalled his brother in size, but altogether lacked grace and fire.

His Majesty's deportment on military occasions was always a source of anxiety to his staff. As the drum-major of each regiment approached, flourishing his silver, balloon-headed cane, it was invariably His Majesty's habit to tear his hat from his head, and hold it in a dramatic attitude by the forecock until that dignitary had gone past. The salutes of Colonels generally received the most perfunctory royal recognition, and those of Majors and Adjutants none whatsoever. Fortunately this morning's programme included no inspection. The Expeditionary Force was due to embark forthwith. The King had not yet breakfasted. He dismounted at the head of the river stairs and the grape-dark square echoed tremendously as rigid lines of scarlet began to move towards the shining river. The Royal Family exchanged greetings, mingled and proceeded indoors to a cold collation reported by those who had seen it to be of singular elegance. The band continued to discourse patriotic airs. Nine transports lying at anchor in the river, began to receive troops carried out to them in flat-bottomed boats brought from Deptford and Woolwich. Each boat accommodated thirty guardsmen and was rowed by eight or ten sailors wearing the picturesque uniform of the Greenwich pensioner. The crowd raised three cheers every time a boat left the shore. At half-past two a slow business was still proceeding, and the re-appearance of Royalty roused the spirits of people who had been standing in Thames-side mud for six hours. The King was observed to wave his hat, the Queen and princesses their handkerchiefs. Knowledgeable persons were able to assure their neighbours that, in spite of assertions to the contrary, the Duchess of York was not present, and that the lady dabbing her eyes was the Princess Elizabeth, the third daughter, who had more influence with her parents than any of her sisters, and having inherited her father's downright nature, relished her family nickname of ' Sally Blunt'.

Last year a far from respectful cartoon had shown John Bull and his family leaving off sugar in their tea. His Majesty's resemblance to a cod had been cruelly exaggerated, while Her Majesty, more like a monkey than ever, adjured her six wry-mouthed spinster daughters, ' My dear Creatures, do but taste it'. Such satires appeared far from representing the feelings of the Thames-side crowd of this February day. Bursts of ' God Save the King ' kept on breaking out from both troops and spectators. ' John Bull ', ' Farmer George ', the King who had announced that he gloried in the name of Briton, was displaying the most affectionate condescension. It was useless for fine ladies to complain that Queen Charlotte retained the outlook and costume of a small German court. She had brought her husband fifteen children, and was joining with them in shedding a tear for the Guards.

Three o'clock sounded, and the dip of oars carrying the last boatload into the river. The Duke of York and his staff left by postchaise and four, for Sheerness, to

board the frigate *Syren*. The Royal coaches rumbled
into action again, and amidst cheers from a thinning
crowd, the short winter's day began to close in.

To a severe critic, the appearance of the force about
to see active service might not have aroused so much
admiration as the setting. The countenances of many
officers and men in the British Army to-day proclaimed
hard-drinking. The ranks contained many characters
who looked rather old or rather young for their profession. The burden carried by the guardsman in
marching order was so great and so awkwardly placed
that the body must be cramped, the head forced for-
wards and the action of the heart impeded. The fact was
that since the close of the American War the army had
decreased in morale and physique. The same carica-
turist who had ridiculed His Majesty John Bull, had
recently published a depressing set of pictures warning
John Bull, the Subject, against listening to the recruit-
ing sergeant. Unfortunate John, who had marched
away, to the sound of drum and fife, as fat as a pig,
was shown in the last picture of the series returning,
with one eye and one leg, to find his wife and children
in rags around a blackened hearth, their spindle, churn,
dog and tea-pot all lodged in the pawnshop.

However, the battalions embarked to-day under the
command of the King's second son contained some of
the best material in the country, and Mr. Pitt had
predicted a short war.

Chapter 2

Peace Negotiation

❦

Everything which Lord Malmesbury perceived through the windows of his travelling carriage as he passed towards Paris, interested him exceedingly. The date was mid-October, 1796, and for three years and eight months the iron veil of War had separated England and France. To an intelligent man, even if he had not been travelling on government business of the first importance, it obviously was extremely interesting to see how the enemy country had fared during this period.

At Calais the officers of the Municipality were most attentive—some affectedly so, thought Lord Malmesbury. There was no question of his being addressed as ' Citizen', although he made the vexing discovery that his passport described him as Envoy Extraordinary. He had to explain that his title should have been Minister Plenipotentiary. When he enquired whether any orders had been given for the passage of his couriers to and from England, the answer was none, but the *Directeur de la Douane* thought that they should encounter no difficulties. There was irritating delay about the departure of the flag of truce. All these characters, calling themselves the Commissary of the Executive, the *Commandant du Civil*, the *Etat Major* of the Garrison, laboured to express their desire for peace. All were clearly dependent on orders from Paris and correspondingly nervous, which was exactly what one would expect of officials of a Revolutionary government. Lord Malmesbury's bill at the *Lion d'Argent* was large, and the landlord a hot Republican, though civil. There were reports of an intended invasion of England, but not many troops visible on the coast road. The roads on the whole were in tolerably good order, and in the fields the usual business belonging to the season was complete, or going on. Some ploughs were drawn by asses and driven by women, boys or old men. The decrease in population was very noticeable, and Lord Malmesbury calculated that he saw four women to every man. A few mothers, tugging children by the hand, called out that they wanted peace, as his carriage rolled past. The majority of the populace did not utter.

At Boulogne, the English couple—Knowles and Parker—who kept the good inn, were not visible. They had been in the Conciérgerie prison for eighteen months. A grand-daughter and a maid were in charge of the house. Abbeville was a depressing sight, practically a dead town. Amiens showed a little traffic and a battered cathedral—its porch plastered with Revolutionary notices. Tales of the destruction of religious buildings had not been exaggerated. Even in villages, only the walls of most churches still stood, and several

were labelled 'Temple of Reason'. Entrances to country
seats had autumn foliage running riot above fallen pillars and twisted gates. Moss-grown drives led to distant heaps of blackened stones. Only occasionally, and
amongst woods recently felled, but in an orderly manner, the traveller might observe a *château* with entrance
intact and glass shining in the windows. Poorly dressed
people were cutting the green undergrowth at will, and
to Lord Malmesbury's amusement, on the republican
highway the post had to give place to waggons and even
farm carts. Never once on his route did he meet soldiers
on the march. At Evreux members of two noisy depu-
tations, accompanied by a band, tore open the doors of
his carriage. They said that they wanted to embrace
the English milor and his companions, shoved in nose-
gays of autumn flowers, crying that they should have
been laurels, and vied with one another in good wishes
for his success. Since they demanded largesse before
they allowed him to proceed, the English Minister
Plenipotentiary did not take this friendly demonstra-
tion too seriously.

He drove into Paris through quiet streets at three
o'clock on the afternoon of Saturday, October 22nd,
and when he came to review his impressions before
writing to England, decided that the thing which had
struck him most on his journey through Revolutionary
France had been the silence prevailing. The poor folk
cutting the undergrowth had looked up as the English
carriage passed, but said nothing, even to one another.
Everyone seemed anxious not to draw attention to himself. At posthouses there was none of the cheerful bustle
and clatter usual when changing horses. The postboys

never shouted on the roads, or asked for money. The universal stillness which pervaded the enemy country did not in the least raise the hopes of the English nobleman come, under circumstances of extreme difficulty, to express his government's anxious desire to conclude a just and honourable peace. He did not judge it to be the placid quiet arising from content and repose. He calmly diagnosed it as the effect of perpetual mental torment and bodily fear.

Fortunately Lord Malmesbury, who had been Ambassador to the court of the Empress Catherine II at St. Petersburg, had strong nerves and an imposing presence. At fifty his waving locks were prematurely snow white, his sharpening features aristocratic, his eye brilliant. Some of the clever young men at the Foreign Office, with whom he was accustomed to exchange the somewhat arid jests permissible between promising beginners and a genial senior, had nicknamed him 'The Lion'.

Lord Malmesbury wrote formally to the Minister for Foreign Affairs, expressing his opinion that the enemy were in a hurry, either to begin this negotiation or end it.

To ' My dear Canning', he wrote a week later, reporting that so far he had escaped the guillotine here, but, as things went at present, did not see how, on his return, he was to escape the Tower of London.

In London, people eager for peace, began to complain that the Lord Malmesbury seemed to be moving very slowly. ' No wonder,' snapped Mr. Burke, ' seeing that he is having to go the whole way on his knees.'

Peace Negotiation

With one notable exception, Britain's prowess in arms during the past three and a half years could not hope to descend to history as glorious.

The career of the Expeditionary Force, part of which had been sped on its way from Greenwich with so much royal attention, had been most depressing. It had fought bravely on several occasions; the French were reputedly lacking in discipline, and Paris was in the grip of the Terror. Nevertheless England waited in vain for news of a decisive victory, and for some weeks in the late summer of 1794 the eyes of all patriots were turned towards Flanders in acute apprehension. The country was faced by the possibility that the entire force under the Duke of York might be cut off and annihilated. This disaster was averted, and on September 6th newspapers were able to announce that the Duke had begun a successful retirement from Dunkirk five nights before, under cover of dark, with the utmost precipitation. It was useless to gloss over the fact that he had been obliged to abandon ' a prodigious quantity of war-like stores '. Popular relief that the worst had not happened was followed by an outcry against the navy for having no squadron to come in to the assistance of the Duke's right flank opposite Dunkirk. What was left of the unfortunate force was hunted to the mouth of the Weser through all the horrors of the worst winter Europe had known for a century. The army was evacuated to England in the following April, and no further Expeditionary Force set foot on the Continent for four years. With its return came dire stories of a commissariat so inefficient that no rations had been served for two days to men marching through heavy snow and across frozen rivers in broken boots. The casualty list for the first year of the campaign numbered over eighteen and a half thousand, and a deplorable proportion of wounded had succumbed in insanitary hospitals. The intelligence and activity of the Commander in Chief and his staff were openly questioned, and bloodthirsty critics pointed out that General Houchard, whose command of the French army had been found unsatisfactory in Paris, had been recalled and sent to the guillotine. A younger son of Lord Mornington decided that he had learnt from his first campaign ' what one ought not to do'. He never forgot seeing despatches from Allied headquarters which happened to arrive at the dinner hour, when the wine was being circulated, thrown aside with the remark, ' That will keep till to-morrow morning.'

English money had been poured forth to assist the land forces of her Allies, and in the course of 1795 two of them—Prussia and Spain—deserted. The Netherlands, an ally on the Declaration of War, had been virtually absorbed by the enemy, and the Dutch royal family landed as exiles from fishing boats at Harwich and Yarmouth.

Fortunately the results of naval actions had not been so disastrous. Since Holland now ranked as a foe, two important strategic points on the route to India were wrested from her. Bells rang in London, and the guns at the Tower and in St. James's Park were fired to celebrate the captures of Ceylon and the Cape of Good Hope. Two months after the outbreak of War, Lord

Hood had been sent to the Mediterranean, with twenty-one sail of the line. In the following August he occupied Toulon, at the invitation of French royalists and accompanied by Spanish allies. His success was much acclaimed, and he was reinforced by a contingent from Naples, but as winter approached his trials were many. His relations with the French Royalists whose immediate task would be to slaughter their countrymen, with British aid, were naturally difficult, nor were the Spaniards whole-hearted. The two thousand men put ashore by him were insufficient to control the land-defences, and presently high ground was occupied by the troops sent by the Convention to expel the invaders. A newly-gazetted Colonel of Artillery, who had his way to make in the world, had arrived to direct the siege. The General whom he found in charge of operations was, in fact, far more terrified of his wife than of the enemy or even the authorities in Paris. Madame Cartaux told her husband to ' do as the young man here said '. When a coachload of pompous delegates from Paris arrived to complain of the lethargy with which the siege was being conducted, Colonel Buonaparte invited them to accompany him to a spot where they found themselves under fire from an English frigate. They did not linger. The few weeks which he had spent recently in the capital had shown the young colonel that the country was torn by the contentions of the Jacobins and Girondists, and he needed a free hand to deal with the unimpressive force at his disposal. His energy and address raised an answering spark. Colonel Buonaparte called impatiently for one man who could write. An enormous fellow named Junot stepped out of the ranks. As he plied his pen at the Colonel's dictation, a cannon ball landed near. ' No need of sand,' he commented gruffly, folding his sheet. By December 17th Colonel Buonaparte's artillery commanded the roadstead, and on January 15th Londoners learnt that a despatch had arrived from Lord Hood explaining his evacuation of Toulon. Readers were assured that the place had been held at great cost, and was of no specific advantage. The Arsenal had been wrecked by the retiring British, and many French ships had been captured or scuttled. The public persisted in the gloomy belief that Great Britain had suffered a loss of prestige. Nothing which she had undertaken since the outbreak of War seemed to have prospered.

Lord Howe cruised about in search of the enemy without bringing them to action. Critics accused the taciturn old Admiral of spending his time dodging in and out of Torbay. He returned to port with the fleet before the first Christmas of the war. In his opinion it was a mistake to keep the fleet at sea in continual bad weather, watching an enemy lying comfortably in port. Not until early May did he put out again from St. Helen's, with thirty-two sail of the line, fifteen smaller ships and nearly one hundred merchant vessels. Off the Lizard, eight line of battle ships and half a dozen frigates were sent southward in charge of the merchant vessels. Revolutionary France was suffering severely from the bad harvest of 1793, and a great convoy bringing corn, and bound for Brest, was known to be nearing the end of its long journey from Chesapeake Bay. Lord Howe considered that to seek this convoy was the surest way to bring the main French fleet to action.

Peace Negotiation

On June 10th the Gazette announced Lord Howe's success, and the newspapers next morning were at last able to dilate on a great naval victory. At six-thirty a.m. on May 28th, amidst early morning haze the British had caught sight of the enemy. A partial action had ensued, after which the French *Révolutionnaire* and the British *Audacious* had been obliged to retire damaged. Next day Lord Howe had made further efforts to force an action from leeward, and by the time that darkness fell had gained the weather gage. For a period, during the 30th, the fleets lost sight of one another, and twenty-four hours of hard weather followed. At eight-thirty a.m. on Sunday, June 1st, the moment for which Lord Howe had been waiting for sixteen months arrived. ' I think we shall have the battle to-day,' muttered one of his crew. ' Black Dick has been smiling.'

First reports of the victory announced six French sail of the line captured and two sunk, with the loss of one British ship. Later accounts contained a correction. Seven ships had been captured, and only one, the *Vengeur*, sunk. Two hundred and thirteen of her crew had been humanely saved by the boats of H.M.S. *Alfred*. The victualling convoy from America had escaped, and French descriptions of the action, which reached London by Midsummer day, made a great point of the fact that all apprehension of famine was now removed, and stated, inaccurately, that the French fleet had been greatly outnumbered.

This time, however, no doubt existed in England that the British Navy had covered itself with glory. For three nights after the news reached London, illuminations were general. A peer who failed to decorate his

Peace Negotiation

house had his windows broken. Lord Howe's victory, gained four hundred and twenty-nine miles west of Ushant, could not be given a place-name. It was christened ' the Glorious First of June'.

With the picturesque return of the battle-scarred fleet to Spithead, towing their French prizes, scenes of enthusiasm abounded. The King and Queen, with three daughters, travelled to Portsmouth, and visited Lord Howe on board the flagship which bore Her Majesty's name. His Majesty presented the Admiral with a diamond-hilted sword, dined twice with Lord Howe and his officers, and showed himself most affable, helping the fish with his own hands. Tales of heroism were eagerly repeated. Admiral Bowyer, having had a contraption called ' a turnicot ' applied to stop the bleeding from his shattered leg, ordered the surgeon to look after the wounds of his men before giving him further attention. A poor tailor, belonging to the land forces aboard the *Barfleur*, who had lost his leg, thereupon refused to have his wound dressed before that of the Admiral. ' My life is of less value. I will wait.'

A flood of souvenirs, destined to fade in the corridors of Adam houses, and on the mantelpieces of bow-windowed marine lodgings, was hastily produced to meet the popular demand. Snuff boxes, plaques, lustre beakers and mugs, and many copper-plate engravings displayed the gallant *Queen Charlotte* passing so close under the stern of the *Montagne* that the French ensign brushed her main and mizzen shrouds as she poured her broadside into the enemy flagship's starboard quarter. In the enormous oil-painting ordered for the Painted Hall at Greenwich, the artist mistakenly depicted the *Queen Charlotte* on the lee-bow of the *Montagne*. In the fullness of time, Mr. Bowen, ship's master of the *Queen Charlotte*, stood before the picture representing this thrilling moment in his career. ' Ah! ' said this excellent character regretfully, in the full dialect of his West-Country birthplace, ' If we could have got the old ship into that position we must have taken the French Admiral.'

In more sophisticated quarters, in the London clubs and drawing-rooms not all comment was so philosophical or free from malice. The chaplain of the *Queen Charlotte*, a person recommended by the Bishop of London, had been so much shaken by his experiences that he had shown a clean pair of heels on reaching Portsmouth, and thus lost dazzling opportunities of preaching before, and being noticed by His Majesty. Lord Howe was at loggerheads with Lord Chatham about the Honours List, which had been published prematurely, with the result that many names had been omitted. ' Black Dick ' was to blame that a slur had been cast on the reputation of some of his officers. After being requested twice by their Lordships to send in details of all actions of merit, he had turned the business over to some flag officers, who had not understood the form submitted . . . Mr. Pitt had had the effrontery to ask our national hero to forgo the Garter promised to him on the deck of the *Queen Charlotte* by the King. The Prime Minister, who needed that Garter for one of his new political supporters, had offered Lord Howe a marquisate, on his own responsibility. Poor Lady Howe had told Admiral Gardner that a marquisate was of no interest to her husband, who had rank enough,

and nothing but daughters. . . . Lord Howe had been
so much hurt by the daily attacks upon him in public
prints during the sixteen months before he brought the
enemy to action, that he had actually been talking of
sending in his papers . . . The Fleet ought to have captured five or six more enemy sail of the line . . . Sir
Roger Curteis had been too cautious . . .

In pillared dining-rooms of country seats, boasting a
flagstaff in the grounds and naval ancestors on the walls,
retired Admirals of the Red, the White and the Blue made
the table-silver leap, as they furiously asserted that Lord
Howe, for his departure from the recognized methods
of warfare, deserved to have lost the glorious First of
June. His startling orders had been only partially
understood and obeyed by his captains, and small wonder. But in humbler homes, such as Steventon Rectory,
where the gentle master of the house had two sons at
sea, who sometimes brought on leave with them young
fellow-officers, the daughters of the family, as they bent
over their satin-stitch, dreamt sea-dreams, wholly happy
as yet. The names of H.M.S. *Audacious*, *Bellerophon*,
Marlborough, *Russell* and *Thunderer* were indelibly
printed on many such hearts, and junior officers mostly
persisted that the ensuing close mêlée, produced by
Lord Howe's daring commands, had been vastly
advantageous to our fleet, possessed of superior sea-
manship and better average gunnery than that of the
enemy.

For three years no further news of a great naval
action gladdened England. The price of the quartern
loaf rose to a shilling, and Mr. Pitt's powder tax dealt
the death-blow to white wigs and hair. Gentlemen gave

dinner parties at which the barber attended in an adjacent chamber to wash and crop the guests after they had feasted. Some of the younger men looked very handsome cropped, but to those for whom the wig had been a necessity, the new fashion was a minor tragedy.

There was trouble brewing in Ireland, and mobs shouting ' Bread! ' and ' Peace! ' assailed the King's carriage as he drove to Covent Garden and to open Parliament. A gentleman of the Royal Household told a Prebendary of St. Paul's that His Majesty had been much agitated, not from any personal fear, but to find such a disposition prevailing. In Paris, the Reign of Terror was a thing of the past. Robespierre had followed the unfortunate Queen of France to the scaffold. Optimistic people thought that in dealing with the authorities of the new French government, called the Directory, Great Britain should lose no prestige and find a great change of temper. An American gentleman, A.D.C. to Mr. Washington, returning from the continent in the late summer of 1796, had said emphatically, ' Peace is the wish of the People of France, and the Army.'

In October, the successes of the Archduke Charles, a gallant ally, led Mr. Pitt to believe that a favourable moment had come for an attempt to end the war. Accordingly James Harris, Baron Malmesbury, described by a famous French statesman, now deceased, as '*ce rusé et audacieux 'Arris!* ', a person, moreover, acceptable to nearly all the royal family, was set on the road to Paris.

Lord Malmesbury's last diplomatic mission had lost

him the friendship of the Prince of Wales. He had been sent abroad last year, with strict instructions to secure in marriage for his sovereign's eldest son, the Princess Caroline of Brunswick. A single interview had convinced him that she was a hopeless choice for a man who was, in any case, only consenting to marriage for pecuniary motives. On their journey the unfortunate Ambassador had done his best. He had hinted to the wild, jolly girl that she should wash more, and that in England sea-sickness and *liaisons* were not permissible drawing-room topics for young ladies. His worst fears had been realized when the moment came for him to introduce bride to bridegroom, and the Prince, after one glance at his future life's partner, had fled to a distant corner of the room, crying, ' Harris! I am not well! Pray get me a glass of brandy.'

Brandy, to the disgust of many observers, had carried the Prince through the wedding ceremony, which had followed all too quickly. No stern critic of that ugly scene knew, though many guessed, that the reeling bridegroom was haunted by compunctious visitings. He could fancy the whisper stealing from Devonshire House to Brooks's and St. Anne's Hill, from White's to Holwood—' The Prince of Wales is a bigamist'. His unacknowledged wife was a Catholic lady, and his previous marriage secret, so the legality was more than doubtful, but some instinct told the eldest son of George III and Queen Charlotte that he was about to inflict irremediable damage on an innocent party, and like most murderers, he was infuriated by the stupidity of the corpse. As soon as possible he escaped from all but the semblance of being the husband of his royal first cousin, the Princess Caroline. He could hardly believe his ill-luck and Nature's cruelty, when she announced, none too delicately, her surprise that she was to be a mother.

III

Lord Malmesbury struggled on in Paris. ' The business of the cockades ' entailed tiresome explanations. The fact was that unless he and his staff condescended to follow the public example, and display tricolour favours, they could not, with safety, go for a walk in the streets of Paris. He explained at length to Downing Street that nobody belonging to him should wear the tricolour when acting in an official capacity. He had many, many interviews with M. Delacroix, Minister for Foreign Affairs, a maddening character. Having been warned to expect a typical rough-mannered Revolutionary, he was at first agreeably surprised to find M. Delacroix a neatly dressed person of about five-and-fifty, who spoke very little and very slowly, listened with attention and answered civilly. The trouble was that as soon as the British Ambassador began to approach terms of business, the French Foreign Minister disappeared like a rabbit into a burrow. He dared not commit himself to anything until he had reported to his masters.

Lord Malmesbury occupied himself in studying Paris under the new *régime*, and picking up information about the men of the moment. The characters of the five Directors were already tolerably well appreciated in Downing Street. Of the five, two were unabashed adventurers, and one was principally interested in opposing all religions, particularly the Catholic. An over-worked military officer of absolute integrity, entirely in-experienced in statesmanship, and his disciple, a non-entity, completed the catalogue. Lieutenant-Colonel Buonaparte, whose artillery had driven Lord Hood out of Toulon, was not at present in the capital. His career since that incident had been colourful, but not unusual for an officer of the Revolutionary Army. He had twice suffered arrest and imprisonment, owing to intrigues or suspicions, and twice regained liberty—on the first occasion owing to the interposition of the younger Robespierre, a connection which had told heavily against him on the second. After a period of eclipse he had been promoted to command the army for the inva-sion of Italy. The price of his general's hat, according to rumour, had been his taking in marriage, before his departure, a cast mistress of one of the Directors. Whether Love or Ambition animated the young General, he seemed to be achieving considerable suc-cess. On the 28th of March of this year he had reported to the Directors that he was ready to take the offensive, and by the 15th of May had ridden victoriously into Milan. Lord Malmesbury made enquiries, and heard much about General Buonaparte that was certainly sor-did and probably untrue. The young man, who was displaying such marked military talent, was said to be a natural son of General Marbeuf, Governor of Corsica, by a Corsican woman. Marbeuf had behaved hand-somely and sent the boy to the *École Militaire*, where, in company with many other gentlemen cadets of pre-Revolutionary days, he had received a liberal education. Lord Malmesbury noted in his diary, on November

8th, that Buonaparte was clever, desperate, Jacobin, even Terrorist. His bride, a well-known figure in Directory circles, was the widow of an *aristo* who had been beheaded, a 'Madame Beauharnois'. Impious Revolutionary Paris now called the wife of the victor of Mondovi, Ceva, Lodi and Bassano, ' *Notre Dame des Victoires*'.

The British Ambassador walked in the Tuileries, beneath trees from which all leaves had now fallen, and thought Paris surprisingly little altered, except that there were fewer carriages visible, and far fewer well-dressed men. Women, on the contrary, were much dressed, and walked about the streets fearlessly. Indeed, judging by the gait of many, other pedestrians should be the persons to experience fear. They all wore dark-coloured stockings, a sensible precaution in autumn weather. In the Imperial Winter Palace of St. Petersburg something was happening to-day which was to render his mission fruitless, but news from Russia at this season took five weeks to reach Paris.

The British Ambassador stepped out of his carriage into fog-scented air, and entered a fashionable theatre. He had taken a box for the month ' *aux Italiens*'. He noted the performance as moderate, not so good as formerly, the orchestra and dresses as good and the company as bad-looking. Every morning he walked early. He bought books and some beautiful furniture, and from a dealer in the Rue Dauphine, who appeared to be honest, some maps.

He saw M. Delacroix nearly every day, and presently had a taste of the kind of manners he had been warned to expect. 'He broke out into what I can really express in no other words than a republican rant'. However, although the Foreign Minister's voice was loud and expression theatrical, he said nothing actually offensive either to the Court of St. James's or the Ambassador as a public character, so his listener heard him out with composure and patience. Lord Malmesbury, whose instructions were to insist on the restoration of the Austrian Netherlands to the Emperor, repeated his royal master's earnest desire for a speedy and honourable peace. Late at night he wrote to Downing Street that although there was general discontent with the present *régime*, he doubted of success in his negotiation. Those at present in power here realized that with peace they would be superseded, but while General Buonaparte continued to win victories the nation could be kept quiet.

The news from Italy continued to be, from the British Ambassador's point of view, 'Bad', and he mentioned to Mr. Canning that he looked forward to 'a *tête-à-tête* roar' over tea and rolls in Spring Gardens.

Portraits of a haggard young General with classic features, gesticulating to admiring troops against a background of snowy Alps, began to fill Paris shops, and the Directors, growing nervous of a possible military dictator, despatched a confidential agent to the headquarters of the victor of Arcola. Lord Malmesbury privately considered that Buonaparte probably very much exaggerated his latest success. From another quarter he heard something which he thought warranted an urgent letter to London. A large body of troops were assembled at Morlaix, ready to embark in eleven sail of the line, lying in harbour at Brest. The expedition was supposed to be meditated against

Ireland, and violent stories of a rebellion in that country were being spread, in order to encourage the invaders.

But while Russia still waited motionless but hostile, Lord Malmesbury would not abandon hope. France certainly dreaded the unknown strength of Russia, and the great Tsarina had a fondness for England. She flattered herself that in the frankness and originality of her temper she resembled the gentlemen of that nation whom she had observed with approbation at her court.

Midnight of a December night in Paris sounded. The boxes for Downing Street were ready, and the courier who was to take them waited below. Noiseless-footed members of the efficient staff—truly a happy family—selected by Lord Malmesbury to accompany him to France, noted with relief that ' the Lion ' had ceased writing. He was seated at ease in front of a fire which burnt well, as fires will when there is frost outside. A kindly light lit snow-white hair and eagle features. His Excellency believed himself to be rather deaf nowadays, and hinted that this should be his last negotiation. Possibly now he was looking back, not forward. His memories should be interesting, for he had known intimately all the more eccentric crowned heads of Europe. Several of them, like himself, were beginning to feel the sword of time. His last description of the King of Prussia—much altered in his looks owing to the loss of his front teeth—had sounded a melancholy note. ' The inside of this court is really a subject fit only for a private letter, unfortunately it is so closely connected with its public conduct, and influences it so much that I wish to give you every information. . . . The female in actual possession of favour is of no higher degree than a servant maid. She is known by the name of Mickie. . . .'

There had been a report to-day that the Tsarina had suffered an apoplectic seizure. She was sixty-seven, and to younger members of His Excellency's staff, almost a legend. They could not reconcile her reputation with the more than life-size portraits presiding over the staircases and mantelpieces of every royal palace they had ever entered. According to court artists, Catherine II had the appearance of a good plain cook, and like many such characters, her features, strongly marked by passion, exhibited consciousness of power masked by apparent affability.

His Excellency said with his usual calm, that the newspapers always killed Her Imperial Majesty about this time of year. But this time the newspapers had not exaggerated.

IV

On the morning of November 8th, 1796, the Empress Catherine awoke in good health and spirits. After being attired by her attendants in a fashionable *négligée*, she took her usual coffee and retired to her writing closet. Although the thermometer in her adopted country had ceased to rise above freezing point, and could not be expected to do so again for five months, her working days began early. It was not true that she was ill after a bout of hysterical fury provoked by the King of Sweden's refusal to marry into her family, nor was it true that she spent her forenoons in Russian costume, wearing a diamond cap on flowing grey locks above a hook-nosed countenance flushed by indigestion. For several generations the rulers of Russia had employed Scottish doctors. The Empress Catherine's first physician had told her frankly that if she wished to survive, she must eat and drink sparingly. Since she desired this exceedingly, she obeyed her expert. False reports in foreign prints that she was afflicted by dropsy as a result of gastronomic orgies, caused her real annoyance.

Unlike many ageing royalties, she did not shrink from contemplation of her inevitable end. Four years past she had drawn up detailed instructions for her funeral. She wished her body to lie in state, robed in a white gown, and wearing a gold crown. She had chosen her place of interment according to which of her palaces provided her death-bed—' In the case of Moscow, in the Donskoy Monastery; in case of Peterhof, in the Sergei Cloister; in case of the City of St. Peter's or Pella, in the Nevsky Cloister.' From Pella the body would have to be brought by water. She left all her manuscripts and papers to her beloved grandson Alexander, together with her jewels and her blessing.

A great many persons in Europe, and particularly in Russia, would have given much for a private view of the last testament of the great Empress. Stories that she was appointing her grandson her successor to the exclusion of his father, were discussed in every embassy. The natural heir of Catherine II, her son Paul, was of doubtful sanity and unquestionably dominated by three favourites, a couple of his wife's waiting women and his

Turkish barber, a state of affairs which sounded extra-ordinary even to Mr. Canning's young subordinates, who were not easily surprised by anything, especially out of Russia.

In the Empress' outer apartments on this sharp morning, her waiting pages and ladies and whippets shifted uneasily. The scene was the Imperial Winter Palace in the city of St. Peter, and from every double window of the immense structure, the view was indeed a winter scene. The building was little over thirty years old, and had been, like several others ordered by the Empress, the work of an Italian architect. Rastrelli's palaces, with façades of rust-red and jade-green, lavishly ornamented with what appeared at a distance to be bride-cake icing, were certainly effective posed against clear skies and snowy landscapes, in company with churches and towers topped by copper and gilded cupolas of onion shape. Such smaller rooms as those in which the Empress penned her private correspondence could be kept warm, but those designed to express magnificence only, harboured a savage combination of heat and draughts.

The Empress, who had appointments this morning, failed to reappear. Her attendants continued to wait uneasily, a business in which they were adept, since all Russians spent so many months of life waiting for the spring, a season in their land exceptionally lovely. The best months of the court year were those spent at Tsarskoye Selo, the Summer Palace, where Her Imperial Majesty, whose power and wealth were boundless, had commanded galleries and chambers decorated in mother-of-pearl and amber and lapis lazuli and silver and gold, and in her park of sixteen thousand odd acres on the Duderhof hills, might wander happily for hours between fine wrought iron gates, kiosks, arbours and pavilions.

She had often proclaimed that since her fifteenth year the greatness and safety of Russia had been her sole aim, and although she declared candidly that she did not appreciate good painting, sculpture or music, she invited to her court artistic foreigners of every nation, and spent largely on works of art and curios. A dinner service of nine hundred and fifty-two pieces decorated with views of English noblemen's seats, had safely performed its long journey from the factory of Mr. Josiah Wedgwood to the mouth of the Neva. It was believed that the ageing lady dreamt now of an Empire stretching from the Thracian Bosphorus to the Bothnian Gulf, from the Vistula to the Sea of Japan. Certainly she had warmly resented the King of Prussia's failure to attack Revolutionary France, leaving her free to annex the remainder of Poland. Her taste for French rococo had not extended to admiration of recent developments in that country. Like all sovereigns, she distrusted political theories which necessitated the decapitation of royalty. Her son was known to have strong French sympathies, and more than a quarter of a century had passed since Lord Buckinghamshire, British Ambassador, had written home that he did not believe the Empress would order her son's assassination. Even her reputation could not hope to survive such a second family tragedy. But the exploits of a possible French military dictator alarmed no one in Russia. Moscow would always be so far from Paris.

Peace Negotiation

Her Imperial Majesty, who could order the use of the knout and sleep none the worse, was not an unkind mistress, yet no servant dared lightly disturb her solitude. No call came from beyond the door through which she had vanished. Whispering grew in her antechamber, drowning the sound of an elaborate ormolu clock, ticking away moments, valueless in a land of sudden alarms and utter disappearances, where the word for 'at once': is 'this hour'. At last a page, bolder than his fellows, plucked up courage to scratch at the door, to strive to open it. His efforts met with silent resistance. Putting his shoulder to the door, he pushed it open, and swept before him on the polished parquet the motionless figure of the Empress. Nobody had heard her fall. While one party of scared attendants carried the heavy and heavily breathing woman to a canopied bed in a vast room crowded with meaningless ornament, another fled to fetch Dr. John Rogerson.

Her Scots first physician saw at a glance that Catherine II, whose detestable husband had died suddenly of official apoplexy four and forty years past, had herself suffered a genuine apoplectic seizure. After being bled twice, the patient showed signs of relief, but did not utter. Since nobody knew what else to do, sledges were sent flying through the snows to the country palace of Gatchina, to summon to her sick bed the creature she most disliked on earth, her first-born son. But the end of Catherine the Great was merciful. She never regained consciousness, and less than two hours after her son's arrival she ceased to breathe.

Peace Negotiation

Exactly a week after the news of the death of the Empress Catherine was made known to the inhabitants of Paris, they watched the British Ambassador's coach roll out of their city. The War with England would have to continue. The negotiation for Peace had been broken off. ' Insurmountable objections ' had arisen.

For Lord Malmesbury the intervening days had been full of incident, mostly irritating but not unforeseen. On December 17th he had a lengthy morning interview with M. Delacroix, who 'talked with an air of triumph'. A Note from M. Delacroix followed during the next afternoon, and another Note twenty-four hours later. Lord Malmesbury forwarded both to Downing Street, accompanied by his own replies, carefully labelled, A,B,C, and D. He sent duplicates to his colleague in Vienna, and ordered his valet to pack for an early start next day. What he did not know as he sat at Calais on a frosty Christmas Eve, waiting for his flag of truce, was that the fleet assembled at Brest, of which he had warned Downing Street on November 13th, had put to sea, at the same time, if not before, he had received M. Delacroix's Note C.

On Christmas Day the flag of truce appeared, but the wind which had been favourable for two days, now changed in the night, and for four further days the unfortunate Ambassador sat at Ducrocq's *Lion d'Argent*, noting dismally in his diary, ' High east wind—great sea—no going.' Not until December 29th was he able to make the comfortable entry, ' Left Dover at nine —got to London at half past four. Dined with Pitt,' and

54

not until that night did he learn that the gale which had shaken the windows of the *Lion d'Argent*, Calais, had proved fatal to Admiral Bouvet's fleet, carrying General Hoche and twenty thousand men ordered to make a descent on the south-west coast of Ireland.

In England, oddly enough, the expedition was not unexpected, even by the man in the street, for a French paragraph, quoted in London on December 23rd, had commented that the Directory seemed almost to invite the British fleet to intercept Admiral Bouvet. The official columns of the *Rédacteur*, as early as December 8th, had chronicled the arrival of the Minister of Marine to accelerate the sailing of the Brest Fleet.

After December 23rd, however, as far as the English public were concerned, a fog thicker than any mid-winter sea-mist descended upon press reports of naval action. Daily the papers headed leading articles ' The Brest Fleet', but the announcements under those headings, sometimes culled from Dutch sources, were confused, contradictory and not as optimistic as facts eventually warranted.

In London a gay winter season continued. Mr. Macready was being great in *Hamlet*. The Opera was crowded, and lead-coloured opera pelisses lined with pink satin were noted as the rage. A Scottish peer, on the first stage of his journey to his Forfar seat, accompanied in his post-chaise by a French *émigré* nobleman, was attacked by highwaymen on Finchley Common. Lord Strathmore shot one of his assailants dead, and the corpse was discovered to be that of the notorious William Lancaster, liberated only last Monday after his attack on Lord Boringdon. At Windsor, the eldest of the six spinster princesses had defiantly announced her intention of getting married, and Mr. Beechey was painting, as a wedding present for the Princess Royal, a portrait of Her Majesty, in a morning dress, walking out in the neighbourhood of Windsor Lodge. In Wiltshire, Mr. Beckford of Fonthill refused to allow the baronial Yule-tide hospitality which he had prepared for his neighbours and tenants to be interrupted. This fabulously wealthy and mysterious gentleman, a Maecenas *manqué*, deemed by his admirers to have been a more suitable personage than Lord Malmesbury to conduct peace negotiations with France, was continuing, in spite of War, to build. Literary visitors to Fonthill detailed with reverence how, when the author of *Vathek* stamped his foot, uttering the magic word ‘ Disclose,’ a mechanical nymph raised a rich curtain, displaying a vista of further galleries, five hundred feet in length. At his ‘inconceivably grand’ Twelfth Night banquet, the author-host arose to make a patriotic speech, ending with a refusal to believe that British ears should ever be assailed within their own walls by ‘the gypsy jargon of France’.

In Cork, since French ships were clearly visible in Bantry Bay, people were not so much at ease. The chief magistrate ordered all citizens to be indoors by ten; carts and carriages were commandeered. Oxford had never known such cold. Even the West Country was getting a white Christmas. The road between Exeter and Launceston was said to be thirty feet deep in snow, but the local yeomanry were displaying zeal.

Gradually the fog of that dark season dispersed, and French papers, which had announced in the last week

of the old year, ' We are now actually in Ireland, if the
expedition has not failed,' were obliged a week later to
admit that the expedition had not succeeded. The best
was made of a bad business by writers who pointed out
that the Elements, not England, had been responsible,
that a fatal blow had been struck at English finances;
already in the greatest disorder, and that the recent surprise attempt had proved how easy it was to invade
Britain. The casualties sustained by the Brest Fleet were
at length known by London readers to be two ships of
the line and two frigates wrecked; one frigate captured.

A patriotic musical piece, called *Bantry Bay*, was put
on at Covent Garden, and received with great enthusiasm, but other news was not so cheerful. His Majesty's
sudden journey from Windsor to St. James's to confer
with his ministers was followed by the announcement
that the Bank of England had suspended payment in
specie. A second expedition was said to be mustering at
Dunkirk. A squadron of British frigates, cruising in the
Bristol Channel, had received a false alarm from a lugger. The North Devon Volunteers, after marching fifteen miles to Bideford, had paraded in an orderly manner, singularly silent but perfectly willing to step on to
Ilfracombe, whence another false alarm had come.
People straining their eyes seawards at Portsmouth had
seen a prodigious French Fleet in sight of Britain. The
town was consequently in the greatest confusion. Next
morning's newspapers were obliged to admit that this
fleet had dwindled, on closer inspection, to a single
cruiser. The next reports of such a sight came from the
Pembrokeshire coast, and were well founded.

Peace Negotiation

The invasion of Wales by General Hoche's ' Black Legion ' under Colonel Tate on February 22nd-24th, 1797, was one of the oddest expeditions in history. Wolfe Tone, United Irishman, who attended a review of the Black Legion before it sailed, noted the force as 'unmitigated blackguards'. They reminded him of Dublin's 'green boys'. The galleys and the gaols of Brest had been searched to stiffen an army designed by acts of sabotage to upset communications and spread panic in England. On their arrival in England, these unfortunates had been informed, they would find a country ripe for revolution. Thousands of sympathisers, yearning to cast off the yoke, would speedily join them. A surprise attack on the city of Bristol, to coincide with a blockade of Irish ports, was ordered. The destruction by fire of Bristol, ' the second city in England for wealth and commerce', was a project described as of the first importance, and carefully planned. The invaders were advised, after reconnoitring the position by day-light, to sail up the Avon under cover of dusk, land on the right bank, within five miles of the town, in the greatest silence, and advancing to whichever side of the city might be to the windward, set fire to that quarter with combustible material. When the port, docks and shipping were irremediably ablaze, the incendiaries were to re-embark ' with dexterity ' and proceed in the same manner upon Chester and Liverpool.

One of the first persons in Great Britain to set eyes upon Tate's alien undesirables was an impressionable lady of nine, named Nellie Phillips, engaged in driving cows in a field at Kilshawe. Wind and weather had again disobliged the invader, and after abandoning an attempt to enter the Bristol Channel, the fleet had made for Cardigan Bay. Troops were disembarked during the night of the 22nd, and met with no resistance. The vessels which had brought them promptly sailed for Dublin Roads, flying British colours, to fulfil the next item on the programme.

But the appearance of the desolate and obscure mid-winter Welsh countryside, from which all life and colour had been pinched by frost, was deceptive. The arrival of strangers had not been unobserved. Colonel Thomas Knox of the Fishguard Volunteers, absent from home, attending a ball at Tregwynt, had received a message from Ensign Bowen. A farm-hand from Crachenllwyd had been sent by his employer to warn the Fencibles, and seventy of the Fishguard Volunteers were already on the march. At Stackpole, Lord Cawdor was roused from bed, and next morning Lord Milford, Lord Lieutenant of the County, ordered Lord Cawdor to advance on Fishguard instantly.[1]

The entire force under Lord Cawdor's command amounted to seven hundred and fifty men, all belonging to the Castle Martin Yeomanry, Cardigan and Cardiff Militia and Fishguard Volunteers. A few sailors, led by a couple of Naval Lieutenants, and a retired officer of the regular army, offered their services. Throughout the night volunteers poured in. The enemy they were prepared to meet was underestimated by local

[1] The Fishguard despatches of Lord Milford and Lord Cawdor came to light some forty years past, in a Birmingham antique shop.

report as numbering about twelve hundred. The sequel was amazing, and so was the length of time which elapsed before the news reached the London press.

At dusk on the 23rd, a French officer, calling himself Tate's second in command, asked for an interview with Lord Cawdor, firmly, but not luxuriously established with his staff at the 'Royal Oak', Fishguard, and by two p.m. on the 24th the entire invading army had surrendered without striking a single blow. They had no hope of re-embarkation and credited Lord Cawdor's statement that he had at his disposal a force of overwhelming numbers, hourly increasing. But not until the night of the 28th did readers of London newspapers learn that a Member of Parliament had risen at Westminster, on the previous evening, to call the attention of the House to the late attempt of the French upon Wales, and that 'Upward of three thousand persons, gentlemen and peasantry of Wales, had with incredible alacrity and zeal, although largely armed with rustic weapons, assisted the yeomanry and Militia to take fourteen hundred French prisoners'.[1]

Lord Cawdor had exhausting experiences before he drove in to London in charge of his principal captives. At Haverfordwest he was obliged to attend personally through the small hours of a February night, while the

---

[1] The picturesque tale of the unexpected appearance, on a headland, of Welsh ladies, wearing their national costume, being mistaken by the alarmed invaders for scarlet-cloaked military, does not find a place in any immediately contemporary account of the Fishguard incident, but was in circulation and generally accepted within a few years.

prisoners were housed in gaols and churches. Few of the civic authorities of Haverfordwest understood the language of their uninvited guests. His hope of a good night's sleep in a private house at Carmarthen was disappointed, for Carmarthen had just been informed—quite incorrectly—that another great French landing had taken place in Glamorganshire.

The inhabitants, and notably the females of Wales, showed a strong inclination to cut the throats of the prisoners, and so threatening were the expressions of the people of Uxbridge, that Colonel Tate, riding in the first carriage of the party, trembled ' almost to convulsions '. Actually the crowd had mistaken the Colonel for the notorious Governor Wall, ' wanted ' since 1784 on a charge of having ordered West African natives to flog to death a British N.C.O. Lord Cawdor himself travelled in the second chaise, with Tate's second-in-command, one Le Brun, alias M. le Baron de Rochemure, a person in whom gentlemen at the Admiralty took great interest. Personally, Lord Cawdor found the Baron ' as dirty as a pig ', but more intelligent and better mannered than Tate's Irish subordinate, Captain Tyrrell, ' a stupid Paddy '. Young Lord Edward Somerset, who brought up the rear of the procession in charge of a Captain Norris and Lieutenant St. Leger, reported those characters so greatly frightened that they had very little conversation.

Lord Cawdor, with British phlegm, wrote to his lady that the weather was extremely cold and Town, he heard, very dull and unpleasant, and the authorities of the Admiralty settled with zest to drawing an incredible story out of the ' Black Legion '.

Peace Negotiation

Intelligent persons began to wonder who had been the originator of an attempt so badly contrived, and to congratulate themselves that the only outstanding General possessed by the Directory was still in Italy. Headlines announcing the Defeat of the Spanish Fleet off Cape St. Vincent by Admiral Sir John Jervis, were as gladly read in London on March 3rd, as those announcing the Fall of Mantua had been in Paris a fortnight before.

Chapter 3

Frigates and Fencibles

Musselburgh sands, at dawn, on a fine August morning three years before the close of the century, presented a scene exactly of the type dear to many contemporary artists. The principal features of the picture were a noble expanse of sea and sky, opalescent in colour at this early hour, a bridge built by Romans, around which clustered a fishing village of many old houses, and, in the distance, smoke arising from the chimneys of a famous city. Moreover, since the military had gone into camp on the spot, and the Quartermaster of a newly-raised volunteer regiment had been crossed in love, the composition was completed by the figure of an interesting and solitary horseman.

The months which had passed since the winds of Christmas week scattered General Hoche's fleet, and Lord Cawdor's volunteers captured Colonel Tate's forces, had not produced any further invasion scheme. Events at home had been rather of a melancholy than a stirring nature. The voice of Edmund Burke would be no more heard in Westminster. The great orator, broken by the loss of an adored son, was beyond cure by all the physicians of Bath. On a July day, the last morning of his life, he spoke with fervour of his belief that this War, which he would not see decided, was for the good of humanity. Mr. Canning wrote to Lord Malmesbury's embassy, ' There is but one event, but that event is an event for the world. Burke is dead.'

Although Britain's only important victories in this war had been won at sea, and the supremacy of her fleet was essential to her existence, serious disaffection at Spithead in April had been followed in May by an absolute Mutiny at the Nore. Patriotic persons, who cherished the warmest feelings for the Navy, but had always realized vaguely that a sailor's life was hard and that ships were largely manned by a process of kidnapping, heard the respectful demands of the Spithead mutineers with a sense of shock. Their rations were maggotty and under weight, their medicines embezzled by their ships' surgeons, their wages and pensions insufficient to support the families they seldom saw. When the Fleet was in Channel ports, no leave was given. The reason was obvious. Desertion must result. There was ' vast discontent ' inflamed by the tyranny of a certain type of officer. Public opinion was roused, Parliament hastily voted the sums necessary to increase pay, and the Admiralty made concessions in every direction. The far more dangerous mutiny at the Nore, which quickly followed, was suppressed with severity but not with speed, and during the days when the situation was threatening, one of the most nervous people in London was General Kosciusko, the Polish patriot. He lay on a couch in his Soho hotel, ostensibly passing the time by drawing landscapes, but eagerly asking every caller whether there was likely to be an English Revolution. If so, he would prefer to go to America in search of peace.

The Mutiny collapsed, and was reported upon. Admiral Sir Alan Gardner, when proceeding to the punishment of an offender in his ship, had been advised by his officers not to persevere. They had believed that if he did so, a signal would be given, and the Fleet watching Brest would return to port. Sir Alan mourned to cronies that a great change for the worse had taken place in the Navy. Sunday schools were much to blame. They gave persons education disproportionate to their situation in life. Newspapers, now regularly received and read on board ship, also did great mischief.

Newspapers, between the dates of the two disturbances in the Fleet, duly chronicled the nuptial weeds of the Princess Royal. A less romantic match could hardly be imagined. The bride, in her thirty-first year, was principally interested in getting an establishment. The ludicrously corpulent widower-bridegroom was, even for a small German prince, remarkably rude during his short stay to the servants at Windsor. By midsummer the honeymoon couple were at home in the pretentious palace of Ludwigsburg, where the Princess Royal of Great Britain nearly burst into tears on hearing ' God Save the King ' played during dinner, but obediently admired the height of the local corn and the size of the local cattle, and did not venture to contradict

her wedded lord when he promised her a novelty in the
shape of a mountain tour, there being, as he kindly explained to the daughter of his first marriage, no such
things as mountains in England.

II

Mr. Walter Scott, Quartermaster of the Royal Corps
of Edinburgh Volunteer Light Dragoons, was a highly
romantic young man. Galloping on Musselburgh sands
at dawn, mounted on his brave 'Lenore', he almost forgot that he was not, and never could be, a regular
cavalry officer, and that his Lady of the Green Mantle
had wedded another. He had perhaps, in his most hopeful moments, scarcely dreamed that he should win his
bright particular star. The lady had made a match
suited to her birth and fortune, and he believed his
heart was broken, but meanwhile, being five-and-twenty
and very good humoured, he had become an ardent
volunteer.

During the past months there had been many meetings, chance and formal, in park and library, between
eminent country gentlemen. The Lord Lieutenant of
Midlothian, the head of his house, had conveyed to the
Government Mr. Walter Scott's offer to serve with a
body of voluntary cavalry in any part of the island, in
the event of invasion. Fortunately for the Edinburgh
Light Dragoons, many years in a stern sire's office had
taught Mr. Scott to write a small legible hand, and
keep accounts accurately. His friends might laugh at
his military enthusiasm, but he delighted to dine in Mess,
and rise at five a.m. to drill, before a hard day of civilian

toil in the Parliament House. He had many friends in Edinburgh, which was at this date a very pleasant place for a young man with literary aspirations. If no invasion came with the early autumn, he planned to depart with a couple of brother officers for a month's ramble into the English Lake land.

Lord Malmesbury was back in France, with slightly better hopes than before of concluding a peace. In Paris, returned *émigrés* were chatting to one another across the boxes at the play and opera, in the tongue which they had learnt during their English exile. Mr. Scott, with two companions, set out on his tour. The weather was good and the scenery all that the most romantic traveller could desire. In the neighbourhood of Thirlwall Castle and the ruins of the Roman Wall, the attention of the Scottish officers was arrested by a solitary *equestrienne* of unusual attractions. When evening came, although both his friends had donned their regimentals, Mr. Walter Scott was the first to lead out the Fair Unknown. It had not been difficult to obtain an introduction, for Gilsland, in Cumberland, was a very small Spa. By candlelight in the ballroom she proved even more captivating than at sunset in the saddle—an arch brunette, fairylike in form, of an olive complexion, with eyes of Italian brown, alternately sparkling and melancholy. She was not travelling unchaperoned. A daughter of the late Dean of Exeter, visiting Cumberland relatives, was her companion at the Spa.

Mr. Scott's empty heart was an easy conquest. After a whirlwind wooing, the struggling Advocate-Dragoon was cheerfully breaking to his circle, the news of his engagement to a young lady with a French accent. Miss Carpenter (born Charlotte Marie Charpentier of Lyons) was of English extraction, he declared. She had the sentiments and manners of an Englishwoman and had received her early education in England. Since her only male relative, a brother, was in India, she insisted that her fiancé must approach her guardian. She was just of age, but Lord Downshire's consent must be asked. The unknown Marquess, duly approached by Mr. Scott, wrote somewhat dampingly, though in flowery language, to the effect that Miss Carpenter's face was her chief fortune. He willingly gave his consent to the match. Mr. Scott's circle was not so enthusiastic, and the vivacious orphan whose lover insisted so strongly on her English blood, wrote pitifully—' They don't perhaps, like me BEING FRENCH.' Little notes signed ' C.C.' occupied Mr. Scott's brain to the exclusion of public events during the weeks that followed. Mr. Scott sat for his portrait, in volunteer uniform, and sent to his bride the likeness of a young man of grand physique, with a flaxen forelock and homely features dignified by an expression calculated to assure the most forlorn orphan that she had found a solid protector. Since the portrait was of head and shoulders only, a lame leg was not apparent. His fiancée wrote coquettishly to acknowledge the receipt of 'the gentleman'. The news of a *coup d'état* by the War Party in Paris, of a peace imposed by General Buonaparte on Austria, and the defeat of the Dutch Fleet off Camperdown, found no place in Mr. Scott's replies to ' C.C.' who said that she was sure her lover would live to be a great rich man.

Frigates and Fencibles

On a cold, dark Christmas Eve, in lodgings in the shadow of the red sandstone cathedral of Carlisle, a nervous bridegroom was tying his stock.

III

About the same time that Mr. Walter Scott in Edinburgh was rapturously re-reading the *billet-doux* of ' C.C.' and Mr. John Constable, at Ipswich, was packing his London introductions and his landscape sketches (mostly of the Dedham neighbourhood), a strong travelling carriage was rapidly bearing a party of French military officers over the Alps.

General Buonaparte had been summoned to Paris, and his sensations as he hastened towards that focal point of intrigue and disquiet were far from pleasant. He was perfectly aware that his phenomenal success at the head of the army of Italy had not endeared him to many members of a Government at once weak, corrupt and violent. He knew that at least one recent guest had been sent to his headquarters with instructions ' to keep an eye on Buonaparte'. In Italy he had been his own master, leader of adoring troops and a staff of whose brilliant qualities any General might have been proud. He had lived in semi-royal state, giving audience to foreign ambassadors and hailed by local poetasters as a second Hannibal. His reason had not been affected, and he clearly perceived himself now in a situation of grave danger. So far he had taken no false step. He could not be convicted of disloyalty to employers whom he thoroughly despised. His reasons for supporting the Directory had been unidealistic. He could not afford to let the royalists overthrow the present régime, for the return of the Bourbons would mean unemployment for General Buonaparte. His new appointment was already known to him. He had been promoted Commander of the Army of England—that is to say, the army for the invasion of England. But although the conquest of Britain was a principal item of his programme, he had strong suspicions that it would not at the moment be possible to make a success of this business, and stronger still that his enemies knew this. Schérer, the Minister for War, would witness the decay of General Buonaparte's reputation with complacence; the egregious Barras would sympathize fulsomely.

The General had done what he could from a distance. On learning of his appointment he had written that although he truly needed rest, he could not refuse to sacrifice himself for the good of France. He had forwarded some helpful suggestions—for instance, that artillery of the same calibre as that supplied to the British army should be ordered in France, so that, once in the country, captured British ammunition could be used against its makers. He had, however, told his employers that four things were essential for a successful invasion—good naval officers, a great army well led, an intelligent and determined Admiral and three million francs in ready money. He had reasonable hopes that the three million francs might prove a fatal stumbling block. General Buonaparte travelled at top speed to take up his new appointment. His companions noticed with interest that he could scarcely control his impatience while horses were changed. But he did not confide in anyone sentiments worth repeating.

Frigates and Fencibles

His welcome in Paris did not appear to please him any better than it pleased his detractors, for the wildly cheering mob were firmly convinced that the Victor of Italy had only to set foot in England in order to vanquish that country. As soon as possible he escaped from the fêtes and speech-making and fatuous flattery. He settled down to several weeks of interviewing colourless characters who brought notes on the stores and equipment at the invasion ports of Brest and Lorient, Dunkirk, Boulogne, Cherbourg, Havre, St. Malo, etc. He also saw, after dark, some characters far from colourless —retired sea-faring men and expert smugglers.

He granted three interviews to a high-nosed, talkative person with a brogue, who gave the Hôtel des Étrangers, Rue Vivienne, as his address, and passed under the name of Citizen James Smith. Wolfe Tone, who brought with him the confidential agent of the United Irishmen, a Mr. Lewens, educated for the priesthood, found that General Buonaparte believed the population of Ireland to number less than two million souls.

The General wrote, in his own untidy, overdriven hand, a number of painstaking reports, and signed many circulars. On the 8th of February he departed from the capital for a personal inspection of the invasion ports.[1]

IV

In London, as usual on January 28th, a court was held to celebrate Her Majesty's Birthday, and Her

[1] The most detailed account of plans for the invasion of England will be found in Desbrière's *Projects et tentatives de débarquement aux Iles Britanniques*, Paris, 1900.

Majesty as usual, according to the writers of fashion articles, appeared very plainly dressed. Queen Charlotte's simple attire consisted of a salmon satin skirt, festooned with ' patent ' lace, and a bodice and train of puce velvet, ornamented with the trimmings known as goat's beard and frivolity. Her only jewels were diamonds, and a miniature of her husband was suspended around her neck by a diamond chain.

Her five unmarried daughters were dressed alike in white crêpe gowns with trimmings of various pastel shades, and it was noted that very few of the high-born females present wore powder or caps. Three tall plumes lashed to the brow by a jewelled bandeau was the headdress now in vogue, and the Princess of Wales sponsored it.

The palm for distinction at the first Drawing Room of 1798 was unhesitatingly awarded by reporters to the Princess of Wales. ' Her Royal Highness looked most beautiful and interesting. Her dress was most magnificent. It was one universal display of elegance and taste; the colours lilac, black and silver.' The ladies of England, and particularly those who had no personal acquaintance with the Princess of Wales, were solid in defence of the deserted bride of a libertine. Unfortunately her errant spouse was entirely unimpressed by the princess's dazzling appearance in half-mourning. The Duke of Clarence said to intimates, ' My brother has behaved ill. To be sure, he has married a very foolish, disagreeable person, but he should not have treated her as he has done. He should have made the best of a bad bargain as my father has always done.'

Every member of the Royal Family was behaving

characteristically. The King was at his desk every morning before breakfast, in a window overlooking Windsor Park, signing the commissions of Volunteer officers. His Prime Minister and the Leader of the Opposition were of one opinion at last. The King said thoughtfully, ' Mr. Pitt is sometimes in the wrong; Mr. Fox often is. But when they agree they are sure to be so.'

Only a few persons in London knew for certain that every morning, during this second week of February, a travelling carriage was drawing up at a dock-head, and General Buonaparte, Commander of the Army of England, was descending to be pompously received by the officials of an invasion port. A secret agent employed by Lord Castlereagh had the good fortune to meet the General, on the road between Furnes and Dunkirk, and sent interesting notes on the number of flat-bottomed boats ordered at Ostend, and already on the stocks at Rouen, Havre and Calais. Every useful tree on the roadsides near Lille had been felled. His progress from Paris, where he found a guard at every important street corner, but the city very quiet, was impeded by troops and ammunition waggons. He forwarded details of an army of fifty-five thousand within twenty-four hours' forced march of the coast, and he believed this number to represent less than a quarter of the available force likely to be employed. He thought the foot indifferent material, badly clothed.

London newspapers announced that at Brest every preparation for the descent appeared in train. At Plymouth an alarm that the French fleet was already at sea was much credited. Firing in the Channel had been heard by the inhabitants of Eastbourne, and extra-

ordinary signals, believed to be warnings of enemy sail
in the Channel, were seen at Brighton. The long Sunday
morning visit of the Duke of York, Commander in
Chief, to Mr. Dundas at Wimbledon was a matter of
fact. After enjoying Sunday dinner, His Royal Highness
inspected the Surrey militia and professed himself
much satisfied. Mr. 'Weathercock' Windham, Secretary
of War, returned home to jot in his diary, ' Saw
Duke to-day. Talk about defence of country. Stated
my plan of opening the country for cavalry. Duke
seemed rather to like it.'

On February 9th many substantial figures, reverenced
in the City of London, deserted their offices for
the square of the Royal Exchange. A public meeting
had been called to support a Lord Mayor's Fund for
the defence of the country. His Majesty headed the list
of contributors with a gift of £20,000, Her Majesty and
the Duke of York followed, with £5,000 apiece; the
royal princesses each offered £100 a year for the duration
of the War. Every street leading to the solemn
square, on that chill and cheerless morning, was
crowded, and after the Lord Mayor had left the temporary
hustings a loyal merchant suggested, ' Gentlemen,
let us give a cheer for Old England,' upon which
' Old England for ever ' was loudly echoed, and ' The
King ' repeatedly cheered.

A series of startling engravings, on view in Fleet
Street and St. James's Street, showed English observers
the types of ' machine ' which they might expect to see
at any moment, bearing down upon their shores. ' The
GIANT raft, drawn from the original at Brest,' had
amongst its salient features four windmills and a battle-

mented wooden fortress, provided at every corner with batteries of 48-pounders. The St. Malo raft was of much the same design, except that its fort was provided with a dome, and it carried two tents, surmounted by fluttering pennons. The smaller Calais rafts, still in the process of construction, but ordered in large numbers, were to be three hundred feet square, and capable of carrying sixty pieces of cannon and four thousand men.

For the comfort of nervous members of the public, portraits of the Semaphore Telegraphs, erected on the Admiralty office and a tower of Westminster Abbey, were also obtainable. Duplicates of this ingenious apparatus, designed to convey news from hill to hill, were already in position on the east coast, and it was claimed that tidings of the approach of the invader could be transmitted from Yarmouth to the Nore in under five minutes. That on the Admiralty had been installed two years past, and a cartoonist unfriendly to Mr. Fox had depicted the large-headed statesman enclosed within the complicated structure of wooden arms and shutters, signalling to France, by the light of a crescent moon which dimly illuminated the dome of St. Paul's, indicated by a baleful timber finger.

Brigadier General John Moore, invalided from the West Indies after his second severe attack of yellow fever, had been ordered last autumn to make a tour of the east coast with Engineer officers. He had been painfully struck by the vulnerable appearance of Clacton Beach, which seemed to him to provide ideal anchorage for the invader, and he found the batteries at the mouth of the Yare very inadequate.

Frigates and Fencibles

Towards the end of February, 1798, the semaphore telegraphs came into action, and a hastily-summoned committee met at the Admiralty. But while the Commander-in-Chief and Prime Minister were still in conference with the Secretary of State for War and Secretary of the Admiralty a despatch arrived stating that the ships seen off Portland, which had failed to reply to signals, had proved to be homeward-bound West-Indiamen.

v

Drills and parades were the order of the day throughout a wet summer, and many new corps, picturesquely named and attired, sprang into being. Military tailors' advertisements filled columns in the newspapers, and miniaturists and portrait painters were much employed. Some of the uniforms chosen were elaborate and expensive, and it is a melancholy fact that the most popular Scottish poet died still owing £7 4s. od. towards the blue coat and nankeen breeches of a Dumfries Volunteer. 'Don't let the awkward squad fire over me,' begged Robert Burns, with a characteristic smile, as he lay on his death-bed.

London produced, amongst many other organizations, the St. George's, Hanover Square, Armed Association, St. Pancras and Marylebone Volunteers, and Hans Town Association, all of whom wore blue, but the majority of the fencibles wore scarlet, with coloured or black and white facings, and the name of their corps engraved on a small brass breastplate. Headdresses were of every description, including ' helmet hats ' and bearskins. Highland volunteers wore the kilt, sporran and feather bonnet. Some wealthy landowners, who commanded their own tenantry, provided clothing and accoutrements, and even offered pay at the rate of one shilling a day for each time of exercise.

Many prominent persons with no physical qualifications thought it their duty to join a local organization, and caricaturists represented the Prime Minister and the President of the Royal Academy drilling Falstaff's recruits. Mr. Pitt, who displayed untiring interest in the volunteer movement, sagely suggested that every effort should be made to enrol gamekeepers, as persons accustomed to the use of firearms and night work in country localities.

On an April night, the weary Prime Minister admitted that, although it had been difficult to rouse the country from lethargy, and the original response to the Lord Mayor's Fund had been languid, public spirit had now risen so as to be 'fairly equal to the occasion'. The Defence of London was taken in hand, and the Duke of York, at a City meeting, approved a set of regulations which had lain too long, in the shape of loose notes, in a government office reading room. Amongst the ' Hints to assist in the General Defence of London ' were suggestions that ' barricadoes ' should be erected at suitable spots, and the inhabitants of corner houses be provided with hand-grenades. Night cellars in the city were to be examined, and all obnoxious foreigners ejected. It was advised that on news of an enemy landing, all barges, vessels and boats should be removed from the Surrey side of the Thames, and large *Corps de Garde* be detailed to defend the waterworks and pipes which supplied the capital. Artillery parks appeared in the centres of stately squares of many-windowed houses, whose view hitherto had been of lime avenues radiating from a bronze equestrian statue in classic costume. In Queen Square, Bristol, once the largest square in Europe, where the masts of ships could be seen down every side-street, volunteers in scarlet coats and blue pantaloons, drilled around a Rysbraek statue of Queen Anne's Dutch brother-in-law.

The organization of country districts proceeded. Posters in which the word INVASION was printed in staring large type, were attached to village oak and lych-gate. Their price was 2d. each, 1s. 8d. the dozen, or one hundred for 12s. The Prime Minister, on long, light evenings at home, tackled a report covering three hundred pages. It had been drawn up at his request, and described the preparations made for internal defence when Queen Elizabeth's ministers expected the Spanish Armada. On that occasion the authorities had exercised the power of calling upon all landowners to furnish vehicles for transport, messengers to convey news of enemy movements had been enrolled, and arrangements been made for the driving of all cattle from the coast inland, and the burning of crops and breaking down of bridges likely to be of assistance to the invader.

On his sixty-second birthday the King, attended by two of his sons, reviewed over eight thousand volunteers in Hyde Park. His Majesty, on enquiring the name of a corps which had kept perfect order, though marching through heavy mire, was told that the Bloomsbury volunteers were mostly gentlemen of the Inns of Court. 'Aye, aye,' nodded His Majesty. 'Lawyers! Lawyers! They make excellent soldiers; very good soldiers indeed. The lawyers were always famous for dashing through thick and thin. Hey, General, were they not? Were they not?'

Queen Charlotte and her daughters witnessed the spectacle from a house in Park Lane. Rain came down steadily, but their indefatigable Majesties proceeded to hold a court at St. James's, and reporters announced that so far certainly the War had not diminished the spirits or wealth of the country. The gaiety and magnificence of the First Drawing Room in Europe had been remarkable. Guests were still leaving the palace at seven o'clock, when the Royal Family appeared on a balcony, and the spectacle of the Prince of Wales handing his little daughter to her grandsire was loudly applauded. The Princess Charlotte, heiress presumptive, was said to be a remarkably sharp child. She always addressed her grandmother as 'Your Majesty', but His Majesty as 'Grandpapa'. The Princess of Wales, still a neglected wife, was sitting for her portrait to Mr. Hoppner, a thing bound to annoy the King, for when His Majesty had said that he did not approve of scarlet and yellow trees in a landscape, Mr. Hoppner had huffily replied that he had studied landscape as much as anybody, after which the King had cancelled his order for a portrait of the Princess. Pacing the studio in high spirits, the Princess noticed a flattering likeness of her husband, and asked when it had been painted. ' Four or five years ago, I think,' said the artist. ' Four or five-and-twenty years ago, I should think,' replied the Princess of Wales cheerfully.

The War continued to penetrate into country life. Individuals calling themselves Directors of Stock appeared to ask for complete returns of vehicles and cattle.

Smiths, carpenters and wheelwrights were enlisted as pioneers, and expert horsemen as guides and messengers. Clergy received a circular letter, signed J. Cantuar, which told them that it would not conduce to the safety and defence of the country if they were to accept Commissions in the Army, but that in the case of actual invasion their duties would include giving every assistance to repel ' the avowed champions of anarchy and irreligion'. They were advised that they must be prepared to superintend personally the evacuation of women and children from a threatened area. Parade services were frequent, and when the Fawley Fencibles presented themselves in St. Thomas's Church, the Warden of St. Mary's, Winton, chose as his text, ' Remember the Lord which is great and terrible, and fight for your brethren, your sons and your daughters, your wives and your houses.'

A heavy stamp-tax made newspapers a luxury. Month-old copies, in the process of disintegration, were passed from hand to hand in shops, barracks and cottages. The pedlar's arrival with his store of lurid cartoons, pamphlets and broadsides was eagerly looked for. A lady writer who condemned as ' poison ' the farrago of ghost stories, horrid murders, sentimental songs and vulgar caricatures brought by the itinerant hawker, turned her talents to aid her country at War. Miss Hannah More, aided by a sister and some friends, produced for the space of three years, three tracts a month, price 1d. Nearly every tale was dignified by the figure of an exemplary parish priest. Miss Hannah More's ' Cheap Repository ' of popular anti-revolutionary literature enjoyed, especially during its first year, a wide circulation, but was eventually not a financial success.

Occasional tables in the drawing-rooms of well-to-do ladies bore recently published volumes filled with beautiful colour plates, displaying the costumes of the volunteer corps. *Town and Country*, *The Gentleman's* and *The Lady's* Magazines, all of which devoted columns of Foreign News, arrived monthly, and families seated in chairs of mahogany and satin-wood beneath stipple-engravings of classic and Shakespearian scenes, talked of Frigates and Fencibles, and ' Raft-weather ' and the Semaphore; but even ladies with relatives in the services were not yet much incommoded by the War. The Commander-in-Chief's wife, a stout and homely Prussian princess, bravely ordered a uniform of scarlet and blue when she consented to present their colours to the St. James's Volunteers. But on the morning of the show a message from Weybridge instructed the Colonel that ' Her Royal Highness desired the Volunteers should not fire', and when she arrived at Calvert's Field, attended by her martial husband, her little speech was utterly inaudible. The Colonel, catching the royal infection, replied in the tones of one within a sacred edifice during service: the St. James's Volunteers marched off without having heard a single word of compliment or encouragement.

Lord Rodney, at his seat near Maidstone, offered a feast to five thousand Kentish fencibles in August heat. Mrs. Fremantle, wife of one of Nelson's captains, a tender wife, a good daughter, a long-suffering sister and a devoted mother, recorded in her diary that rain prevented her and her companions from witnessing the

Yeomanry sword exercises which were the reason for a large gathering of local gentry at Stowe; however, their dinner in tents was not postponed, and a charming ball and supper was enjoyed by twenty-four couples till four a.m. ' Nearly all the county was there.' In a month when dismal War news was reaching Mayfair, Mrs. Fremantle was so much engaged in the agreeable business of painting handscreens that she never stirred out of doors. To be a woman of fashion was still considered sufficient occupation for an intelligent female. As piety was unfashionable, most important weddings took place in drawing-rooms. ' Me and Mine ' was the motto of the lady of fashion, and in homes where the spouse was neglectful and the infants were fretful, the motto was simply ' Me '. But since a divorce necessitated an Act of Parliament, and a divorced woman was, unless possessed of exceptional advantages, a pariah, families held together in name. The lady of fashion who had lost horrid sums at the gaming table, saw nothing disgraceful in giving the grocer a large order in return for £50 in cash. Wives of penurious officers were perfectly prepared to follow their husbands on active service to distant climes, attended by an annually increasing nursery, but those who had the opportunity to stay in a comfortable home generally did so, and since intellectual attainments were not much considered when choosing a bride, many a gallant husband in cabin or barracks clasped his brow in dismay as he read sprightly or lachrymose accounts of disaster in dairy, stable, coverts and kitchen of his country estate. The conduct of two daughters of a Scottish peer, who augmented their incomes by using their brains, was deplored by their

acquaintance. Lady Margaret and Lady Anne had discovered that buying or renting houses, furnishing them
with what their detractors called ' second-hand furniture, pieced and patched by themselves to look fashionable ' and then letting them for the Season, was a
profitable business. Lady Anne, cheerful and bustling,
interviewed clients and struck the bargains. Lady Margaret, elegant, gentle and sweet, provided the ' tasty '
background. 'I wish to God', said a scandalized friend
to their compatriot, Lord Glenbervie, ' that those two
very agreeable women would leave off being uphol-
sterers and begin to be women of fashion.'

VI

Shortly before three o'clock on the afternoon of Sunday, May 27th, 1798, a number of vehicles converged
upon an unfrequented quarter of Putney Heath. In
spite of the fact that open rebellion had broken out in
Ireland four days past, and foreign invasion was imminent, the Prime Minister had felt it his duty to afford a
gentleman's satisfaction to Mr. Tierney, M.P. More
than his customary frigidity marked the Prime Minister's features as he drew towards the rendezvous in a
hack post-chaise, accompanied by his second, a son of
Lord Harrowby. Colonel the Hon. George Walpole,
second to Mr. Tierney, had travelled to the scene with
his principal in a hackney coach. Two surgeons were
already present, and several gentlemen from London,
including the Speaker of the House of Commons. Some
chance pedestrians, recognizing all the makings of an
unexpectedly interesting Sunday afternoon, discon-
tinued their stroll.

What followed was slightly ludicrous and very boring. For over forty minutes the seconds stalked to and fro, endeavouring to bring about a reconciliation. At length, a large crowd having gathered, the combatants took up the positions indicated to them. The awe-inspiring order to fire was heard, and the sound of the discharge of firearms broke the Sabbath calm. Neither gentleman secured a hit. A second case of weapons was brought to each duellist, and again they fired—Mr. Pitt in the air this time. The seconds then recommenced stalking and talking, and while they argued Mr. Pitt and Mr. Tierney were left in conversation. Presently the seconds declared that the affair must terminate. Honour had been assuaged. A third long wait took place, while the account to be given to the newspapers was drawn up. The facts were not very interesting, and mainly demonstrative of War nerves.

The Prime Minister had accused Mr. Tierney, who had spoken very aggressively against hurrying the bill for manning the Navy, of desiring to obstruct the defence of the country. The accusation had been ruled unparliamentary, but Mr. Pitt had refused to withdraw it.

Four cases of pistols were re-strapped. The vehicles from London drove up and prepared to receive their occupants, and the duellists shook hands. The crowd began to melt away.

Public comment was much as might have been expected. When Mr. Pitt's slight illness was announced a few days later, Opposition newspapers gleefully asserted that he was now raving mad. Mr. Pitt's admirers said that it was a pity Tierney had such a nasty tongue, and was not quite the gentleman. Mr. Tierney said that the Speaker was much to blame. If Mr. Addington had not taken up Mr. Pitt's words, no duel need have resulted.

Meanwhile, the Prime Minister's doctors urged him to take a complete rest, preferably at Bath, and newspapers announced the unfortunate termination of a secret expedition to Ostend and the very alarming aspect of affairs in Ireland, where martial law had been proclaimed. General Moore, now on service in Ireland, was gloomy. ' Should an invasion be attempted, there will be no head to direct, and no previous arrangements made; the scene will be disgraceful, and I wish to retire from it.' Unaccountably, the enemy failed to take advantage of their opportunity.

The rising in Ireland had been a rising of despair, and with the signal defeat of the insurgents at Vinegar Hill all immediate danger passed, but the Prime Minister and Cabinet now knew that General Buonaparte was embarking troops at Toulon, and did not know their destination. The south coast of England was thought to be the likeliest spot. Many people believed that an attempt, intended to synchronize with the Irish revolt, had been accidentally delayed. Naples was another possibility. The most thrilling rumour declared that Buonaparte was about to cut a canal through the Isthmus of Suez. Sir Horatio Nelson had sailed from Portsmouth, in the *Vanguard* of seventy-four guns, to join St. Vincent's fleet, but news from that quarter took a very long time to reach Downing Street. Although by midnight of August 1st a famous naval action had been won, and all communications between Buonaparte's army and France effectively severed, the victory was not announced in London until October 2nd.

The King was still lingering at Weymouth with his family, when a despatch, forwarded by the Secretary of the Admiralty and headed '*Vanguard*, off the mouth of the Nile, August 3rd, 1798', was placed in his hands. He read the opening words—' My Lord, Almighty God has blessed His Majesty's arms in the late battle,' and before reading more was observed to pause, and stand silent a moment with his eyes raised to heaven, as if returning thanks. Few officers in His Majesty's service could better convey in an official document the unmistakable imprint of character, and Sir Horatio's two terse but eloquent descriptions of the Battle of the Nile, published in a Gazette Extraordinary on the day of their arrival, exactly hit the popular taste . . .

' Sir, Herewith I have the honour to transmit to you a copy of my letter to the Earl of St. Vincent, together with a line of battle of the English and French squadrons, also a list of killed and wounded. I have the pleasure to inform you that eight of our ships have already top gallant yards across and ready for any service; the others, with the prizes, will soon be ready for sea . . . The island I have taken possession of, and brought off the two thirteen-inch mortars, all the brass guns and destroyed the iron ones . . . I attacked at sunset on the 1st of August, off the mouth of the Nile. The enemy were in a strong line of battle for defending the entrance of the bay (of shoals) flanked by numerous gun-boats, four frigates and a battery of guns and mortars on the island in their van. But nothing could withstand the squadron your lordship did me the honour to place under my command. Their high state of discipline is well known to you, and with the judgment of the captains, together with their valour, was absolutely irresistible.

' Could anything from my pen add to the character of the captains, I would write it with pleasure, but that is impossible . . . The ships of the enemy, all but their two rear ships, are nearly dismasted . . . The support and assistance I have received from Captain Berry cannot be sufficiently expressed. I was wounded in the head, and obliged to be carried off the deck, but the service suffered no loss by that event . . . I had the happiness to command a band of brothers . . . '

After the long strain of waiting for an invasion which did not come, and was now, at least, indefinitely postponed, the people of England gave vent to jubilation. In London the Park and Tower guns fired and joy bells rang. Club members subscribed ten guineas a head towards celebratory entertainments. Every householder who could afford to do so, lighted his windows and the decorations on some façades were elaborate. Ladies and gentlemen ordered their carriages, and drove around the streets until the small hours to admire the ' transparencies '. In the neighbourhood of Covent Garden the mob got completely out of hand, and at dawn decorous streets were still disturbed by the voices of cup-shotten revellers chanting that popular song, ' The Snug Little Island '.

At last the gentlemen of the pen had a worthy subject, and pens became busy. *The Mouth of the Nile, a new Serio-Comic Intermezzo of Pantomime, Song,*

Frigates and Fencibles

Dance and Dialogue, produced at Covent Garden on October 24th, was a brilliant success, and soon earned a command performance from the King. On the appearance of the Royal Family in their box, so much cheering took place that the rise of the curtain was delayed. Every seat in the house had been taken within a few minutes of doors opening, and noisy plaudits continued throughout the piece, especially when reference was made to the victory of Baron Nelson of the Nile and Burnham Thorpe. Theatrical critics dealt indulgently with ' a motley composition, brought forward from the most laudable motives, and on the spur of the occasion', and while condemning the ballet, praised the songs by two leading comedians disguised as British Tars, the representation of the engagement between the two fleets and the explosion of the French Admiral's flag-ship.

The Lady's Magazine, or Entertaining Companion for the Fair Sex appropriated solely to their use and amusement, always catered for a public warmly interested in the Navy, and the November issue offered as frontispiece an elegant engraving showing Lord Nelson engaging two Spanish ships of superior force off Cape St. Vincent, faced by a sketch of the national hero's life. On later pages, the Admiral's ' Mouth of the Nile' despatches appeared, and an Ode on the late glorious victory by a young resident of Lynn. The Ode was full of colour and included mention of Neptune's heroes, proud Gallia's tarnished laurels, and death-dealing thunders shaking oozy caves where hoary billows crimsoned beneath a purple sky. The sketch of Lord Nelson's life was somewhat deficient in vitality.

Frigates and Fencibles

There was no mention of the picture familiar in so many nurseries, of a frail little midshipman alone on an Arctic ice-floe, defying a Polar bear. Readers learnt that his lordship was the son of a respectable clergyman, and had a brother in the church. Lady Nelson, the widow of a West-India gentleman before her second marriage—on which occasion she had been led to the altar by the Duke of Clarence—was at present settled at Roundwood Farm, near Ipswich, with her father-in-law, a person beloved and respected by all his neighbours. Her ladyship had one son by her previous husband—Lieutenant Nisbet, R.N.—no issue by Lord Nelson. The author certainly did not succeed in making the Admiral's family sound interesting, and Londoners who had met them confirmed this impression. An invitation from Lady Inchiquin (a good hostess when not fussing over the complicated will of her uncle, the late Sir Joshua Reynolds) brought a few favoured intimates hot-foot to meet the Nelsons, who had come up to London for a short stay. Lord Nelson's wife, a small lady somewhat sharp-featured, in the late thirties, seemed quite startled by the attentions being paid to her. After dinner she diffidently showed her fashionable fellow-guests the drawing sent to her from Constantinople of the tremendous diamond aigrette, valued at £18,000, presented to her husband after the late victory by the Sultan. Her father-in-law was a martyr to asthma.

Three more French attempts at invasion took place in the latter part of 1798, but all were upon Ireland, and followed the previous unsuccessful pattern. Three weeks after the defeat of his countrymen in the Battle of the Nile (of which event England was quite ignorant), General Humbert landed in a remote corner of Mayo, and disembarked one thousand men. Much to his disappointment, only a few hundred natives rallied to him, and on the road to Castlebar on August 25th he was informed of the approach of General Lake, the dreaded victor of Vinegar Hill, in command of vastly superior numbers. He courageously attacked, and at the cost of heavy casualties took the town, although nearly all his Irish recruits vanished when the English opened fire. No further Irish joined him, and on his road to Dublin on September 8th, caught between Lake's cavalry and regular troops commanded by Lord Cornwallis, he surrendered.

The third expedition, despatched in October, reached Sligo Bay, but ' hearing there news which it did not like', set sail and regained Rochefort swiftly. The news which so discouraged Captain Savary concerned the Brest squadron which should have combined with General Humbert. The fleet had sailed late for the sordid reason that the government had not produced the pay in advance promised to the troops on board. On October 12th, Sir John Borlase Warren, with three ships of the line, five frigates and a sloop, having fallen in off the west coast of Ireland with a French fleet of one ship of the line, eight frigates, a schooner and a brig, had captured the ship of the line and four of the frigates. Amongst those discovered aboard the *Hoche* was Wolfe Tone. ' He was disguised, but known.' The eloquent United Irishman who had been so much disappointed by General Buonaparte's ignorance of Irish affairs, died on November

18th in the Provost Marshal's prison, Dublin, from pneumonia, after an attempt to cut his throat.

So the Old Year wore out, and unlettered folk who had enlisted because the French were coming, heard with very little understanding that Buonaparte, after several hard-fought battles, had made himself master of Grand Cairo in Egypt, and presently that Buonaparte's army was suffering much from the climate, bad water and repeated attacks of the natives of Egypt. A Viennese report asserted confidently on October 17th, that accounts had arrived of the surrender of Buonaparte and his troops by capitulation, but the English editor wisely added that this required further confirmation.

At a grand ball and supper, offered at Ipswich in honour of Lord Nelson's victory, Lady Nelson was welcomed by Admiral Sir Richard Hughes, Bart., and Admiral Reeve, who led her, attended by the venerable father of his lordship, to the top of the room. Captain Bourchier, leading Miss Berry, sister to Captain Berry of the *Vanguard* followed. On the ladies entering, they were welcomed by the grateful respects of the whole assembled company, and the dance band struck up ' Rule Britannia '.

A privileged visitor to Windsor mentioned a faintly disturbing fact. After his dinner, which he took at four-thirty, His Majesty did not join the ladies for coffee. He preferred to retire to his study for conversation and any public business necessary. His Majesty, when offered documents, complained of insufficient light, and murmured, ' We are not quite so young as we were, and eyes will fail '.

Frigates and Fencibles

A brief paragraph under the heading of 'Foreign News' in the November number of a fashionable magazine, announced that the lady of the unfortunate Lord Edward Fitzgerald had arrived at Cambray, and tender-hearted people who had seen an exotic trio in the streets of Dublin, spared a sigh for 'La Belle Pamela'. Even before her light-hearted young husband had become a declared revolutionary, she had not been much liked in Vice-regal circles. She was said to have been a daughter of the Duke of Orleans, by the notorious Madame de Genlis, and authorities in Paris seemed to believe this, for they had not received Lord Edward's offers to raise Ireland with much enthusiasm. However, little Lord Edward, so handsome in the Irish style, with his long lashes and melting eyes, had died horribly in prison, of wounds received when resisting his arrest, and his bride, who had shocked Dublin ladies by appearing at a ball in a white gown spangled with scarlet, intended to represent the gore of guillotined *aristos*, had returned to foreign parts. What had become of their large Black, history did not relate. The faithful 'Tony', who had saved Lord Edward's life, when his master was still an officer in His Majesty's service, had been a constant attendant on the dashing couple.

French emigrants were still a care to benevolent societies. In England, on an autumn day of this year, the same columns which had noticed the wanderings of Pamela, recommended the deserving case of a Madame Desparre, safely delivered last week in Welbeck Street by Dr. Poignant, of three children (one male, two female). 'Madame Desparre is from St. Domingo, where her father had an estate of 20,000 a year. Of all this they are deprived by the Revolution. They were fourteen in family before the present addition.'

Lady Nelson, whose anxiety had been relieved by the arrival of several letters from her husband, spent Christmas quietly at Roundwood Farm. Her husband's triumphal reception in the Bay of Naples, where he had been greeted by the English Ambassador leading a procession of boats, had evidently been a beautiful scene. Many writers chronicled the picturesque effect of brilliant terraces of ochre and coral buildings, rising under plumy trees, in tier upon tier, beneath a cloudless sky, above crowded wharves echoing to the strains of Italian airs. The King of Naples, who had immediately followed Sir William and Lady Hamilton on board the *Vanguard*, had pressed the Admiral's hand, saluting him as 'Deliverer and Preserver!' Lord Nelson told his wife that Lady Hamilton, on meeting him, had exclaimed 'Oh God! is it possible?' before swooning into his arms. 'Tears, however, soon set matters to rights.' Good Lady Hamilton had given a magnificent fête in honour of his birthday. 'Dear Lady Hamilton is an Angel.'

He was recovering from his wound, and his letters were still affectionate, but his wife began to suffer from a new anxiety.

VII

The reason why no invasion of England took place in 1798 was not fully understood in that country for many years, though the truth was quite simple. But as yet people in England did not realize the difference between dealing with the Directory and dealing with General Buonaparte.

After his mid-February tour of the invasion ports, the General returned to Paris. His brief inspection had shown him clearly that a successful invasion was improbable under present conditions. He had always suspected this, and he did not wish to be associated with a failure. He intended, in good time, to compass the ruin of both the present French Government and the British Empire, but in his own words 'the pear was not ripe'. He reported to his employers conscientiously, and at length. The condition of the Navy caused him the gravest alarm, and to make a descent upon England without the command of the sea would be one of the boldest and most difficult things ever attempted. A surprise crossing was the only hope, and this could only be effected either by raising the British blockade of Brest and the Texel, or by landing an expeditionary force in small boats during the night, after a seven or eight hours' passage. Kent or Sussex would be the most suitable areas for disembarkation, but such a business demanded long nights, and therefore entailed all the hazards of winter weather. It could not be done later than April, and the date on which he wrote was February 25th. Invasion by means of sloops in calm weather would not be practicable. The British Fleet would hinder both the passage and the disembarkation. ' The English expedition seems to me, therefore, impossible until next year. . . .' He suggested that the appearance of invading England should not be abandoned, but that there were other ways in which England might be wounded—' We might well make an expedition into the Levant and threaten the commerce of India.' A conquest of the north-west German coast would be destructive of English trade with central Europe. If none of these operations were deemed feasible, he could but suggest that, for the moment, a peace with England should be concluded. He imagined that the terms refused by Lord Malmesbury last year would now be very acceptable. Also, once at peace with England, it would naturally be possible to make fresh large demands upon the German Empire. He wrote comfortingly to General Berthier—who he had known would not be a success filling his place in Italy—' I should greatly like to have you with me in England.' He continued to sign himself ' Commander of the Army of England'. Two months later he was still writing, ' We ought to be able to defeat England, and we can do so', but his estimates for the reorganization of the fleet were devastating to a government already short of money, and ' the expedition to the East ' appeared as a settled fact in his calculations. To the Minister for Foreign Affairs, a person with whom he had an understanding, he explained a programme which began by the seizure of Malta and occupation of Egypt, to be followed by the invasion of India. ' We may change the face of the world.' The Foreign Minister, who was indeed a man of parts, was at the moment little more than the head clerk of his department. His reputation for public morality had been under a cloud since some supposedly lucrative dealings with American envoys. Nevertheless, while the Commander of the Army of England toured invasion ports, Charles-Maurice de Talleyrand-Périgord had been the official to bring to the favourable notice of the Directory schemes which included the cutting of a Suez canal in order that French armies should march to rouse the Mahrattas to expel the English. There was, however, in General Buonaparte's opinion, always the possibility of a successful invasion of England before tackling India. If the British fleet was kept busy around Alexandria, he might manage a surprise return to the Channel. Alternative suggestions, after the seizure of Egypt, were for the invasion of Syria, the capture of Constantinople and the destruction of the Ottoman Empire.

The Directory, so carefully and gradually approached, consented to the Egyptian expedition. It was recollected that the mastery of the Nile valley had been a favourite project of *le Roi Soleil*. The alien government of Egypt was unpopular with the natives, and the army was believed to be weak. The Directory also considered that in Egypt, General Buonaparte, whether he succeeded or not, would be out of sight and fully occupied. Money to equip the expedition was obtained quite easily by a callous attack on Switzerland, and on May 19th the General set sail from Toulon. His last weeks in Paris had been nerve-racking. He did not wish to leave his fascinating wife, of whose loyalty to him during his absence he had doubts, but in his more neurotic moments he had believed that his rivals would not stop at poison. His brother, after his departure, managed to convey the impression that a great patriot had been virtually banished.

The army for the invasion of England was unostentatiously dispersed to Switzerland, to the Rhineland, to Belgium. Malta, well prepared by propaganda and corruption, surrendered to General Buonaparte on June

13th, and twenty-three days after landing in Egypt, he won the decisive battle of the Pyramids. Cairo and Lower Egypt, with all their possibilities, were his. He had carried with him on his Oriental campaign a band of mathematicians, historians and geologists, ordered to inspect the antiquities and develop the resources of captured territory. Near Fort St. Julian, four miles north of the town of Rosetta, an engineer officer called Boussard discovered a basalt stele inscribed in hieroglyphic, demotic and Greek, with a decree of the priests of Memphis, praising Ptolemy V, Epiphanes, and his wife, Cleopatra. But an ironical fate decreed that the Rosetta Stone, which supplied a French *savant* with the key for deciphering Egyptian monuments, should become a valued exhibit of the British Museum.

The English Cabinet still suspected General Buonaparte at Toulon, of English invasion schemes, and when he had been months in Egypt, reviews of fencibles still continued. By the time that Sir Horatio Nelson had severed its communications with France, General Buonaparte's army was already disappointed in Egypt. He put his forces into action again without delay, and at first his invasion of Syria was a progress from strength to strength. El Arish, Gaza and Jaffa fell, and by the 19th of March, 1799, he was encamped before Acre. After two months' ineffectual attack, he raised the siege. Commodore Sir Sidney Smith and a French royalist engineer, rather than the Turks, resisted his pressure solidly. Plague had broken out in his camp, ammunition was running short, torrents of rain descended, the approach of a Turkish fleet was reported. By mid-June the army of Syria—or what was left of it—

was back in Cairo, and by mid-July it had won a victory over the Turks at Aboukir.

On August 21st, after dark, and attended by only a few chosen officers, the Conqueror of Egypt sailed for France. The secret of his departure had been so well kept that even the General appointed his successor learnt the news by letter too late to ask for explanations. General Buonaparte had excellent excuses to offer for his desertion of men who had followed him with heroic courage. But he did not think that many excuses for his reappearance in France would be called for. During his absence their inevitable fates had overtaken the incompetent rulers of that country. By means of newspapers which had reached him *via* Sir Sidney Smith, he had learnt that his conquests in Italy had been reversed; French soil was in danger of invasion. At last the pear seemed to be ripe.

VIII

During the Egyptian campaign, hundreds of letters from General Buonaparte's army were intercepted at sea, often under dramatic circumstances. Although French Headquarters ordered that, when capture threatened, all despatches must be thrown overboard, quick-witted and hardy British sailors plunged after them. Now and then a ship coming from France was the prize, and important instructions from Paris, and such trifles as the miniature of some fair one, destined for her lover, were deflected to Whitehall. A first collection of captured letters, published in London in the year of the Battle of the Nile, aroused so much interest

that a second volume followed in 1799. Reprints were
made in several towns on the continent, including
Hamburg and Frankfort. The editors announced that
their reason for publishing private as well as official
correspondence was to undeceive the world as to
France's motives, and correct exaggerated accounts of
her success. Delicacy had been observed, and they had
refrained from printing passages from the epistle of
General Buonaparte to one of his brothers, complaining
of his wife's infidelity, or one from her son, expressing
filial hopes that Madame Buonaparte was not behaving
as badly as was represented.

Actually the captured correspondence of the Army
of the East, taken as a whole, was rather Anti-War
than Anti-French propaganda. It included many simple
screeds, expressing the young soldier's homesickness
and longings to be once more in the centre of a complicated family circle. Julies, Adélines and Joséphines,
residing in Paris streets, thatched cottages and country
châteaux, received tender or burning protestations of
fidelity. A distracted Colonel yearned for news of his
expectant lady, who hoped for a little Camilla, but was
resigned to the prospect of another boy. A worried
archæologist lamented that he could get nothing but
chopped straw for his gallant mount, 'Milord'. A
young officer had left a favourite dog behind, asleep, in
a tavern at Malta. There was a furious note from a
Commissary, asking the Agent for Military Hospitals
to explain why an establishment with four hundred
patients possessed neither bedding, sanitation, dres-
sings nor drugs. One and all, officers complained
agonizedly of the ravages of many forms of insect, lack

of transport and lost baggage. The English editors pointed out that, amongst the mass of correspondence, there was not a single letter from any man in the ranks. An interesting fact, to which they did not draw attention, was that, although the writers grumbled unceasingly against the Government which had sent them on this expedition, no word of criticism was ever directed at the Commander-in-Chief. Indeed mentions of General Buonaparte were generally something in the hero-worshipping line. A private letter from the General himself, in which the editors took great pleasure, told his brother Joseph that Egypt was a barbarous country, and that he had no pay for his troops. ' I may be in France again in two months. Please arrange to have a house in the country, either in Burgundy or near Paris, ready for my arrival. I reckon on passing the winter there in solitude.'

Accounts of the impressions made by their new colony on General Buonaparte's army were even more cheerful reading for English homes.

' We are arrived at length, my friend, in the country so much and so eagerly desired! It is far from being what even the least enthusiastic pictured. This execrable dog-hole, Cairo, is inhabited by a set of lazy wretches who squat all day before their filthy huts, smoking and taking coffee, or eating pumpions and drinking water. It is perfectly easy to lose oneself for the day in the stinking narrow streets.' The results of drinking Nile water were soon apparent. ' In the name of God, bring us our baggage and our brandy! The whole army has dysentery from being obliged to drink the local water. In the name of God, WINE, BRANDY and RUM!' ' I fear we have been horribly deceived in this vaunted expedition. The most uncultivated district in France is a thousand times more beautiful than this promised land. Nothing could be so gloomy and unhealthy as Alexandria, the chief port of Egypt, with its mud houses, windowless, except for a few holes in the walls, covered with a rude latticing, and entrances so low that you stun yourself entering. In a word, picture to yourself a collection of dirty, ill-built pigeon-houses, and you have a fair idea of Alexandria.' Alexandria was universally accepted as detestable. At first hopes were held out that Rosetta would be an improvement. But officers stationed there said that Rosetta was only a shade less wretched than Alexandria. The Delta was the rich and fertile part of Egypt. ' I have just passed through it, and I can assure you that it is nothing of the kind. As for Cairo, the wealthiest, the largest and most magnificent city of the world, it is the vilest and most miserable kennel on the face of the earth.' Even the boasted houris of the East were a disappointment. Veiled women of the poorer sort, whose clothing was shrivelled and stained, reminded young French officers of nothing but hobgoblins. The handsome and opulent ones presumably stayed indoors. ' This infernal Egypt is nothing but a waste of sand. Since we have been here we have done nothing but suffer.' After August, gloom deepened. ' Before you receive this, the destruction of our fleet by the English will be known in France. All here are horror-struck . . . Since the action the enemy's cruisers are masters of the whole coast and interrupt all our communications . . . The English, as usual, have suppressed their casualties, but we are assured that

Admiral Nelson has a dangerous head-wound and has lost two of his captains.'

The first volume of intercepted letters ended on a despairing note. ' To tell you the truth, after such a disaster as we have experienced, I can see no hope of our consolidating our position in our new colony except by a Peace. May our governors procure us a solid and honourable one! '

The second volume bore as frontispiece the facsimile of a letter covered with small, slanting, overdriven handwriting, marked by blots and erasures. It was signed 'Bonaparte'. Since 1796, for his own reasons, the General had abandoned the Italianate version of his surname. Across the cover the words ' found on the person of the courier ' appeared in large, rather unformed characters, which tended to fall backwards. The editors were sure that every Englishman would be interested to see a specimen of Lord Nelson's writing—performed, of course, with the left hand.

The second volume covered much the same ground as the first, since, after the Battle of the Nile, few French had much hope of communicating with home. The same pictures were drawn again and again, a nightmarish medley of marches across burning sands under pitiless skies. Hunger, thirst, heat, and fear of assassination were the constant theme.

Already, in France, stirring sketches and lively engravings depicting the triumphs of the Army of the East were solacing eager purchasers. In later years large smooth oil-paintings, destined to grace the walls of a conqueror's palaces, showed the Victor of Egypt, motionless on horseback, under serene skies, regarding the Sphinx, urging handsome cavalrymen to the destruction of writhing tan and ebony-skinned Eastern enemies, commiserating with plague-victims in the heat and horror of a hospital square, or looking down upon Nazareth by moonlight.

But the letters of the Army of the East intercepted by Lord Nelson's fleet tell a less glorious story.[1]

[1] *Copies of Original Letters from the Army of General Bonaparte in Egypt, intercepted by the Fleet under the Command of Admiral Lord Nelson*, London, 1798–9.

Chapter 4

The Experimental Peace

When a Gazette Extraordinary announced on October 2nd, 1801, that preliminaries of Peace had been signed, between Great Britain and France, not only the general public but also many well-informed and influential persons were taken by surprise. They affirmed solemnly that no State secret had ever been so well kept. Even the newspapers, whose influence was growing, had been kept in the dark.

It was fairly widely known that as long ago as Christmas Day, 1799, the Ruler of France had forwarded to King George a personal letter, containing peace proposals, to which Lord Grenville's haughty reply had been, even in his royal master's opinion, ' much too strong'. Ten days before that date, General Bonaparte had been elected First Consul for a term of ten years. He described himself to His Britannic Majesty, quite justifiably, as ' called by the will of the French people to hold the highest office in the Republic'. In England, the man in the street had a very hazy notion of the

104

delicate and at last desperate intrigues which had ended in Bonaparte's predominance. From the press and French engravings, they had received a confused but colourful impression of a scene full of sound and fury, in which scarlet-cloaked Republican Deputies, threatened on a November evening by the bayonets of a number of grenadiers, had fled pell-mell from a large-windowed council hall, formerly the Orangery of the palace of St. Cloud. The Deputies had every reason to be nervous, for General Bonaparte's brother, Lucien, had called upon inflamed troops to deliver the Assembly from the hirelings of Mr. Pitt. His youth made the Victor of Italy and Egypt ineligible for a place in the Directory: the Directory therefore was abolished—or more exactly, all members being obliging enough to resign simultaneously, a provisional government was established. A month later, supreme power was placed in the hands of Napoleon Bonaparte. His new title, redolent of republican Rome, satisfied a people weary of internal strife, and grateful that no bloodshed had accompanied or followed his *coup d'état*, but few thoughtful persons believed that they had submitted themselves to anything but a Dictatorship.

England, too, was ready for peace. She was tired of waiting for an invasion which did not come, and of lavishing money on defective allies. Some not inconsiderable recent successes on land and by sea made her hope that a peace arranged this winter might be far from ignominious. Eight months ago invasion had again appeared imminent. The First Consul had brought the Continental War to a close, his reputation enhanced by two more spectacular victories. In the early summer of

1800 he had performed a remarkable passage of the Alps and shattered the Austrians. Austria, strongly urged by England, had refused to accept defeat, but one of his Generals completed in the miry winter woods of Hohenlinden the business begun by him in June on the plain of Marengo. By February, 1801, the Peace of Lunéville had been signed by a disconcerted Austria, and France was at liberty to reconsider plans for the destruction of England.

On March 7th the First Consul sent a typically peremptory despatch to his Minister of Marine. He asked how long it would take to collect certain gunboats at Boulogne, what were the present stations of these boats, and what was their condition. He also wished to know how many men they would carry, how many Boulogne harbour could accommodate, and how many could leave on a single tide. A fortnight later, M. Forfait had failed to satisfy his exacting master, but the English public had taken alarm, and once more shop-windows and newspapers displayed horrid likenesses of invasion rafts, propelled by gaunt windmills revolving against lurid sunset skies.

Lord Nelson's defeat of the Danish fleet at Copenhagen put an end, for the moment, to the First Consul's preparations, but Admiral Latouche-Tréville, disobeying orders, continued to collect a fleet at Boulogne. He asked in vain for seventy-five thousand men, and permission to land in Kent or Sussex. Once more confidential circulars concerning internal defence reached commanding officers in southern England, and fencibles breathlessly awaited the message of the Semaphore Telegraph. The garrison was doubled at Brighton, where the Prince of Wales was enjoying sea-breezes, and all leave was cancelled.

By mid-May the news of the surrender of the French forces in Egypt had reached London, but the brilliant success of General Abercromby's expedition was not at once appreciated, and Mr. Fox, writing to his military brother, could only say that something which might be called a victory seemed to have taken place. ' Here we are all in a state of uncertainty about it, and unfortunately all we know about it is that our killed and wounded amounted to near two thousand before the famous action.' Why, said Mr. Fox fretfully, Egypt should be of such importance either to the French or us, was a thing he had never been able to discover. Personally he had always considered Bonaparte's expedition there the only foolish act of his career, unless, of course, Bonaparte had at that time some knowledge of French internal Politics hidden from us, or—as Mr. Fox had always suspected—a desire to be out of the way at that moment, and relieved of his command of an army for invading England. Mr. Fox added that the best news he had was that wheat had fallen in price, for the misery endured by the poor, and indeed by those a little above the poor, during the last twelve months, had been remarkable.

Lord Nelson was not at first inclined to believe in the latest invasion scare. ' This boat business may be part of a great plan of invasion; it can never be the only one.' Still, puzzled by Admiral Latouche-Tréville's persistence, and remembering that ' it is perfectly right to be prepared against a mad Government', he forwarded to the Admiralty a vigorous memorandum full of underlinings, dealing with the defence of the Thames. He believed that the waiting flotilla, with forty thousand troops aboard, might cross from France in twelve hours. ' If a breeze springs up our Ships are to deal DESTRUCTION, no delicacy can be observed. . . . Whatever plans we may adopt, the moment the Enemy touch our Coast, be it where it may, they are to be attacked by every man afloat and ashore; this must be perfectly understood. NEVER FEAR THE EVENT.'

Royal inspections of volunteers, blessed by much better weather than those of the previous danger period, enlivened the later months of the summer, and at a review in Hyde Park it was reckoned that thirty thousand spectators gathered to watch the London corps go through their exercises. ' Innumerable fair forms, sheltered from the scorching rays of the sun by the protecting parasol, were seen, escorted by their *beaux*, tripping over the turf. The surrounding walls were covered with men, women and children. Every eye sparkled with animation; every heart beat with loyal fervour.' A bombardment of the French invasion port of Boulogne, which took place a fortnight later, did not do much damage. The heights above both Boulogne and Dover were crowded, and as the day was very clear, spectators of both countries were able to watch the operation. Eleven days later, a night attack on the French fleet in harbour was equally disappointing, and somewhat costly, and in after years it became known that Lord Nelson's ill success in this expedition had given Bonaparte a more favourable impression of the possibilities of Boulogne. Lord Nelson, undaunted, reported to the Prime Minister that he found in his

command much zeal and good humour, and should
' Mr. Bonaparte ' put himself in the path of the British
Navy, he believed that the gentleman would soon be
wishing himself even in Corsica. For his own part, Lord
Nelson sincerely hoped that if an invasion was coming
it might be upon a date before September 14th, because
nowadays his frame was not suited to exposure to
equinoctial gales. He was not getting on with the First
Lord, who refused to meet him to discuss a raid on
Flushing: the Admiralty would neither accept his suggestions nor his resignation. ' None of them cares a
d—— for me and my sufferings,' complained the
victor of the Nile, who had domestic sufferings in his
catalogue.

II

While Madame Bonaparte was interviewing her head
gardener on the subject of carnations at her new country-
house, ' La Malmaison', and General Baird's army, after
a six months' passage from Bombay, was preparing to
march from the Red Sea to the Nile in nine days, in a
temperature of 115° in the shade, something was happening in Russia which was to have a direct influence
on the course of England's struggle with France.

The court of St. James's was no longer represented
at St. Petersburg. Paul I, successfully wooed by the
First Consul, had abruptly dismissed the handsome and
tactful Sir Charles Whitworth. History seemed to Sir
Charles to be repeating itself. Nine years had passed
since he had reported to London that a French adventurer had arrived at the court of Catherine the Great,
with a plan for invading Bengal by way of Kashmir.

The Experimental Peace

Sir Charles, whose last years in Russia had been marred by the necessity of continual complaints of outrages by the police on British subjects, reached home, *via* Copenhagen, in September, 1800. By March, 1801, Russia was openly preparing for hostilities. The First Consul, although he realized the personal undesirability of an ally who allowed no blue sledges or red liveries in his capital, and expected ladies in the latest Paris fashions to descend from their carriages and kneel in the snow as he passed, saw great possibilities in the might and resources of Paul I's Empire. Russia, said the First Consul, held the key to Asia. He hoped with her assistance to drive the English out of India, to hold Egypt and advance into the Balkans. These projects were as yet visionary, but the Tsar's League of Northern Powers, directed against England, was of immediate value. An embargo had already been laid on all British vessels in Russian ports, and incidentally Russian merchants were groaning at the result.

That loud sounds of revelry should be issuing from the palace of Platon Zubov, last favourite of Catherine II, towards midnight on March 23rd, aroused no special interest in the capital. The week was that of the Maslanitza carnival. Festivities had been taking place in connection with the marriage of the Tsar's second daughter, the Grand-Duchess Elena, and Count Pahlen, the bland and calming Governor of St. Petersburg, had persuaded his master to mark the happy occasion by recalling several banished personages.

In the days of his ascendancy Zubov had been rather disliked. He had been in the habit of admitting less fortunate courtiers, and even princes and ambassadors, to morning *levées*, at which he made languid appearances, wrapped in a rich dressing-gown, with a pet monkey grimacing on his shoulder. The Empress's generosity had been proverbial, and her affection for her ' Little Blackie' had been great. Since the residence of a favourite included a winter garden, a theatre in which plays and concerts could be performed, and immense vestibules separated by rows of marble pillars, entertainment on a large scale was within his power.

Zubov's guests on the night of the 23rd numbered a hundred and twenty, mostly officers in, or dismissed from, the Imperial service. Amongst those seated at a table loaded with gilt plate and foreign delicacies, and lit by thousands of wax candles in crystal chandeliers, were Count Feodor Vassilievitch Rostopchin, once Minister for War, whose lady was of the Orloff family, Count Nikita Ivanovitch Panin, once Minister to Berlin, and a member of the Council of Foreign Affairs. Generals Ouvaroff and Benningsen, Colonels Tataramoff, Jesselowitz and Jaschwel, and two of the host's brothers, all still held important court appointments.

Wine had flowed freely for some hours, and most of those present were in a bemused condition, when the doors of the room were locked and the host arose to make an impassioned speech.

The scene which followed could only have taken place in Russia. Zubov reminded his listeners that for four and a half years they had writhed beneath the tyranny of an autocrat whose behaviour rivalled that of the most insane and vicious Roman emperor. The first act of the recluse of Gatchina had been to repeal his mother's law exempting the populace of Russia from corporal punishment and mutilation. Under the present régime, nobody, whatever his rank or character, could for a moment feel safe from brutal ill-treatment, or banishment to Siberia. Count Pahlen had, in the course of his duties, seen recently an order for the arrest of the Tsar's eldest son, Alexander, chosen successor of Catherine II. The Grand Duke, interviewed privately by the Count and warned of his peril, had agreed to a scheme for his parent's dethronement. All that remained to be done, therefore, was to secure the Tsar's signature to his abdication. But time pressed, for Count Pahlen had also seen, this very morning, an order superseding him, and summoning to St. Petersburg the notorious Araktcheyeff, Governor of Moscow, and General Alexei Araktcheyeff was known to be in the command of troops within twenty-four hours' march of the capital. Zubov did not add, or did not know, that Pahlen, having in the course of his duties noticed this order passing through his department, already sealed and signed by the Tsar, had opened it and boldly detained the messenger.

The matter of Zubov's speech was, of course, familiar to his listeners. A plot for the deposition of Paul I had been formed some months past, and would have been executed before, but for the death of a principal conspirator, Admiral Ribas. The Tsar himself had heard of it. He had said to Count Pahlen, ' I hear a conspiracy is being formed against me,' to which his well-liking chief of police had replied with aplomb, ' Such a thing is impossible, sire. It could not be formed unless I belonged to it.'

The Experimental Peace

Fortunately for the peace of mind of the company at Zubov's table, they were also unaware that twice to-day written warnings had reached the Tsar. The first had been presented to him as he dismounted outside his palace after a morning ride. The Tsar's horse had reared, and the proffered document had been accepted by his attendant Grand Envoy, once his Turkish barber. This official, being of Oriental indolence, had slipped the letter in his pocket and forgotten it. A second warning had actually been laid in the Tsar's hands during the evening, but on the entrance of a mistress he had laid it aside, unopened.

The nerves of the feasters, although well fortified, were not in a steady condition, and when Zubov's peroration was interrupted by a sound of peremptory knocking, many countenances changed. The late arrival, however, was an essential figure of the conspiracy, Count Pahlen, Commander of both the Garrison and Police of the capital. The Count explained that he had been detained by His Imperial Majesty, who had now retired quietly. His consort and sons had also retired for the night. Unless Mademoiselle Lopukhin was still with him, his visitors should find the ruler of all the Russias alone. But no time must be lost. Already midnight was striking.

Two parties, each numbering sixty, one led by Nicolas Zubov, the other by Pahlen, thereupon set off for the Mikhailovsky Palace, latest freak of a sovereign who lived in constant dread of surprise and assassination. It had been built according to his own plans, and was surrounded by canals. Its gloomy walls contained decoration and furniture of the first order, but damp was streaming down them, for the building had been occupied in mid-winter weather, as soon as it was completed, less than a month before.

The night was calm and moonless. A large number of gentlemen in uniform, who had evidently dined well and were lighting themselves to duties at the new palace on foot, passed through the streets unremarked by late-faring pedestrians. The Semenovsky regiment, of which the heir-apparent was Commander, was on guard. When an aide-de-camp was told that a fire in the city must be reported to the Tsar, he did not oppose the entry of General officers. Nicolas Zubov, Grand Equerry, at present on daily duty at the palace, was well known to the sentries, and also well acquainted with the intricate passages leading to the Tsar's apartments.

On reaching the Imperial dressing-room the conspirators received a shock. A light was still burning behind a closed door. A young valet, surprised in the act of attending to his master's clothes, cried out that soldiers were coming to murder the Tsar. He was quickly silenced, and the company pressed towards another door, upon which Nicolas Zubov knocked gently, announcing his name. No answer came, and without delay he led his party into a large and lofty room, apparently empty. Evidently the Tsar had heard the valet's cry, and made his escape. An officer, placing his palm on the tumbled linen of the great bed, called out that the bedclothes were still warm. Sixty officers, mostly flushed with wine, some roaring drunk, ransacked the dim and damp chamber. Another door to it did exist, but unluckily for Paul I, he had ordered that it should be kept locked, and the key removed. It communicated with his wife's apartments. Presently a brocade portière or, according to other accounts, a screen, was observed to tremble in a manner unaccounted for either by the passage of so many midnight visitants or the draught caused by an open door. The covering was torn away, and a meagre and ghastly figure, clad only in a nightshirt, was dragged forth. Paul I, his dark features, always hideous, distorted with rage or terror, was propelled towards a writing-desk. The heavy hand of General Benningsen fastened on his shoulder.

For obvious reasons, descriptions of the events of the next few moments differ considerably. An aide-de-camp on duty, called Argamakoff, was careful afterwards to say that, hearing a scream of treason, he had hurried to call the Cossacks to repel intruders. He was never in the death-chamber, but believed that the Tsar had made a sudden dash to an alcove in which captured banners and arms were stored, and providing himself with a sword, attempted to defend himself. All accounts agree that the Emperor, although shaking in every limb and rolling his eyes horribly, never uttered when General Benningsen presented him with a pen and the paper containing his abdication. Nikita Ivanovitch Panin stood by his side. One of the Zubov brothers is credited with having broken the victim's arm.

Only one utterance of Paul I descends to history. Like Caesar, he thought he recognized one of his murderers. But he was mistaken when he believed that an officer in uniform, bearing down upon him, to whom he addressed abject appeals, was his second son, Constantine.

The Experimental Peace

No record tells whose was the officer's sash, of richly dyed supple silk, heavily fringed, by which the deed was done, either by being formed into a noose and cast from behind upon the neck of the seated figure, or as he lay writhing on the floor.

There was no blood shed. General Benningsen, who had left the room on hearing noises without, returned to find a limp corpse being buffeted and kicked by assassins, who cried aloud that Paul Petrovitch was dead. Count Pahlen, the next arrival, explained breathlessly that he and his party had lost their way in the park. The Empress, who evidently remembered the history of another small German princess, afterwards Catherine II, made a brief and somewhat hysterical appearance, during which she paid small attention to the body of her husband, but announced that she was now the ruler of all the Russias. Her pretensions were supported by nobody, and she was removed from the scene of horror.

Downstairs, awake and not undressed, Alexander, eldest son of Paul, renowned for his ' heavenly ' blue eyes, and the splendid stature which he had inherited from his mother, was awaiting news. When Nicolas Zubov stood before him, repeating the words ' It is over', the murdered man's child was overcome by a passion of remorse. Naturally the conspirators had taken care to implicate Paul's successor, but Alexander ever afterwards regretted that he had not insisted that his insane father's abdication was all he required.

The sudden death of Paul I from apoplexy was officially announced, and a young and popular Tsar, with Anglophile tendencies, proceeded to dissolve the

The Experimental Peace

League of Armed Neutrality. By June, a treaty between England and Russia had been signed, and the First Consul's dreams of driving Britain out of India had perforce to be laid aside. His disappointment was great, for his plans had been carefully laid. One of his first Generals, Masséna, had been ordered to proceed *via* the Danube and the Black Sea to Astrakhan. Every day's march had been scheduled, and proclamations to the Mahrattas printed. Even the balloon *personnel* and the *savants* who were to rouse India, had been mobilized. The Russian forces, marching by way of Bokhara and Khiva, had been told to meet General Masséna at Astrakhan and proceed with him to Herat and Kandahar. The Hetman of the Don Cossacks had actually set forth to meet the French.

The First Consul believed, or affected to believe, that English agents of surpassing ingenuity and iniquity had been responsible both for the gruesome scene in the Mikhailovsky Palace and an unsuccessful attempt, made a few weeks previously, on his own life. On Christmas Eve, 1800, as he drove to a performance at the Opera, an ' infernal machine ' was discharged from a handcart by some French royalist desperadoes. The explosion killed three passers-by and wounded many others, but the First Consul and his party, which included his wife, continued their journey to the theatre, where the audience, knowing nothing of their escape, received them at first with no more than usual marks of respectful loyalty. The First Consul said, ' The English missed me on December 24th. They have not missed me at St. Petersburg! '

The Experimental Peace

A French agent, in London on business connected with the exchange of prisoners, was the person to draw up, together with His Britannic Majesty's Foreign Secretary, the preliminaries of peace between England and France. He was a M. Otto, and throughout early October, 1801, his name, and that of Colonel Lauriston, *Chef de Brigade* in the Artillery, and First Aide-de-camp to Bonaparte, were prominent in English newspapers and conversation.

On the night of October 2nd, M. Otto hung out on the face of his Mayfair lodging an illumination bearing the single word 'Concord'. A patriotic sailor, whose notions of spelling were phonetic, roused a mob to attack the house of the foreigner who believed Britain conquered. M. Otto, from a balcony, endeavoured to make an explanatory speech. The crowd only dispersed when the motto deemed offensive had been taken down, and one saying 'Amity' had been substituted.

Colonel Lauriston, bringing the First Consul's ratification of the treaty, arrived in London on the 10th. He had been expected two days earlier, and his non-appearance had caused anxiety. It was occasioned by the fact that the superb casket, appropriately engraved, ordered by the First Consul to contain the portentous document, was still in the hands of the Paris goldsmiths.

Colonel Lauriston, having travelled night and day, reached M. Otto's house in time for breakfast, after which he proceeded with his host to Downing Street. Their short journey was marked by demonstrations on the part of the London mob, who took the horses out of their equipage. The First Lord of the Admiralty, from his garden gate, adjured his exuberant countrymen not to overturn the French gentlemen. When Colonel Lauriston appeared at a window of the Foreign Office, bowing and smiling, the populace shouted 'Long live Bonaparte!'

The French military envoy had been carefully chosen. He was a person of good family, son of a General de Lauriston, of Scottish extraction. He had been a gentleman-cadet with Bonaparte, resigned his commission during the Revolution, and returned to the service only a year ago. On the morning after his first appearance in London, a Gazette Extraordinary announced that while the Colonel, with M. Otto and his brother were at Downing Street, such an enthusiastic concourse had collected outside that they had been obliged to change their clothes, and take their departures singly, through the garden gate into the Park. For some unknown reason, a number of those who had given Colonel Lauriston so rousing a welcome believed him to be a brother of the First Consul.

All the transparencies and illuminations which had been lying in boxrooms since the Battle of the Nile were brought forth and refurbished. As there had not been much time in which to prepare fresh decorations, the effect was noticed as indifferent. Bond Street and Piccadilly were 'exceedingly brilliant', and the Post Office put out six thousand lamps, for which the taxpayer would provide. Many a large G.R. had been hastily provided with a pendant F.R. 'Peace and General Happiness,' was a popular form. M. Otto, playing for safety, contented himself with a multicoloured star, a G.R. and F.R. surmounted by an olive branch, a big P, and ' Peace and Universal Happiness ' clustering around a highly un-republican crown. A daring transparency showing Mr. Pitt and the First Consul, attended by satellites, dancing the fandango to ' Union bagpipes ' roused guffaws. The late autumn day was close and hot. During the afternoon, Mr. Fox, walking in Cockspur Street, looking cheerful and thinner, with Mrs. Armistead on his arm, received many greetings. Mr. Fox had personal as well as political reasons for looking cheerful. For eight years he had been needing to consult documents in the French archives for facts essential to his biography of his ancestor, James II. Towards dusk, the growing reddish dimness gave place to a terrific thunderstorm, which, to the dismay of croakers, demolished the illuminations.

Coaches leaving London bore placards announcing 'Peace with France'. As they dashed through high-road villages, their postilions waved caps decorated with sprigs of laurel. Relieved from the threat of invasion, from the prospect of an eighth war winter, simple folk rejoiced. At Ipswich, some soldiers from the barracks issued forth to hug the wheels of the vehicle which brought such glad tidings. In market towns many careful tradesmen, believing that dearth and high prices would now disappear, gave vent to unusual jocularity. At Hull sailors volunteered for the same duty performed by the citizens of London for the carriage of M. Otto. They were not so skilful or so lucky, and after a three hours' passage, upset the coach in the principal square, fatally injuring one inhabitant and wounding others. At elegant Brighton, the Steyne was

The Experimental Peace

beautifully lit, and at Plymouth contributions towards a bonfire produced a result visible for forty miles. *The Times* announced that the unexpected news, which should have cheered every heart, had not been received with general enthusiasm at Sheerness. The Jewish traders of that port had been conspicuous for their long faces. These astute characters suspected that the Treaty did not contain any stipulations with regard to commerce. The continent, guarded by a system of prohibitive tariffs, would be even more firmly closed than it had been during the years of declared war.

Not only the Jews of Sheerness were doubtful. In London a fashionable diarist noted the scenes of jubilation as ' to the eternal disgrace of John Bull'. 'There is ', said Lord Nelson, 'no person in this world rejoices more in the peace than I. Yet I would burst sooner than let a d——d Frenchman know it! ' The Secretary for War had written to the Chief Secretary for Ireland, as long ago as August, ' In the present state of France, I would not give a twelve months' purchase for any peace, however fair upon the face of it. . . . France on her part (I mean the military despots of France) may possibly incline to a *truce*, with a view to throwing us off our guard, and procuring the laying up of our navy, and disbanding the greater part of our army.' The King shouted his opinion to poor Lord Malmesbury, now sadly deaf. ' D'ye know what I call this peace? An Experimental Peace! It is nothing else. I am sure ye think so, and perhaps ye don't give it so good a name! But it was unavoidable. I was abandoned by everybody —allies and all.' Mr. Sheridan gladdened fellow members of the House of Commons by an epigram, ' This is a peace which all men are glad of, but no man can be proud of'.

The Prime Minister, to whom Lord Nelson had reported in August, was not Mr. Pitt. Mr. Pitt had gone. By an ironical chance, he, who had been rather swept along by, than director of, the tide of opinion in Great Britain since the declaration of War, had come to grief on the subject of Catholic Emancipation. The insurrection of 1798 had convinced him of the desirability of the Act of Union passed in 1800. His attempt to remove Catholic disabilities had failed. The King, at his most intractable, remarked, ' I count any man my personal enemy who proposes any such measure! ' In spite of the decision of the lawyers whom he consulted, His Majesty considered himself bound by his Coronation oath to maintain the Protestant ascendancy in Ireland. Mr. Pitt considered himself committed to the Catholics who had not opposed the Union. In the month when the news of the Peace of Lunéville carried gloom into the hearts of many loyal subjects, the King sent for Mr. Addington, who was ' sound ' if not conspicuously able. The new government was said by a wit to be deficient in three things only—brains, blood and gold. Not everyone who took a close interest in Mr. Pitt's retirement realized that the circumstances were equally honourable to him and his royal master. Enemies noted with satisfaction that the Prime Minister, as he proceeded to his last Royal audience in that capacity, had looked much shaken. The taste of the day did not deter friends from chronicling with equal satisfaction that Mr. Pitt had wept profusely after that interview. Paris news was that the First Consul and

The Experimental Peace

Madame Bonaparte had been to breakfast at the select boarding school of Madame Campan, where Madame Bonaparte's daughter was a pupil. A few days later, whispers that his worries had provoked a return of the King's mental malady brought a string of concerned callers, in carriages and on foot, by every avenue, to his London residence. Bulletins were guarded, and not until June was the King able to leave the seclusion of Kew for Weymouth.

The terms of the Treaty which blossomed into the Peace of Amiens on March 27th, 1802, proved a source of annoyance to every reasonable person in the United Kingdom. It was generally recognized that England had no claim to interfere in the settlement of the continent, but Britons had not been prepared to hear that England had surrendered all her colonial conquests, except Ceylon and Trinidad. The First Consul, alive to the weakness of Mr. Pitt's successor, and fully advised of the scenes which had greeted the news of peace in England, had asked largely. Malta, which had capitulated last year to Lord Nelson, was restored to the Knights of St. John, Minorca to Spain, Martinique and Guadeloupe to France, and the Cape to the Dutch. The French Royal Arms, borne by every English sovereign since the third Edward, were relinquished. France, for her part, agreed to evacuate Egypt, where she was already beaten, and Naples, always ripe for re-conquest. She recognized the integrity of the Turkish Empire and Portugal, and promised an indemnity to the House of Orange. The bargain was unbelievably advantageous to France, and France in gratitude elected Napoleon Bonaparte Consul for life. Thereafter he signed only his Christian name, or its initial, on all documents.

In his pleasant London studio, a well-known Academician told a sensible Englishman called Smith, who had lived for seven years in Paris, that he had for some time fancied that Bonaparte aimed to be Emperor, or at least King of France. Mr. Smith agreed, but said that in Paris Bonaparte was much disliked and not respected. Mr. Pitt, in the House on February 3rd, 1800, had spoken prophetically—' I see various and opposite qualities—all the great and all the little passions unfavourable to public tranquillity—united in the breast of one man, and of that man, unhappily, whose personal caprice can scarce fluctuate for an hour without affecting the destiny of Europe.' Even before the preliminary treaty had been ratified, secret agents of Bonaparte had established French influence in Holland and Italy. The First Consul for life did not display any signs of relinquishing the policy of aggression which he had found so successful.

But with childlike innocence, Great Britain proceeded to disarm. Within five months the militia had been disembodied and the fencibles had been disbanded. The Regular Army was reduced to a strength of about forty thousand, and Lord Nelson received orders to quit his station off Boulogne and return with his fleet to the Downs. The new Prime Minister was defensive and apologetic. He was said to have explained that the necessary supplies for two further years' prosecution of the War were simply not forthcoming, and that the Income Tax had been monthly less productive and more disliked. The Princess of Wales, whose inability to joke on any but serious subjects was becoming noticeable said that as far as she could see, she was the only gainer by Mr. Pitt's resignation. She had inherited his first-class cook.

IV

Although by the summer of 1801 England had been at war for eight years, and he suspected Napoleon Bonaparte of aiming at a tyranny, Mr. Joseph Farington, R.A., thought the date perfectly suitable for an extensive tour in North Britain. His companions were a London wine-merchant and his wife, and one of those unexplained, unoccupied spinster ladies who make frequent appearances in contemporary diaries and fiction. The party took with them a landaulet, two riding horses, a coachman and groom. They spent a delightful three months visiting celebrated houses, scenes and personages, and Mr. Farington never once found it necessary to mention the War in his journal.

In the picturesque village of Nuneham Courtenay, in Oxfordshire, they observed a large letter M accompanied by a star, decorating the doors of several cottages. Lord and Lady Harcourt had for many years bestowed these distinguishing marks upon such of their tenants as were remarkable for industry and moral conduct. The M stood for 'Merit', and some cottages bore two and even three M's and stars. Their guide told the interested Londoners that Lord Harcourt had been obliged to discontinue the Spinning Feast held annually in his park. Some unworthy creatures, presumably never likely to achieve an M, had made the occasion an excuse for rowdy behaviour. It was even

The Experimental Peace

feared that at the last Feast, the stately Lady Harcourt, personal friend of Her Majesty, had been knocked down by boors carousing. But his benevolent lordship had substituted for the historic Spinning Feast, a Harvest Banquet to the people of his village.

Next day Mr. Farington and his friends proceeded to inspect the splendours of Blenheim. The ducal family were not in residence. The afternoon was excessively hot. The tourists admired the 'Drunken Silenus' by Rubens, and Vandyke's 'Earl of Strafford with his Secretary', which Mr. Farington thought one of the finest pictures he had ever seen. Five other companies of sight-seers arrived during the three-quarters of an hour which they spent in the palace.

Late Georgian England was looking very typical. The Londoners rolled soothingly past thatched cottages, outside which, under rose-garlanded porches, white-haired women were fingering the spinning-wheel, leathers for the glove-making, or the lace-cushion. Smock-frock and bee-hive hat were busy in the fields. Accompanied by their dogs, harvesting parties dined in the shade of enormous trees. Between loaded branches could be seen blue distances. In August Oxfordshire the harvest was naturally an engrossing topic. Landlords and innkeepers discoursed much on the prices of wheat, corn and barley, but nobody seemed disturbed by the machinations of Bonaparte.

At the entrance to Dovedale, a week later, while Mr. Farington was engaged making a landscape sketch, a fellow artist similarly employed came up and offered his respects. He was young Mr. Constable of Ipswich staying for the second time in a district he admired.

The Experimental Peace

It was satisfactory at Cromford to see that the children employed at one of Mr. Arkwright's Manufactories were mostly very healthy-looking. Some well-meaning people, ever since the introduction of the Spinning Jenny, had been spreading rumours that the children in the new factories were not happy. Local enquiries into conditions, mostly by medical men, had therefore been instituted by Lancaster Justices of the Peace. Most foremen, to be sure, preferred to employ children whose homes were not in the district. Mothers had a tiresome habit of sending messages to say that boys and girls felt ill to-day. At one mill there had been complaints owing to the harshness of a certain foreman, but he had now left. Mr. Farington and party arrived outside the Cromford factory at an evening hour when the children were leaving work. Sunset lighted rosy faces and sturdy forms. The sound of rushing waters harnessed to industry was exhilarating. The children's working hours were from six or seven in the morning until near seven in the evening. At noon they were allowed a forty minutes' rest, during which time they dined. A well-mannered lad of ten or eleven told Mr. Farington that his wages were 3s. 6d. a week, and a little girl said that she got 2s. 3d. a week. The sightseers, who had given the Duke of Marlborough's servants tips amounting to 8s. for showing them over Blenheim, made no comment. As the next day was Sunday, no respectable travellers could take the road. The tourists went to the local church where the children engaged by Mr. Arkwright occupied a whole chapel specially built for them. The children, all boys this Sunday, were decently clothed and clean. On alternate

Sunday mornings and afternoons boys and girls attended divine worship or received education. The whole plan appeared to Mr. Farington to do Mr. Arkwright great credit.

By Tuesday the travellers had reached Harewood House, and admired four large pictures by the Italian Zucchi, a number of portraits by Sir Joshua, two Hoppners, and a house which, while magnificently situated and of imposing size, gave the impression of being a home. A newspaper which was one of the amenities of the very good inn at Catterick Bridge, told them something of interest which had occurred since they left the south. The Duke of Devonshire's horse ' Childers ' had broken a record at Newmarket.

They crossed the Border on September 16th, and amidst fresher airs and heavy showers, heard talk about the price of salmon caught in Tweed. It looked extremely odd to see women of the lower orders striding along bare-legged and bare-headed. Only a few wore shoes and a mob cap. Children, whose high cheek-bones were not yet pronounced, were often very handsome. Inns in Scotland, even those on the high-road to the northern metropolis, proved, alas, much less neat than those in England, and even houses seemed to ' have something very disagreeable to the sense of smelling'. Drysdale's Hotel in Edinburgh New Town, however, was all that could have been desired. Comfortably settled in a handsome sitting-room on the first floor, with three adjacent well-proportioned bedrooms, all overlooking St. Andrew's Square, the Londoners almost fancied themselves in their own capital. Prices were high—a fire in a bedchamber cost 9d. a day, breakfast with cold meat was 1s. 9d. a head, and afternoon tea 1s.

The portrait painter most esteemed in Edinburgh was Mr. Raeburn, whose servants had instructions to display his studio. He lived in a house in the New Town designed by himself; his showroom had a strong overhead light and his painting-room commanded a view of the Firth of Forth and distant mountains. He was at the moment on holiday with his family at his country home near the Water of Leigh. His prices were one hundred guineas for the whole length, fifty guineas for the half length and twenty-five for the kitcat. Mr. Raeburn, whose work showed a true appearance of nature, and great firmness but inequality, was always eager to learn what prices London artists were asking. In Edinburgh, according to his friends, he said that as far as news of the artistic world went, he might as well have been at the Cape of Good Hope.

The daughter of Mr. Boswell of Auchinleck, biographer of Johnson, visited the same day, also assured her guests politely of the disadvantages of living so far from London. Edinburgh society, she said, was very limited. Indeed in Scotland the age of feudalism might be said to be still in progress. One convenience she must claim. In the New Town, as in Bath, single ladies might pass from street to street in perfect security. Nearly every family with pretensions to rank or fortune lived within a few hundred yards of one another.

In Perthshire, while Mr. Farington, obsessed by memories of bed-hangings worked by Queen Mary and legends of the Young Pretender, was recording dark purple-hued hills softened by mist, a male child, attired only in a waistcoat and kilt, obligingly held down the corner of his sketching paper. An elderly woman, who addressed the child in the Erse tongue, explained to Mr. Farington that she was calling her charge in to his porridge. He was Captain Campbell's son, heir-presumptive to the Earl of Breadalbane. Mr. Farington asked why was such a child at Killin, and the gude-wife answered smilingly, because there was a good school at Killin. Mr. Farington was inclined to be impressed by the fact that even scions of the nobility were thus accustomed early in Scotland to Highland hardiness.

The news of Peace with France reached Perth when Mr. Farington and party were staying there, but was not noticed in the artist's journal. They had happened upon Perth in an unfortunate week—that of the annual County Meeting, when every inn and house was crowded by local gentry and their ladies, gathered to enjoy three balls.

v

The Dover and Calais mail-packets began to run again on the 18th November, 1801, and one of the first brought to the shores of France no less than sixty-three English ladies, all burning for a glimpse of Paris novelties, including the First Consul. For the next eighteen months, accounts of the French capital published in English journals continued to disturb the repose of innumerable families.

Two thousand ballrooms and twenty-four theatres were inscribed on the registers of the Paris police. At these haunts of gaiety the bright blaze of waxen tapers displayed the charms of nymphs dressed *à la sauvage* or *à la Grecque*. But it was at official and private entertainments that the *connoisseur* of fashion saw most to delight him. The fêtes of the late court were but tawdry splendour compared with the classical elegance of those offered by Republican contractors. Many fair widows or daughters of titled *émigrés* had consented to marriage, or less, with such persons, who kept them in Asiatic luxury. At a dance given recently by one of them, in his spacious *hôtel*, all the decoration had been in the latest style. Etruscan vases and Athenian busts had abounded; even the chimney irons had been supported by bronze sphinxes and griffins. The *Valse*, never omitted at a Paris ball, had been performed, and a supper of Attic taste served. Towards the close of supper, doors had been flung open, disclosing a garden, lit by coloured lamps, where trees bent beneath the weight of crystallised cherries, peaches and apricots, above fountains of iced orangeade and liqueurs. The female guests who wandered in this paradise, had been appropriately attired, with naked arm, bare bosom, sandalled foot, circling zone and curled tresses. A fashionable hairdresser kept a selection of antique busts on his premises, and asked clients to choose between coiffures *à la Cléopatre*, *la Diane* or *la Psychée*. The last rage had been the Niobe. To dress *à la sauvage* was simple, since the only necessaries were some drapes of flesh colour, a knitted silk shift and a quantity of jewellery. But this costume was declining in popularity, as gentle savages had been mobbed, even in Paris. Periwigs now adorned only the heads of shopkeepers, and the cavernous four-poster beds, fading Gothic tapestries and heavily gilded suites upholstered in floral brocades, which had satisfied the courtiers of Marie Antoinette, had been banished to the garret or stable. Some noblemen's houses, long uninhabited, and now emptied of their furniture, had been redecorated in the prevailing bare style at small cost, by enterprising confectioners, and re-opened as *glaciers*. A *glacier* was a sort of coffee-house where light refreshment might be had during the half-hour between the play and supper. A number of persons, now gorgeous in uniforms, and giving themselves great airs, who under the old order would never have penetrated further than the hall, were ready to pay an exorbitant sum for a cup of coffee or an ice enjoyed in the ballroom of an *hôtel* with an historic name. They sometimes carried on their persons exquisite baubles. Since the costume of a *Psyché* or a Niobe admitted of no pockets, ladies used as purses pouches of Oriental leather, thrust through their belts, and delivered to their attendant cavaliers the custody of fans spangled with *fleur de lys*, and *bonbonnières* whose sliding lids hid likenesses of forbidden royalty. To claim intimate connections with the late court was still *chic*. It was even rumoured that when the First Consul retired heavily to his study, leaving his lady, widow of a Vicomte, alone with a few old friends, Madame Bonaparte, after a glance to see that all doors were closed, would murmur in her fascinating Creole voice—' Now let us talk about the old days! Let us make the party to Versailles! ' Ineffable English dowagers knew that Madame Bonaparte had never been presented to Marie Antoinette at Versailles or anywhere else, and wondered whether the First Consul shared their knowledge. He probably did, for his police were wonderful. No letter, however private, was safe from his eye; he knew how much the wives of his officials paid their servants, and had been furious when his own wife commissioned a picture of his Egyptian campaign without fixing the price. He was said to be contemplating divorcing a partner several years his senior, who showed no signs of bringing him a family. At any rate, this affectation of recalling tender memories of the old court would soon die a natural death, since it must become a mark of old age.

Fireworks began in Paris every night at ten p.m. Gentle explosions startled the scented air, and in the skies above the city arose enchanted palaces, brilliant arcades and classic columns. Rockets surmounted them. A stranger entering the capital at night by the bridge of Neuilly must suppose some victory being celebrated. On his right, the lights of Bagatelle gleamed through bosky foliage, on his left the illuminated façades of the Idalia and Elysium dazzled his weary eyes. The Théâtre Français had been re-opened as the Odéon. Parties bound for Frascati and Tivoli would obstruct his progress.

It was quite easy and cheap to reach Paris. For £4 13s. a traveller might obtain a through ticket, either from the City, at four-thirty a.m., or from the new Charing Cross Posting-station, whence coaches left 'for the Rue Notre Dame des Victoires, Paris', at both morning and evening hours. A cheaper route, for those who enjoyed the sea passage, though without through tickets, was by Brighton and Dieppe. That crossing should take ten to fifteen hours. The Calais passage seldom took more than eight hours, but family parties were urged to provide themselves with facilities for a picnic meal. English arriving at Boulogne at low tide were advised that they might be landed in an amusing fashion. Those on board a recent packet, unable to enter harbour after nightfall, the tide having ebbed, suddenly perceived their boat-head surrounded by a throng of muscular sea-nymphs, up to their breasts in breakers. With clamour and gesture the *citoyennes* invited John Bulls to leap into their arms. Some timid persons who lingered at the stern were deluged with sea spray, but those who leapt boldly were safely and quickly carried to shore. Only one gentleman escaped the clutches of the waiting mermaids and was eventually delivered at his equipage soaked to the skin.

Amongst interesting émigrés just returned to their native capital was Mademoiselle Rose Bertin, *modiste* to the unfortunate Marie Antoinette. Patriotic English fashion writers told that at Her Majesty's last court hoops had decreased in size. 'Nothing very new appeared in the style of dressing the hair. We were glad that no one introduced the French fashion of antique dripping locks.' But of course more than half the English ladies who had rushed to Paris had done so in hopes of seeing something more interesting than the shapeless Caroline wrapper so long in vogue at home. The shades most worn in Paris this season sounded lovely—*fumée de Londres, Terre d'Egypte, Nègre, gris-antique* and *point du jour*. Lebrun's new hat was of velvet, with straw beads. Sable, swan and silver bear muffs were much carried, and in the evening square shawls embroidered with gold or silver acorns, sprigs, stars and spangles, fringed with light silver or gold tassels. Only Cashmere shawls were still long-shaped. Since the colder weather had set in, ring and screw curls were not so much displayed, and grey beaver hats were quite out. It had been observed that when a woman of *ton* entered her box at the play, she took off her hat and hung it up. Ribbons were either tartan or covered with hieroglyphics and known as 'Mameluke'. At masked balls dominoes were most prevalent. Some young men of fashion had adopted very high collars to their shirts. The angle of the latest French collar rose above the neckcloth as high as the nose. Duffle greatcoats had five collars falling one over the other. Some *beaux* wore spencers of the same colour with their coats. All young men, even in full dress and without powder, were cropped.

An English lady of title, ordering a winter velvet pelisse, made with a high collar, and lined with satin or taffety, at an establishment of the first fashion, might be charged £15 15s. but the cost of a seven weeks' visit for a single gentleman, including hotels, sightseeing and restaurants, need not exceed £30.

The *diligence* from Calais took fifty-four hours on its journey, but a handsome carriage, something on the same lines as the English post-chaise, could be hired at the port by one or two families, and would proceed at the rate of six miles an hour. The fine road from Calais rebuilt last year by the First Consul's order, to facilitate the journey of Lord Cornwallis, Ambassador Plenipotentiary, was loaded every day now by mail-coaches, post-chaises and private carriages. They toiled or charged past thinning woods and still waters, through muddy villages and cobbled markets, sodden with rain or sparkling with frost. All were hurrying towards the chief centre of attraction in Europe—the lights of Paris. The young people wanted to see. Their elders wanted to see what was left. A number of persons really past travel, roused themselves from wing-armchairs, stirred by sudden memories of an unmistakable scent of sun, dust and flowers, or the mention of a great house, now a shop, which recalled an ardent host or a tender hostess.

Noblemen and gentlemen shipping their own vehicles were warned that arrangements for steeds must be made beforehand at the port. No horses were allowed to land.

VI

The High Tories were not pleased with a peace which they considered built on Jacobin principles. To them Bonaparte represented the Revolution. The Whigs, on the other hand, viewed with despair a despotism established over the country which had declared for political liberty. Nevertheless, during the second season of the Peace, eighty-one members of Parliament, sixty-one peers and thirty-three peeresses, many accompanied by large families, arrived in Paris. A serious epidemic of *grippe* devastated French homes in January, but the visitors were lucky. Paris newspapers supposed the English habituated to humidity.

Officials of the British Embassy passed exhausting days and nights. They knew that the First Consul was provided every morning by his police with an exhaustive bulletin, and by his librarian with a digest of everything of importance in every French newspaper, except

The Experimental Peace

the eleven political journals. Once in ten days he received an analysis of all books, pamphlets and plays produced during that period. Every evening between five and six he settled to the study of bills, posters, advertisements, accounts of literary, fashionable, educational meetings, sermons, and 'anything that may be of interest from the political or moral point of view'. He could, if necessary, work eighteen hours out of twenty-four.

Paris hotel- and inn-keepers struggled nightly with the lists, demanded by their police, of every visitor under their roofs. During this season their lists included such names as Baring, Bentinck, Bathurst, Chichester, Cholmondley, Cust, Egerton, Gurney, Hely-Hutchinson, Stanhope, Wyndham. . . .

Lord Cornwallis had merely come over to arrange the definitive treaty. Sir Charles, now Lord Whitworth, appointed Ambassador as early as April, 1802, did not arrive until November of that year. He was no stranger to the Paris Embassy. His reappearance as bridegroom of the last English Ambassadress to the court of Louis XVI, caused some confusion in French minds. The Duchess of Dorset insisted on retaining the title of a cold and magnificent spouse, with whom she had not been happy. Wits declared that Lord Whitworth had, in Paris, the same house, the same wife and the same horses as his predecessor of 1789. Less intelligent persons firmly believed that Lord Whitworth and the Duchess of Dorset were not man and wife. The Duchess whose hauteur was pronounced, had scruples about calling on the lady of the French Foreign Minister, who, according to rumour, had been scolded into matrimony by the First Consul only a few weeks before her arrival. In fact, rumour was being too charitable. Lord Whitworth, for his part, was continually vexed by the problems of ' rascally countrymen ' who should never have got passports, and important ones who came over, took good houses and entertained largely, but refused to take the slightest notice of the First Consul. He had to shut his doors against people whose hysterical admiration of the First Consul must appear to justify French belief that a strong pro-Bonaparte party existed in influential English circles. Miss Mary Berry, authoress, said mildly that she hoped Bonaparte would not be assassinated. He seemed so simple and unaffected. If he could only keep his position, he was obviously doing his country a great service. He had ended Revolution. Other ladies echoed this opinion with additions. They called upon their friends to look at the condition from which he had raised France. He was not naturally a war-monger. He made a point of cultivating the Peace party in England. And after all, his desire for colonies was very natural. It seemed so strange that he was, actually, not French. They could not shut their eyes to the superiority of his talents and amazing ascendancy of his genius. His restoration of the Church, his recall of the poor exiles, filled them with confidence. It certainly seemed unlikely now that he would retire in favour of the Duke of Angoulême. France required the vigorous hand of a Dictator. Lady Oxford considered Bonaparte her ideal of manly beauty—an opinion, said a French royalist spy, held by no French lady. The Duchess of Gordon was a perpetual thorn in the flesh of the Embassy. At a dinner, when seated between two French Ministers, she delivered a right and left. ' I am

always frightened when I look at you,' addressed to
General Berthier, 'but when I look at you', turning to
Decrés, representative of the far from alarming Navy,
' I always feel reassured.' She was a matchmaking
mama, and a law unto herself. The Duke of Bedford
had just slipped through her fingers. He had died.
Eugène, stepson of Bonaparte, was said to be her next
choice for her daughter. Lady Georgina, attired in the
latest Paris fashions, and fashionably pale after an illness, danced beautifully with the handsome young
Beauharnais. English journals of the baser sort credited
the Duchess with designs upon the First Consul himself, and thought that ' Lady Godiva, we mean Lady
Georgina, Bonaparte, would sound very pretty '.

A certain number of the English were going on to
Montpelier or Nice and Italy. Although the majority of
visitors were bent on nothing but pleasure, amongst
the five thousand in Paris calling for attention, there
were, of course, serious characters. There was a stoutish
gentleman of Hanoverian birth, with a wise eye and a
firm jaw, who had discovered a planet. Mr. Herschel,
whom the French Institute had elected as a foreign
associate, had come over to acknowledge the compliment in person. Mr. James Watt found the Marly
aqueduct, on which he had advised, out of repair.
Lord Elgin's physician, Dr. Maclean, was anxious for
information on French suicides. Dr. Gregory Stapleton
wished to recover the property of the English college
at St. Omer. Miss Mary Linwood wanted to study old
masters in the Louvre. She was performing a remarkable Bonaparte in woolwork. Brook, head of the London
police, had been sent over to report on French methods,

while his opposite number from Paris visited London.

Not all those who professed to have come on business were as honest as they sounded. An Enclosure Commissioner, employed by the Board of Agriculture, turned out to have left behind him in England an indignant wife and five children, and removed a large sum belonging to Lord Digby. An Irish peer who had escaped his creditors, brought with him as supposed lady, an unmistakable Frenchwoman, of whom the French authorities knew too much to make any enquiries. The party from Devonshire House looked correct on paper, but included the sister of the Duchess travelling in amity with the Duke's mistress. Lady Bessborough, whose kind heart was, as everyone in the Embassy knew, her undoing, had felt so unkind when she found herself in company with Madame Bonaparte. Not having paid her respects at the Tuileries, she could not address a word to the poor lady, who really looked very pleasant, holding quite a little court, beautifully dressed, and not at all assuming. Joseph Bonaparte, whom she ran into at a picture gallery, did not look a gentleman.

The Devonshire House party revisited familiar scenes, sighed at the sad fates of great houses, where they had once been well entertained, now destroyed or turned into lodgings, shuddered at the remains of *La Guillotine* in the Place de la Concorde. They performed all the usual expeditions open to visitors who declined to call at the Tuileries—saw Bonaparte at a parade, mounted on a white charger once the property of Louis XVI, Madame Récamier in bed, and only one captured English standard in the Invalides, 'Thank Heaven!'

The Experimental Peace

Lady Bessborough, like all English who refused to be presented to the tyrant and despot, was deeply interested in him. ' He has ears everywhere! I believe he spies on one's thoughts . . . He hates Liberty. He hates the English from the bottom of his heart.' All the great Whigs suspected the First Consul of monarchical tendencies. He was said to be terrified of plots against him. He saw all his principal officials singly, and took care that they never met. Madame Bonaparte's blonde *débutante* daughter, looking scared, and pushed forward, occupied the most prominent box at the Opera. Her step-father sat in a box below, nearly concealed behind a gilded grating. He always left the house before the curtain fell, and set off, escorted by Mamelukes with torches and a very strong cavalry guard, for *La Malmaison*, where he slept.

Until the Peace, people in England had very little idea of the personal appearance of Napoleon Bonaparte. Caricaturists repeated an imaginary picture of a typical French Republican officer, a perfect scarecrow, small, very thin, all nose, jackboots and tricolour cockade. An official portrait of the First Consul, exhibited in the Paris Salon of 1802, showed (even allowing that M. Ingres was a flatterer) the likeness of an undeniably interesting and handsome young man in a carnation velvet suit. His eyes were hazel—no, grey, and black as night when his Corsican temper was roused! A Royal Academician, who had obtained a sitting during the First Consul's supper hour, owing to the kindness of Madame Bonaparte, settled this point for his circle. Bonaparte's eyes were blue. His voice was like thunder, and seemed to issue from a cavern. On the contrary, his voice was well modulated and most agreeable. Lord Whitworth, whose trials were increasing, reported confidentially to London that when the First Consul got through his manners of ceremony he used expressions more suitable for the mouth of a hackney coachman. He developed a vulgar Italian accent, and could not listen to anyone. At close quarters, the British Ambassador found the First Consul not formidable. He seemed to have a growing fear of assassination, reminiscent of Paul I. 'His literary taste', said a blighting man of letters, ' may seem to give some insight into his character. His favourite author is Ossian.'

Bonaparte's manners were as much a subject of dispute as his voice and the colour of his eyes. He was not well bred. His manners alternated between a coarse familiarity—as when addressing his troops—and a professional dryness. He lacked aristocratic repose. He could not keep his hands still when addressing a lady or gentleman. Usually Bonaparte was rigid with vitality, but when forming one of his grand resolutions, he had a habit of squeezing his cheek with his right hand, or pulling his mouth. His look, grave and thoughtful, was not at all ignoble, his sudden smile most engaging. The consular garb did not become him. He appeared most himself in the plain uniform of the National Guard—his features strongly marked by melancholy reflection and deep thought. His complexion, though sallow, was not unpleasing. He was said to be impenetrable, even to his intimates.

In vain William Wordsworth, all of whose memories of France were painful, apostrophized his countrymen from Dove Cottage, Grasmere, ' What is it that ye go

The Experimental Peace

forth to see?' Great ladies, talking fluent but incorrect French, stayed on in Paris, enjoying themselves, and criticizing everything. More and more tourists, famous and obscure, arrived daily. M. Talma was seen, showing England's greatest actor over the Louvre. Mr. Kemble looked thoughtfully at Bonaparte's veterans, glaring triumphantly at their spoils of Italy and Flanders. Sir Edward Berry, whom Lord Nelson called his 'right hand', was one of a party of naval officers. The President of the Royal Academy was accompanied by his son, hopefully christened 'Raphael'. The Industrial Exhibition opened, and scores of tradesmen brought over their wives and offspring.

On their return, the comments of visitors varied. Paris had been wonderful! The fashions were as Anti-Jacobin as possible. Everything was returning rapidly to that gaiety, splendour and urbanity characteristic of the French nation. A young officer wrote home solemnly after a visit to the Opera, 'The Bishop of Durham would expire at seeing some of the performers' dresses.' A great lady said that at the Tuileries, the other night, she had seen the whole of the ancient monarchy, except the Bourbons. The atmosphere of Paris was very bad—void of amusement, because void of security! Conversation was poor, because everyone was afraid of their remarks being repeated and bringing them into trouble. Consequently, asking riddles had become a feature of insipid evenings. Madame Junot, wife of one of the First Consul's ranker Generals, now Governor of Paris, was herself an aristocrat, but a mere schoolgirl. At Madame Fouché's receptions one saw muddy boots and soiled linen. The *nouveaux riches* vied with one another in asking English out to their country estates, but had not succeeded in becoming country gentry. Their houses were magnificently furnished, but their gardens and woods were unkempt, and their stables often in a lamentable condition.

Young officers repeated stories of finding themselves tapped on the shoulder at the Salon or Exhibition. Bonaparte was quite well up in regimental history. He knew that the 42nd had served in Egypt, seemed interested in the siege of Seringapatam, but had been baffled by the uniform of the Wiltshire Militia.

On a penetrating but less resonant note, French tradesmen complained that, as far as spending went, the *milords* were not what they had been. Even nabobs haggled about prices, and frequented inferior restaurants. The English only came to see the parades, the fireworks, the Venetian horses. They stayed for two or three weeks and then departed, leaving France not much the richer. Clearly they did not mean to spend their money in France.

The weeks wore on. Lady Cholmondley got herself arrested for driving in the Champs Elysées at forbidden hours. A naval officer, who declared that his elbow had twice been jogged by a French bully when taking a stroke at billiards, threw the native out of the window, and then, at the urgent request of the proprietor, ran for his life.

General Fox, younger brother of the great Fox, broke his long journey from Minorca in Paris. He was much annoyed with Lord Cavan, another homeward-bound officer, who, having raised out of the sand of ages at Alexandria, a pink granite monolith weighing one hundred and eighty tons, expected the British navy to bring it to London. General Fox had been firm, and Cleopatra's Needle had to wait another seventy-seven years for transport.

Presently the great Fox himself appeared upon the scene, bringing with him Mrs. Armistead, at last acknowledged as Mrs. Fox. His nephew, Lord Holland, had engaged a house in the Faubourg St. Germain. He moved from it to the fashionable Hôtel Grange Batelière, and then to the Hôtel Richelieu, where many years past he had been guest of an aristo of the most deplorable type. He seemed determined to spend his days consulting documents in the National Archives. He was very much obliged to M. Talleyrand for the promise of a complete set of some seventeenth-century despatches. He visited the Exhibition, and bought some cheap knives and watches. He was seen at the theatres, and went shooting with General Berthier, who was mentioned as Bonaparte's successor. All this was disappointing to gossip-mongers who knew that the First Consul kept busts of both Fox and Nelson on his dressing-room mantelpiece. They were reduced to spreading a story that Mr. Fox had taken tea with Helen Maria Williams, who was a colossal talker and oddity, even as authoresses go, and who, as a matter of fact, had not marched exultantly over the bodies of massacred Swiss in 1792.

Had the gossips but known, Mr. Fox's failure to call upon Consuls Cambacérès and Lebrun had caused a flutter at the British Embassy. Lebrun could be quietened down, but Cambacérès insisted that when a call was made it must be quite informal, so as to give the impression of being a second visit.

The Experimental Peace

At last the great day came when Fox and Bonaparte must meet, and Lord Whitworth, after presenting some English noblemen, spoke the name of his most distinguished guest. The First Consul, evincing great emotion, possibly even slight disturbance, made a polished little speech of welcome, highly complimentary, but on strong propaganda lines. Mr. Fox, who had refused to eat with the brewer Santerre, infamous for his part in the execution of Louis XVI, tersely accepted an invitation to the Tuileries.

Amongst the two hundred guests present at the table of the First Consul, and attended by an army of servants in green and gold liveries, several heard him compliment Mr. Fox as the greatest man of a great nation. Little Madame Junot thought that the burly Englishman, with his hanging cheeks and brows, and his long, dark grey coat, looked like a Devonshire farmer. Not until he spoke, did his countenance shine with intelligence, sagacity and eloquence. At the Embassy they knew that Mr. Fox, who had not at all liked the First Consul's recent behaviour to the Swiss, and in any case was immune from gushing compliment, had summed up his host as ' a young man considerably intoxicated with success'. He said, however, that he thought Bonaparte was sincere in his desire for peace.

Only a Bourbon secret agent was present when the ageing statesman returned to his lodgings after his pretentious entertainment by the First Consul, and subsiding heavily, muttered, ' It's all up with Liberty! '

The Experimental Peace

Messages from His Majesty to both Houses on March 8th and 11th, 1803, announced his intention of calling out the Militia, in view of the very considerable military preparations and increasing armaments in the ports of France and Holland. Soon afterwards, English in Paris were shocked by hearing that the First Consul had been very rude to Lord Whitworth at one of Madame Bonaparte's Sunday receptions at St. Cloud. The *Allgemeine Zeitung* affirmed that the First Consul had said, in the presence of the Russian Ambassador, 'If War be renewed, let all Treaties be covered in crape. God and Europe will judge us!' He had ordered the Bayeux Tapestry to be brought to Paris for display. English in Paris were comforted by hearing that the Embassy was to be spring-cleaned, which did not look as if Lord Whitworth expected to leave, and that the young Duke of Dorset was coming to spend his holidays from Harrow with his mother. A fortnight later, Mr. Stuart, counsellor of legation to the British Embassy, set off in great haste for London, with despatches supposed to relate to Malta. A letter sent to the French consul at Hull, intercepted by the Post Office authorities, had contained a plan of Hull harbour and full details of its approaches. Angry English were glad that their countrymen had not yet evacuated Malta, as agreed in the Treaty.

For Bonaparte's aggressions had never ceased. During the Experimental Peace he had already annexed Elba and much of Northern Italy. He was now demanding the suppression of all English journals which made attacks on him, and the expulsion of French royalists. His agents were busy in Ireland.

Prudent persons cancelled their plans for remaining in Paris over May, the month when the capital was at its most attractive, and began to pack. Crowds began to assemble in the Rue de Roulers, outside the British Embassy, to judge from appearances there whether to stay or go. Still a few bold or careless visitors continued to arrive. The *Argus*, a French paper published in London, had promised that British tourists in France would find their rights respected. The country was no longer the prey of a Robespierre. The editors of English magazines, who had laid in a large stock of French fashion plates, began to publish notes and pictures of summer toilettes. With the approach of warmer weather, a new short coat of many colours, known as a 'Joseph', was the vogue. It was worn over light gowns of embroidered India or Cambrai muslin. Very large yellow straw hats, trimmed with tufts of poppies, marguerites and cornflowers, colours of England and of France, were being shown. On May 10th readers of London newspapers learnt that the conduct of the French Government had obliged His Majesty to recall his Ambassador from Paris. Six days later England declared War on France. The Peace of Amiens had lasted one year and sixteen days.

Once more the fine road between Calais and the capital was thronged by post-chaises, mail coaches and private carriages, filled to capacity. Some unfortunate persons who had come over to collect relatives, could not get a vehicle or even a seat in a vehicle. The Duchess of Gordon and her daughter, now *fiancée* of

The Experimental Peace

the new Duke of Bedford, were only just in time. The Ambassador had preceded them by four days. Miss Berry and party, warned by Lord John Campbell, were lucky, but in their haste or flurry had not time, or were too cautious, to pass on the warning to the Elgins. The consequences in that household were disastrous. They led to the divorce court.

On the morning of May 2nd, Bonaparte struck his first blow, and struck hard. After all his friendly advances, he was infuriated by the conduct of England. He had never believed that the peace party there was so weak. At one a.m. the Governor of Paris was summoned to the First Consul's study. According to Madame Junot, her husband attempted in vain to reason with an old friend, and pointed out that the action he proposed defied all International courtesies and must blemish his reputation. The order delivered to Junot read—'All Englishmen from the ages of eighteen to sixty, or holding any commission from His Britannic Majesty, who are at present in France, shall immediately be constituted Prisoners of War.' The First Consul said peremptorily, 'This measure must be executed by seven this evening. I am resolved that to-night not an Englishman shall be visible in the obscurest theatre or restaurant of Paris'.

The measure was enforced with such rapidity that at Calais the cutter *Nancy* and packet *Prince of Wales*, just in from Dover, were seized, and their crews detained. Sir George Burrell's young son and his school friend got out by making their *valet* pose as a rich American, to whom they were attentive flunkeys. A future physician to the parent of Queen Victoria was not so fortunate. Augustine Sayer, aged thirteen, was obliged to earn his living as a teacher in exile for more than a decade. French newspapers described the haul, in Paris alone, as numbering over seven thousand five hundred. In fact, the First Consul was disappointed by securing only seven hundred, of whom more than half were small tradesmen doing business at the Exhibition. In their zeal, police of both the capital and the provinces secured many victims of over sixty, and some under the age of twelve, who could not produce birth certificates. All over the country, travellers who either had not read the news on holiday, or had read the *Argus*, were electrified by a demand for their papers of identity from officials of suddenly ferocious bearing. Nervous characters who had been on their way home with all speed, but suffered unavoidable delays, deemed their last hour come, and dreamt of *La Guillotine* as they found themselves hustled from coach or bedroom for interrogation. Although women were not included in the decree, some suffered arrest, and great annoyance in getting home, and to the horror of English parents, who had been determined to give their darlings the best of everything, dead silence fell for weeks upon a boarding-school at Rouen.

The sweeping up of the *détenus* was a tedious business, a fair foretaste of what was to come. By July 2nd, a contingent of military and naval officers held at Fontainebleau, were given the choice of residence at Melun, Meaux, Nancy or Geneva. Civilian *détenus*, whose conduct was suspicious, were ordered to the fortresses of Bitche, Sedan, Lille and Valenciennes, and presently service captives joined them at these places.

The Experimental Peace

And there they remained, to fulfil the usual destiny of the British Prisoner of War. They carved 'Rule Britannia!' on the walls of their prisons, got up theatricals, quarrelled with one another, formed escaping clubs, wrote diaries and longed for news and exchange. When news from home came it was not always good. Not all wives had been able to stand the strain of separation. Some ladies obtained permission to share their husbands' captivity in provincial towns, but not all such experiments were a success. Christmas, 1803, was long in coming, 1805 passed, 1810. . . .

As the years dragged by, the *détenus* received fresh companions, drawn into the net from Italy, from Hamburg, from ships wrecked or captured at sea. Officers, noblemen and Members of Parliament, home-bound planters and Government officials from the Indies, merchants, large and small, teachers, students and medical men, schoolboys, rogues and vagabonds, herded together, with very little news of anything but Napoleonic victories, had ample leisure in which to curse the day upon which they had decided to visit France, and the very name of the Experimental Peace.

Chapter 5

East India Reflections

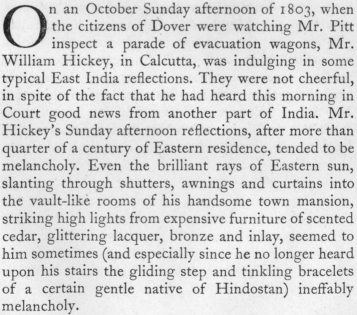

On an October Sunday afternoon of 1803, when the citizens of Dover were watching Mr. Pitt inspect a parade of evacuation wagons, Mr. William Hickey, in Calcutta, was indulging in some typical East India reflections. They were not cheerful, in spite of the fact that he had heard this morning in Court good news from another part of India. Mr. Hickey's Sunday afternoon reflections, after more than quarter of a century of Eastern residence, tended to be melancholy. Even the brilliant rays of Eastern sun, slanting through shutters, awnings and curtains into the vault-like rooms of his handsome town mansion, striking high lights from expensive furniture of scented cedar, glittering lacquer, bronze and inlay, seemed to him sometimes (and especially since he no longer heard upon his stairs the gliding step and tinkling bracelets of a certain gentle native of Hindostan) ineffably melancholy.

Mr. Hickey never could decide whether he felt at

his worst during those breathless nights when the Monsoon was overdue, or towards the end of the ensuing weeks of steady dripping. The breaking up of the rains was commonly a very sickly season in Bengal, or to be exact, a fatal season. To do Calcutta justice, although there was a considerable amount of sudden death within its walls, there was not much lingering illness. Mr. Hickey had, like most Europeans in the Company's service, snatched moments from Court and Club to wait pressed against a neighbour's stairhead for the verdict of the medical man issuing from the sick-chamber. But such calls upon his time were not often made, and since it was advisable in this climate that the funeral took place within twenty-four hours of decease, he more often heard of the sudden illness, death and burial of an acquaintance in the same moment.

Marquis Wellesley's younger brother had, it appeared, gained a considerable victory at a place called Assaye, a village of the Nizam's dominions, just beyond the Berar frontier. The exploits of General Lake, much nearer home, were better appreciated by Mr. Hickey, but everyone in Calcutta with pretensions to military knowledge assured him that General Wellesley's action was of first rate importance and highly significant.

Letters from England took about six months to arrive. The news of the execution of Louis XVI in January, 1793, had reached Calcutta in the July of that year. A nine months' passage was considered an unfortunate experience. Consequently, in the autumn of 1803, although Mr. Hickey knew that Revolutionary French agents had long been tampering with native potentates, the name of General Bonaparte did not embody French aggression. For all that he knew, Mr. Fox might still be dining at the First Consul's table.

Five years past, a French invasion of India had been a general topic amongst the Company's servants. In the north-west, the troops of Sindhia were officered by French adventurers. The Sultan of Mysore, son of Britain's ancient arch-foe Hyder Ali, had allowed the French officers who trained his troops to plant a tree of Liberty, and display a Cap of Liberty on their uniform buttons. He had certainly been the recipient of several flamboyant epistles written by Bonaparte from Egypt. The Battle of the Nile and the fall of Seringapatam had relieved the English in India of fears of Tipú or French invasion. For the last two years, however, British officers with knowledge of Oriental languages, cool customers, accustomed to go disguised as Faquirs into Mahratta country, had brought back strange tales. According to these resourceful and fearless characters, French revolutionary mania was hourly extending its harmful influence. The Mahrattas were going to rise again. Their information proved correct, but fortunately for the English in India, two principal native chiefs were not friends, and the Peshwa of Poona had asked for English assistance against the Mogul Nizam. The news of General Lake's success at Aligahr had been received with relief in Calcutta. General Wellesley's sanguinary action at Assaye was evidently of even greater significance.

Mr. Hickey, who liked to be acquainted with prominent persons, remembered General—then Colonel—

Wellesley perfectly. Indeed he might, without exagger-
ation, describe the magnificent Governor-General's
younger brother as having been quite a chum, although
that word, somehow, did not seem appropriate applied
to Colonel the Honourable Arthur Wellesley. Mr.
Hickey had all sorts of memories of the Colonel. . . .
Colonel Wellesley, most kindly and patiently reasoning
with a young clergyman who had exceeded at table, and
next morning tried to destroy himself—Colonel Wellesley most irritably and violently complaining of his disgraceful treatment by the War Office and honourable
agents of the Company—Colonel Wellesley practising
the violin. . . .

Mr. Hickey, who loved entertaining, remembered
with satisfaction a very snug party at which he had been
host some six seasons past. The occasion had been His
Majesty's Birthday (June 4th, an uncomfortable date
in Bengal), and the guest he had been anxious to impress, a General St. Leger, man of fashion, reputed
bosom friend and crony of His Royal Highness, the
Prince of Wales. Calcutta gossips said that the elegant
St. Leger had come out to Bengal to recruit his health
and his fortune. General St. Leger's appearance at the
races, where, as he watched high-blooded Arabians
pour past, he had murmured affably that the sport
could not have been excelled at Newmarket, had caused
a considerable flutter in Calcutta society. There had not
been such a stir since an East Indiaman had come in,
bringing fifteen new ladies from Home, ten of them
General's daughters, all very fine, dashing, showy
women, all in their teens. Every one had married before
the year was out. General St. Leger had brought his

staff to Mr. Hickey's Royal Birthday party, a Major
Maxwell of the 76th Regiment, acting as Brigade
Major; Captain De Lancy, aide-de-camp. Other guests
had been the Dutch governor, the Judge of the Supreme
Court and the Governor-General's younger brother.
They had sat down sixteen to a very fine turtle and half
a tolerably fat deer, followed by ice-creams, and Mr.
Hickey, who knew that the General was a professed
judge of every circumstance connected with good living,
had summoned a French *chef* to the Garden House,
Chinsurah, to dress the meats. The wines served had
been champagne, claret, hock and madeira unsurpassed
in Bengal. They had sat down at three p.m., the General
on his host's right hand, Colonel Wellesley on his left.
At three-thirty next morning they had all been singing
'The British Grenadiers', with arms linked. At noon,
the aide-de-camp, aged eighteen, had been the only
man not suffering from headache.

Mr. Hickey had heard this morning that poor Maxwell had fallen at Assaye, gallantly leading the 19th
Regiment of Light Dragoons, of which he was in command. The 74th Regiment was said to have suffered
beyond example. It had lost eighteen out of twenty
officers, killed or wounded, and four hundred privates.
Sindhia, well aware how dearly the victory had been
gained, had done his best to get the Rajah of Berar to
attack again next morning, and said that if they did
so, he would answer for it that not one Englishman
survived. But Berar, with typical native duplicity and
sudden irresolution, had turned his troops off into his
own country.

A wonderful escape! Mr. Hickey could not feel

sufficiently thankful that the future of England in India
had been secured by General Wellesley. In his darker
moments, like most of his fellow exiles, he could not
help sometimes considering how few were the English
in this country, how many the natives, how large the
Continent, and that a passage Home took six months,
if you were lucky. There was in this very city—up in
the disused old Fort around the Custom House offices,
a certain Guard room measuring eighteen feet by fourteen feet ten inches, into which a native prince had once
thrust one hundred and forty-six Europeans on a June
night. Only twenty-three had been alive next morning.

Relatives in England did not understand the feelings
that sometimes afflicted even the strongest-nerved servants of the Company on hot nights in Calcutta, causing
sudden makings of wills and booking of passages.
Female relatives at Home liked to display to acquaintances the procession of ebony elephants, the ivory ball-
within-ball (marvellous evidence of Eastern ingenuity
and persistence), the supple Cashmere shawl, sent by
the Nabob brother. They wrote regularly and affec-
tionately, expressing their longing for the moment
when he arrived home to the modish hotel just off Bond
Street, with his faithful native servant on the box of his
post chaise.

Mr. Hickey ought to retire. He had long ago settled
to retire as soon as he was assured of capital which
would bring him in £1,000 a year. He would not be
able, on such a sum, to set up in style—a neat cottage
in a large landowner's park was his ideal. On panting
hot nights he saw it in his mind's eye. It would be very
dull and very safe. He would occupy his mornings

writing his memoirs and his afternoons in poking the pigs and receiving callers. He might even, garbed in an Eastern dressing-gown and turban nightcap, with the dusky Munnow in attendance, sit for his likeness in oils. He intended to ask his youngest unmarried sister to keep house for him. A young wife would render him ridiculous, if not worse. A lady of his own age would not entertain him. Judging by the miniature which she had sent him last year, poor Anne had grown into a regular old maid. Indeed, he had thought the likeness so bad that he had given it back to Lady Russell who had brought it out for him. The addition of a frame of brilliants had made it an acceptable gift to an influential and respected friend. But Mr. Hickey's trouble at present was that he could not yet afford to retire. The days when Bengal agents might acquire a large fortune by plundering natives were passing. Living in Bengal was so expensive. His Garden House, twenty-five miles up the Hooghly, was a continual drain. He never went there for more than the two or three months, when Calcutta was impossibly dusty and disagreeable. He had bought it to please his poor native favourite. It was filled with painful memories of the departed girl and her son—such a fair child. But he could not give it up. His Calcutta house, too, entailed living quite beyond his means. Its capital billiard room made by Seddons, its noble dining-room and breakfast-room, and truly spacious sitting-room (or drawing-room, as such an apartment would be termed at Home) had been ordered by the late Chief Justice, regardless of expense, and had been a real bargain. Mr. Hickey's own addition of the verandah had made all the difference to the exterior.

East India Reflections

And then, when he had gone through all the weary business which he had witnessed so often—dismissed a staff which fell upon its faces and clutched the feet of the Burra Sahib, entreating not to be left behind, made arrangements for a kind home for the terrier, Tiger, got the helpful Captain Larkins to secure a passage for him in the *Warren Hastings*, the *Lord Thurlow* or the *Albion* —when all this was done he might not be happy. He had old, but very vivid, memories of travel in England —bad inns and surly servants. In the East, travelling was so easy. One simply told one's head servant where one was going, and for how long, and the business was done. Mr. Hickey was sometimes not at all sure that he would really like Home when he got there. But laudanum was beginning to lose its effect on his spasms. A horrible couplet which he had once seen on the tombstone of a Dutch gentleman, recurred to him—

' *Mynheer Gludenstack lies interred here,*
Who intended to have gone home next year.'

Mr. Hickey, who had enjoyed a full meal, closed his eyes and composed himself for his afternoon nap. But before he began to breathe heavily and regularly, he saw a horrible picture of officers in powder and scarlet, singing *The British Grenadiers*, set upon suddenly at table by turbanned figures brandishing scimitars; and an improbable vision of Miss Anne Hickey, carried aloft in a palankeen stuffed with bags of sicca rupees; and a muddled and darkish scene, showing himself and friends at one a.m. on January 1st, 1800, singing in the new Century, to the sound of bells ringing; and presently, sane and comforting, a view of big-nosed Colonel Wellesley, stretched in his shirt sleeves on the verandah at Chinsurah, watching budgerows and sampans sail up the blue river—by his side Major Maxwell, with a long cheroot between his lips.

Now that the destiny of an Empire was confirmed, Mr. Hickey would certainly go home next year.

Chapter 6

England Expects (I)

The news of the Peace of Amiens had taken England by surprise. The news that War had recommenced surprised few people. Even the most hopeful Ministers had for some time realized that they had misconceived the First Consul's intentions. The colonial expansion which he evidently desired was impossible so long as Britannia ruled the waves.

An Engineer officer, ordered to Portsmouth on the declaration of War, was so much struck by the scenes that he witnessed there, that he recorded them in his memoirs. The result was an inimitable crowd picture, suggestive of 'Derby Day', 'Ramsgate Sands', or 'The Railway Station'. Only the brush of the yet-unborn Frith could have done justice to Captain George Landmann's impressions of Portsmouth, in May, 1803.

Many ships of war were being recommissioned. In streets and squares, volunteers whose uniforms showed signs of having been laid up in loft or trunk for twelve months, were beginning to drill again. The disbanded sea-fencibles had been recalled to duty. Merchant vessels awaiting convoy filled the harbour, and more, which had run for the nearest port on hearing the news, arrived every hour. Pavements, shops and markets were thronged by sailors carrying their kit on their shoulders, and naval officers were followed by hallooing porters trundling luggage on wheelbarrows over cobbled descents. The route to the landing-stage at the Point was further impeded by the passage to and fro, at top speed, of butchers' vans. The high wheels of light carts, delivering crates of poultry, vegetables, groceries, liquors and crockery, became interlocked, with disastrous results. Near the Bank at the corner of the Point, and at the open doors and bow windows of the Crown and Fountain Inns, officers of both services hung about, discussing the situation. Lord Grenville did not believe that this country would be invaded. He was peacefully watering rhododendrons at Dropmore. Mr. Pitt, on the other hand, had told the House that this time the struggle must be for existence, and that Bonaparte intended to break the spirit of Britain. Mr. Fox said, firstly that he did not believe Boney would venture, next, that if he did he would be destroyed, and lastly that if he landed he would frighten more than hurt us.

In Portsmouth there were hearty handshakes between old friends, and introductions, by stately relatives, of young members of the family about to see action for the first time. A staff officer with despatches for London called for a post-chaise-and-four at once. He could not even wait to change a travel-stained uniform. As many as a dozen attached ladies, each bearing in her hand a parting gift, accompanied some embarrassed Ensigns and midshipmen. Suddenly the sound of firing from Spithead added to the commotion. Officers hurried to the platform to make enquiries. Females who had swooned, or threatened to do so, were revived by being told that the signals, which continued throughout the day at intervals, were merely salutes to Admirals or Generals returning from, or leaving for, foreign service.

Motley's select Library was overfull. Officers, young and old, needed copies of the last Army and Navy Lists. Ladies in light summer dresses and frivolous headgear, clamoured for the latest *Hampshire Telegraph* and any London papers. As the spring afternoon wore on, the hubbub on the Point increased, and all along and behind that famous thoroughfare, harassed and voiceful midshipmen could be seen and heard, collecting boats' crews from dining and dancing houses. If necessary, these determined gentlemen forcibly separated their charges from gaily-dressed but tipsy sweethearts.

Hired coaches paraded the streets, carrying sailors who waved tarpaulin hats and shouted witticisms to admiring pedestrians. With dusk, a regiment came down from Hilsea Barracks to embark, with its colours unfurled, flapping in the breeze, and its band playing a country dance. A one-armed colonel on horseback preceded it. The sounds of marching boots, military music and distant gunfire, vied with that made by dogs barking, and women tugging children, all screeching or sobbing. Simultaneously, troops moving in the opposite direction were sighted, and recruits just landed from the Isle of Wight and Southampton trod up towards the barracks in good style, as merry as larks, their headgear decorated with streaming red, white and blue ribbons. On the heels of both processions followed gangs of Jewish pedlars, pressing the sale of ' real ' gold watches at twenty shillings, wedding rings of the same metal, price 4d., and silver pencil cases and penknives, ' all as cheap as dirt '. The parting embraces of stiff officers and tearful or tight-lipped ladies were disturbed by the antics of jugglers and pickpockets. Here and there a skulking sheriff's officer surprised an ill-fated warrior who had hoped to sail, leaving his tailor's bill unsettled. A pink-cheeked young officer, with too bright new buttons, was stayed with one foot on shore, to offer his palm to a gabbling fortune-teller. Itinerant musicians plagued families for orders to play the favourite air of a dear one already embarked.

At length the expanse of sky deepened from green to darkest blue, and only the glow of ships' lanterns, and star lights above and at sea, pierced black darkness. Captain Landmann returned to his inn to spend a disturbed night. With dawn the clamour grew again. Britain was at war again.

II

At first, in political circles, opinions as to the future differed. Lady Stafford, speaking for the High Tories, was relieved that a peace in which they had never believed, had come to an end. ' So much the better for us ! ' Lady Bessborough, for the Whigs, sighed, ' Poor us ! ' Bonaparte's first move roused the indignation of both parties, though it must have been obvious to anyone who had studied his methods. The Sovereign of

England Expects (I)

Great Britain numbered amongst his titles that of Elector of Hanover. The present King had never even visited a possession in which foreign policy had for some years diverged from that of his native land. In May, 1803, the First Consul mentioned to the Austrian Ambassador that he could at any moment quieten and secure Prussia by giving her a bone to gnaw. On June 1st, English newspapers stated that the Electorate had been thrown into a state of the greatest perturbation by the arrival of French troops at Bremen. The jewels, plate and archives of the capital were packed, ready for evacuation. A week later the cities of Hanover and Osnabrück capitulated to the Bonapartist General Mortier. Lady Stafford wrote, ' That vile, proud, ambition-elated villain! Oh, dear! It is truly vexatious and mortifying.' Lord Nelson, who had always expected the worst of Bonaparte, also expressed himself in customary vein. ' It is really shocking that one animal should disturb the peace of Europe.'

The occupation of Hanover, the seizure of English visitors to France, united England and made the resumption of the War popular. Theorists who had sympathized with French Revolutionary ideals were at last convinced that military despotism threatened them. The War was now definitely anti-Bonapartist, not anti-French, and the least educated understood that he was being called upon to fight for hearth and home against ' Little Boney ', who had a huge army and didn't play fair. To the Englishman in the street, the loss of Hanover had little meaning, but the blow to national pride and affront to His Majesty were deeply resented.

England Expects (I)

An incident much reported in contemporary journals showed that Britain's awakening had not come too soon. On an April morning, a few weeks before the resumption of War, two officers of His Majesty's service appeared in the Row, on horseback. By an unfortunate coincidence both were accompanied by favourite dogs of Newfoundland breed. The large dogs closed in battle. In vain Colonel Montgomery of the land forces and Captain Macnamara of the Royal Navy shouted to one another to call off your dog, sir. Words of such heat followed that a meeting was appointed. Accordingly, on Primrose Hill, in the valley under the rise, at five p.m. next evening, shots were discharged, and His Majesty's service was deprived of two officers of valuable pugnacity. Colonel Montgomery did not long survive his removal to Chalk Farm. Captain Macnamara, crippled by a wound in the groin, was carried by coach from the fatal scene.

On the 1st July firing was heard at Dover most of the day. Some listeners said that it celebrated Bonaparte's arrival at Boulogne, others that the invasion fleet had left the shores of France, others that Sir Sidney Smith was bombarding Calais. The midsummer seamist was so thick that no Briton could see above a mile or two from his white cliff top. Three weeks later, Bonaparte was still inspecting invasion ports. The next sound of gunfire heralded a piece of good news—the capture of the West India isle of Santa Lucia, but to counter-balance this, a report from Antwerp declared that France had refused to receive any vessel cleared out by an English port or any which had even touched at an English port. Little Boney had begun his threat-

ened task of starving Britain. 'You may confine us to
Europe, but I can confine you to the seas.' The captain
of a Prussian galliot, which arrived in mid-August,
bringing the fluttered inmates of the best Rouen
finishing-school, and despatches for the Spanish Ambassador, said that all the talk in France was of the
Invasion, but that Bonaparte's fleet was so closely
blockaded by our cruisers that a smack scarcely ventured out to get fish. A new battery on Boulogne sands
received repeated attentions from British cruisers, and
on one occasion a daring landing-party satisfied themselves by collecting and casting into the sea the mat-
tocks, shovels, engines and baskets used to repair their
depredations. Boulogne was continually in the news.
Two houses in the lower town had been demolished
by British gunfire. Two hundred bombs caused greater
havoc, a fortnight later. Still the new forts replied to
visiting cruisers. A stout-hearted sea-dog who had come
over in the last flag of truce from France was asked by
the harbour master of Boulogne, 'What news in England?' He answered that England was all impatience
to see the French, and had got everything ready for
their reception. 'But sure you are a d———d long while
preparing! We expected you a month ago. However,
this I can assure you. Not one of you will go home
again.'

On October 5th, the Tower Hamlet Militia received
orders to be ready to march at an hour's notice for the
coast, and a grand sham fight was staged in the fading
glades of Epping Forest. The volunteers who took part
bore full camp equipments. A Mentz correspondent
said that no person in that area doubted any longer that

the expedition against England would take place. The tramp of French troops marching towards the coast shook the soil of Alsace, Lorraine and Burgundy. Bonaparte had selected the large vessel in which he was to sail, and even his marine guard. Although he had now retired to St. Cloud, he spent several hours every day in his cabinet studying details of the English expedition. The exact date of his departure was a dead secret. The Mentz writer concluded by promising readers that ' at any rate the forthcoming winter must be productive of very important decisions'.

On October 9th, Mr. Pitt, Lord Warden of the Cinque Ports, escorted by civic dignitaries, made a slow progress down a parade decorated by wagons of all descriptions, neatly ranged. The ex-Minister took the greatest interest in the vehicles destined to carry British women and children of a coastal area to scenes of safety. Job-masters had promised their stables. ' Pickford's ' and other large firms had offered their vans. At Dover, no officer was being allowed to sleep out of camp, and every soldier slept with his accoutrements handy at his bedside, ready to be assumed in the dark when the alarm sounded.

III

On a late autumn evening of 1803, an elderly gentleman retired quietly to his study to write an important letter. Although he had just dined in the bosom of his family, and the letter he meditated concerned them closely, he had not thought fit as yet to take them into his confidence. The letter he was about to despatch was the result of some agonized private communings.

England Expects (I)

Three months had passed since Paris newspapers, quoted in England, had described Bonaparte's arrival at the invasion port of Boulogne. The Boulonnais had decorated their steep streets with green boughs and triumphal arches. Since that date, Bonaparte had been to and fro between Paris and the coast, but there seemed no doubt that he was in earnest. And an invasion engineered by him would be a very different thing from the fumbling and ineffective attempts directed by members of the Revolutionary government which had preceded him. This time, Britons knew, the struggle must be for life or death.

The elderly gentleman, like most persons of his day, had raised a large family, and during the past weeks had realized with dismay how dear and how many were the hostages he had delivered to fortune. For his sons he had no particular pangs. They would be with their ships and their regiments, and in his less indulgent moments he considered that a whiff of active service might improve all of them. His seven sons had long been a source of uncertain pride and joy, and certain anxiety and expenditure. His own plans, also, were quite simple and settled. He was sixty-six, and his sight was not what it had been, but his place would be with the armed forces of the realm. Unfortunately for his peace of mind, the study in which he sat was situated above a small Thames-side town not twenty-five miles from London. In his heart he could not believe that the wicked invader would ever get there, but no conscientious head of a family could leave unprotected females to run such a risk. He must make immediate preparations for the removal, in case of need, of his wife and daughters

England Expects (I)

Although he had been a romantic young man, and he had married young, his marriage had not been romantic. He had obediently wedded the partner chosen for him by a very masterful widowed mother. His bride had been young, healthy, quiet in manner and dress, well-connected, but not sufficiently so to make herself a nuisance. She had not brought him a fortune, but since he had enough for two, that did not matter. Now that she was no longer young, his Charlotte was still remarkable for the sterling qualities which had commended her to his mother, at the age of sixteen. She was an untiring economist. She was always correct in behaviour. She had been consistently faithful and fruitful. She had brought him, besides the seven surviving sons, six lovely daughters. Once when reading Shakespeare's *Lear* aloud, he had been obliged to break off to remark that his daughters were all Cordelias. Even allowing for parental partiality, he believed himself to be singularly blessed in this respect. In the quiet of his candle-lit study, he recalled their charms and differences—Augusta, so handsome, so nervous, always kind . . . Perhaps it was for the best, after all, that his eldest had married. He had not liked parting with her, and his wife had been definitely against the match. The fact remained that when the Corsican monster threatened the homes of Britain, five unmarried daughters was a sufficient responsibility. Elizabeth, third of the beloved group, was at the moment engaged upon a series of designs inspired by patriotic fervour. She was drawing Cupid supplicating Minerva to let him become a British Volunteer. Elizabeth had inherited her father's sense of humour. Mary would have been considered a beauty, even had she been born in a cottage. He saw in his mind's eye the bright faces and sweet smiles of his poor, poor Sophia and consoling Amelia. . . .

Words began to flow from his pen. ' We are here in daily expectation that Bonaparte will attempt his threatened invasion . . . As it is impossible to foresee the events of such a conflict, should the enemy approach too near . . .' He had thought the matter out carefully, and decided that the best person to take charge of his jewels, should scenes of horror threaten, was a clergyman and an old friend. Luckily he had just such a person in his acquaintance. Richard Hurd, born the son of a substantial Staffordshire farmer, had for some years acted as a tutor in his family. Hurd was not too young—eighty-three—but in full command of his faculties, a delightful companion, and last, but most important, owner of a residence safely across the Severn.

' Should this event arise, I certainly would rather have what I value most in life remain, during the conflict, in your diocese and under your roof, than in any other place in the realm.'

George III completed his strictly private note to the Bishop of Worcester, and rang the bell. Before despatching his letter he added a last thought. It had occurred to him that the sudden arrival of a Queen Consort and five princesses might cause some inconvenience in a bachelor household. He was careful to assure the Bishop that the ladies should be attended by a proper servant, and some furniture.

England Expects (I)

That no invasion came during the first winter of the resumed war did not convince waiting English that no such attempt was to be made. Many people who had visited France during the year of peace were certain that the First Consul had needed another eighteen months in which to complete his preparations for attack. England's declaration of War had thrown out his plans. He was now working tirelessly, but he would probably not be ready until November, 1804, at earliest.

Meanwhile he performed two actions which confirmed his growing unpopularity in Great Britain, and earned him a new collection of abusive nicknames. In February, 1804, during investigations of a royalist plot, the police of Paris discovered that the arrival of a French royal prince in the capital had been timed to coincide with the disappearance of the First Consul. Their suspicions fell upon the Duc d'Enghien, who was living very quietly in Baden, just over the frontier. In fact, the prince had chosen his residence and unostentatious style of life for two excellent reasons. He was devoted to hunting, and to a fair niece of the Cardinal de Rohan. He was two-and-thirty, and had been an exile since he was sixteen. Portraits of Louis-Antoine-Henri de Bourbon Condé, last of his house, showed a brittle, fine-drawn young aristo, with the eyes of a spaniel and a lamentable deficiency of chin. He was said to have inherited the warlike spirit of his ancestors, and certainly had served with credit against Revolutionary French troops. He was not on French territory, but the First Consul ordered his arrest and seizure. A strong party of mounted gendarmes crossed the Rhine secretly, surrounded the prince's house after dark, and carried him swiftly to the château of Vincennes, on the outskirts of Paris. At two-thirty a.m. on the morning after his arrival, he was led into the castle moat, shot dead by a firing party, and interred in a grave which had been ready before he stood his brief trial at a late hour on the previous night. The First Consul's action was the more inexcusable because during the interval between the kidnapping and the death sentence, he had been convinced that the prince had no connection whatsoever with the recent attempt on his person. But an example was needed to show the Bourbons and their followers the dangers of plotting against the new *régime*.

In France, and even in Paris, the news was at first scarcely credited. Popular fancy throughout Europe was struck by the tragic accessories of the act, all performed in darkness and secrecy—the gallant young sportsman surprised in his country retreat, dragged four hundred miles chained hand and foot, the ghastly procession, before dawn, to the frozen ditch of the frowning fortress. . . . With royal *sang-froid* the innocent victim had refused to allow his brown eyes to be bandaged. He had sent a lock of his hair to his lady love —'Adieu! my Clementina!' In St. Petersburg a memorial service was held for the murdered Condé. The Tsar ordered court mourning and broke off diplomatic relations with Paris. A Hamburg correspondent told that when the First Consul made his first appearance at a theatre after the tragedy, half the audience left. In England, all the tales that Bonaparte had poisoned his sick at Jaffa and committed atrocities at El Arish revived, and gained fresh credence. He was the Fiend of the Bottomless Pit, the Serpent of Corsica, the Brigand Chief and the Beast of the Apocalypse.

But the crime which was worse than a crime, because it was a blunder, succeeded in its immediate object. Henceforward no Bourbon prince ever dabbled in a plot for the removal of the First Consul, and a few weeks after this strong evidence of his power, Napoleon Bonaparte abandoned all lesser titles for that of Emperor of the French. Indignant English monarchists drew what satisfaction they could from learning that when the new Emperor's Proclamation was read at the appointed high places of the French capital, there had been some laughter and few cheers. The President of the Legislative Body, who had been unable to hold his horse, had said that the mummery had resembled a Shrove Tuesday masquerade. But no voice had been raised in dissent. France had long ago decided that the life of Napoleon Bonaparte alone stood between her and civil war. Rather than face a renewal of the Terror, she was ready to acknowledge every minor member of the Bonaparte family as an Imperial or Serene Highness. Napoleon I began to plan pageants.

v

At a date between the murder of the Duc d'Enghien and the proclamation of Napoleon I, Mr. Pitt's return to office was announced. The majority of English voters agreed with Mr. Canning that—

> ' *Pitt is to Addington*
> *As London is to Paddington.*'

England Expects (I)

The late government had proved incapable of dealing with a serious situation. In civil parlance, ' the king's health was uncertain'. A strong ministry was essential for the vigorous prosecution of the War. But although War had, as usual, united a nation, the prospect which the new Prime Minister surveyed in May, 1804, was not a cheerful one. He had much desired to include Mr. Fox in his cabinet. The King, threatening a seizure, had refused point-blank to accept the man who, besides being the Votary of Vice, had coolly declared, 'If the French land our slavery is decided. The only question is " Who is to be tyrant? " In this question I should prefer George III.'

The King demanded a pledge to maintain the Test Act. Mr. Pitt renewed his promises to the Catholics, and, still hoping to bring in Mr. Fox, tried to persuade that brilliant intellectual to employ his talents awhile in Russia—a wonderful picture. Mr. Fox refused, and all his talented friends refused to take office without him. The government eventually formed was after the King's heart, but demonstrably deficient in merit. Disasters crowded upon it. Henry Dundas, now Viscount Melville, resigned after an awkward and protracted enquiry as to Admiralty funds paid into his private account for Secret Service. Dudley Ryder, Lord Harrowby, who at any rate understood finance, who had been, six years before, Mr. Pitt's second on Putney Heath, must needs delight juniors at the Foreign Office, who had suffered beneath his caustic tongue, by literally falling downstairs in that establishment. Severe concussion made his retirement inevitable.

Amongst the Prime Minister's lesser pressing duties

was an effort to bring about a reconciliation between his sovereign and the heir to the throne, who complained in print of his exclusion from high military command. The Additional Force Bill narrowly escaped defeat. Volunteer officers were complaining that two months had passed since they had asked for muskets for their patriot followers, watching on lonely heaths in unconsciously heraldic attitudes, armed with pitchforks to meet the legions which had captured Holland and Italy.

The complaints of Naval officers were more alarming. On the day after the renewal of War, Admiral Cornwallis had sailed from Ushant to mask the enemy fleet at Brest, and Lord Keith and Vice-Admiral Collingwood had taken charge of the defence of the island. Both commanders reported that few vessels of the blockading or defensive squadrons were in good condition. Vice-Admiral Lord Nelson, from the Mediterranean, said that he had never seen a fleet so well officered and manned. 'Would to God the ships were half so good!' He asked for 'More frigates, the eyes of the Fleet', and denounced Lord St. Vincent's 'Penny wise and pound foolish' policy. Vice-Admiral Collingwood, from his flag-ship rightly named *The Venerable*, mentioned resignedly, 'We have been sailing for the last six months with only a sheet of copper between us and Eternity.'

While politicians at home refused to meet, and gentle souls in country rectories waited, heartsick, for a letter from Captain Wentworth or Lieutenant Rowed, the protectors of Britain's shores endured a terrible winter. Admiral Cornwallis, hugging the French coast in gale and hailstorm, was obliged to detach sail-of-the-line to convoy homeward-bound merchantmen. His only comfort was that his spies told him that the Brest fleet was not ready to put to sea, far less to engage a blockading squadron. The Admiral wrote of a week without the chance to change his clothes, and many whole nights on deck. Lord Nelson, to the annoyance of his officers, would not station his fleet near Toulon. He believed that it was more valuable out of the enemy's sight. The Victor of the Nile, whose eyesight was causing him agony, refused to obey his physicians and return home. ' I must not be sick until after the French fleet is taken . . . I never did, and never shall, desert the service of my country, but what can I do more than serve till I drop? ' He believed the Toulon Fleet to be bound for the Levant, or Egypt or Ireland. In April, 1804, he noted, ' We are on the eve of great events.' Admiral La Touche-Tréville was beginning 'to put heads outside harbour'. A couple of months later, Admiral la Touche-Tréville ' took the trip foreseen ', and after a miniature skirmish, announced to his Emperor—who saw that the French press made the most of the triumph—that the British in the Mediterranean had fled from him. When Lord Nelson heard in August that the Admiral had succumbed to fatigue, he commented that he had always said watching the British Fleet would be his death. ' One thing is perfectly clear. We shall never have a solid Peace until the Invasion is tried and found to fail.'

English propagandists were not idle during these critical months. The idea of an appeal to their compatriots by French refugees in England was considered worth a trial, and a pamphlet addressed, 'To the French soldiers on the Coast of France ' was duly dispersed. It was signed 'An old French soldier', and ran—

England Expects (I)

' My brave and generous fellow-soldiers,

' Your Despot, that Corsican who sets no value on the Lives of Frenchmen, calls on you to be prepared for an Expedition against England of the most desperate nature. Reflect seriously, brave Frenchmen, what has been offered to your Consideration. Tell the Corsican Tyrant that you are Soldiers and not Robbers: that you are Warriors and not Thieves and Assassins, that you know how to engage with an Enemy in the Field of Battle, but that you cannot Murder him in his Bed. Tell him that, if he will fit out a Fleet to protect you in your Passage, and cover your descent on the British Coast, and if he will furnish an Army to engage with British Troops on their own Ground, you are ready to embark, but that you are not willing to be sent to Disgrace yourselves by plundering and wantonly murdering peaceful Citizens and Farmers, and laying waste their Habitations, exposing yourselves to a Vengeance which a conduct so mean and execrable would most justly deserve.'

But to soldiers whose Leader was providing them with opportunities for fresh victories, naturally such an appeal produced no response.

VI

The Emperor's pavilion on the heights above Boulogne sounded to English readers an extraordinary affair. Its site had been chosen so that he could survey, in a sweeping glance, his four principal camps, the town and the harbour. It had arisen amongst pale, salty grazing land within forty-eight hours. This suggested that it must present a somewhat shoddy and temporary appearance, but nothing, declared extracts from French descriptions, could be further from reality. All the timbers and glass had been brought to the obscure spot ready cut and numbered. All the work that had remained for a large body of skilful engineers, was to fix the timbers to a firm brick basework. They had been delighted when, during their first day's work, their picks struck the foundations of an earlier building. They guessed it to have been Roman, and evidence of an older attempt to invade Britain. A battered bronze eagle, presently disinterred, was carefully preserved for inspection by their master.

His Imperial Majesty's ' Baraque ' was painted pearl-grey without. Within, no refinement of modern luxury was lacking. The large and lofty Council chamber, principal apartment of the structure, was lighted by many long windows and hung with a silver-grey paper. It had a remarkable painted ceiling, on which an eagle moved through golden clouds in an azure sky, directed by Bonaparte's Star to discharge a thunderbolt at England. Only His Imperial Majesty sat at Councils. Weary officers, at meetings lasting more than three and four hours, had to prop themselves on their sword hilts. A single chair, of plain wood, with upholstery of green morocco, was drawn up to the long oval table, covered by a cloth of the same colour. All the decoration was suitable for a marine situation, and exposure to strong seaward light. An enormous map of the Channel and coasts was the sole ornament on the light-tinted walls.

In the Imperial bedroom the same combination of simplicity and expense was noticeable. A small iron bedstead was shaded by a green sarcenet canopy pendant from the ceiling. The windows, which looked towards the Right Camp and the sea, had short curtains of the same material. All the furniture took to pieces. At night, the Emperor placed beside his bed on a straw-seated chair, his candlestick, his green morocco pocket-book with steel corners, and his snuff-box, laid on a fine clean cambric handkerchief. He wore instead of a nightcap, a scarlet bandana. His only table was loaded by the contents of a splendid dressing-case, and included a porcelain jug and basin with a gilded border of Etruscan design. On a nail on the shell-pink walls he hung his favourite old grey overcoat and plain black hat. In the adjacent room stood a telescope, through which he could clearly distinguish, on fine days, the walls of Dover Castle. The instrument, which had cost twelve thousand francs, travelled in a mahogany case of its own, in size suggestive of a grand piano. Yellow leather trunks containing three complete sets of uniform, and a store of underlinen, completed the furniture of this apartment.

The drawing-room was spacious and airy. The dining-room, in the extremity of the building, possessed a window bow thirty feet wide, with a panoramic view of the harbour. When the Emperor entertained guests, his two principal stewards had no objection to superintending some of the cookery in the open air. The wines were brought from his cellars at Headquarters in the Château of Pont de Briques.

Between the Imperial Baraque and the smaller pavilions of the Minister of Marine, Admiral Bruix, and Marshal Soult, stood the Signal Semaphore, an apparatus singularly reminiscent of the gibbet. The Marshal's pavilion was in the grotesque style. It was thatched down to the ground, but glazed at the top. It possessed a single entrance, and all its rooms were below ground level. It was intended to resemble the dwelling of a savage warrior, but seen in silhouette against the skies of dusk or dawn, looked like a giant extinguisher.

The immediate surroundings of the Imperial Baraque were purely functional. A plain wooden fence, lighted after dark by reflector lamps, placed four feet apart, railed it off from the remainder of the cliff top. Marines of the Imperial Guard, and Grenadiers of the old Consular Guard, were on sentry duty day and night. But beyond the jealously guarded fence, engineers had relieved the monotony of the prospect by an ornamental sheet of water, on which floated two black swans, and a garden with sandy yellow paths, flower beds, and clumps of ornamental shrubs.

During the many months that the ' Iron Coast ' had been populated by the expectant *Grande Armée*, its face had been considerably changed. Trees from the forests of Boulogne and Hardelot had supplied the timber for thousands of thatched, mud-walled huts, covering an area of over ten kilometres. Broad highways ran through the four camps, and sign-posts, placed at street-angles, bore such names as ' Avenue de Marengo ', ' Rue de St. Bernard ', 'Avenue de Campo Formio'. In the small gardens of their home-made dwellings the heroes of Italy and Egypt had arranged, amongst annuals and vegetables, rockeries, formed of specimens from the adjacent shore, pyramids, grottoes, rustic benches and arbours. Some officers' quarters, complete with aviary, duck pond and poultry yard, really looked like solid country houses.

The *Grande Armée*, through the fine summer months of 1804, grew additionally bronzed and muscular, digging, hewing and building in the intervals of drilling and practising embarkation. They marched to songs about sailing for England, where there was more money than shells, and to a droning litany composed of the strange village names of the Iron Coast—Alincthun, Florincthun, Terlincthun. . . . Commanding officers not only permitted dancing and fencing after dark: they encouraged such exercise, which kept waiting men active and good-humoured. From the noble bow window of his dining-room the Emperor was seen to smile, as he watched veterans of his campaigns holding out their tunic skirts between finger and thumb, and curtseying daintily to their partners. A Madras scarf tied around the locks, or a fishwife's frilled cap, indicated that a grizzled warrior was acting as lady in quadrille or gallop. On most fine nights, large groups of men might be seen, gathered around a rough-hewn table, playing, by the light of the moon and a few tallow dips, a popular gambling game called 'Loto'. Only a few fellows could hold cards, but dozens strolled up to stake rations and tobacco.

The theatre, down in the town, was a great attraction, for good companies had been summoned from Paris. Sometimes accounts of the Imperial Court and Staff at the Boulogne playhouse reached England by quicker means than the smuggled French newspapers. In spite of the Iron Guard kept on the Iron Coast, English spies kept on slipping in and out of Boulogne.

England Expects (I)

Some of them had the coolness to sit between French rank and file, roaring pleasantries at attractive members of the Paris Vaudeville. There were recurrent whispers of small boats covered with tarred canvas, found on the beaches at dawn—fires on the cliffs, and rockets. . . . On a fine June morning of 1804, eight English gentlemen, described as 'well-dressed', who had failed to regain their boat, faced a firing squad. Those that did return, and could be persuaded to confide their impressions, in the quiet of some London dining-room, over a bird and bottle, by candlelight, after the last coach had rolled past, had plenty of interest to report.

The road out of Amiens was labelled 'To England'. Believe it or not, Dessin's Hôtel d'Angleterre at Calais was still doing a roaring trade under that name. . . . Boulogne, to everyone who had known it in the old days, was almost unrecognizable. Only the ancient citadel, into which the second Henry Tudor had ridden victorious, under an archway bearing the royal arms of England and France, was completely unchanged. The Cathedral, of course, had been brought down in the Revolution. Scores of new shops were making hay whilst the sun shone, amongst the army for the invasion of England. The whole coast bristled with guns, and fresh troops in fine condition kept on pouring in. Bonaparte was everywhere. He had, besides his theatrical cliff-top eyrie near the Tour d'Odre, a Headquarters in the decent old château of Pont de Briques, two and a half miles out of the town on the Paris road. He enjoyed playing Haroun al Raschid, and appearing unexpectedly at strategic points, taking snuff with veterans, dazzling recruits, snubbing or scarifying incompetents. It was quite useless to rely on notices in the official *Moniteur* for judging whether he was in Boulogne or Paris. The *Moniteur* only dared mention him when authorized to do so, and every other organ copied the *Moniteur*. He had said himself, four years past, 'were I to give loose rein to the Press, I should not remain in power three months'. Since then, sixty out of seventy-five French newspapers had died or been suppressed. 'Give the Editors to understand', wrote the Emperor, 'that I shall end by retaining one newspaper only.'

South of the harbour, three batteries defended the entrance to the Channel. There were six more between the cliff range and fishing village of Le Portel, and four around the fort of l'Heurt and Cap d'Alprech. The most formidable crowned the range on which the pavilion had been erected. Its mortars were of the largest calibre ever cast. The Emperor had discharged the first 'monster' shell from the Tour d'Odre Battery. In consequence he had been deaf for two days, and many windows of his pavilion had been shattered. Farther north, the 'Battery of the Republic' guarded all access to the port, and close to the harbour entrance stood the famous 'Wooden fort', subject of continual attentions from British frigates. It was not unusual for the Emperor's dinner to be disturbed by the sound of gunfire, or bombs and rockets rattling into the lower town.

The Boulogne powder magazines were near a timber bridge, and very strictly guarded. Wimereux and Ambleteuse harbours were being enlarged by two thousand workers. All the way from Etaples to Cap

England Expects (I)

Gris-Nez the story was the same—an unending catalogue of new forts, batteries, quays and jetties.

One hundred and seventy-five thousand men was a
popular estimate of the troops encamped at the moment
in the neighbourhood of Boulogne, and a Corps of one
hundred and seventeen Guide-Interpreters, all of whom
spoke and wrote good English, were ready to perform
their duties as soon as the Army of England landed in
that country.

The Emperor's days were long. He was capable of
spending twelve consecutive hours reviewing infantry
from all four camps, drawn up in échelon over four
leagues of coastal plateau. He was often seen by six
a.m., riding amongst the Condette sand-hills, scaring
the rabbits. He had sent twenty-seven pairs of riding
breeches to Paris for repairs. He 'skated' in the saddle.
His first official visit to the Upper Town had been enlivened by an unrehearsed effect. His horse, stumbling
on a wooden peg amongst the cobbles, had nearly
thrown him. The peg represented all that was left of a
fence protecting the Boullonais Tree of Liberty, which
had died a natural death.

Bonaparte took piping hot baths whenever he felt
tired, and ventured out again, even into night air, without
the least injury to his health. A humble sanctuary stood
close below the Imperial pavilion. Fisher folk who re-
paired after dark to the little sailors' chapel of Terlincthun, told stories of the appearance amongst them of an
unknown worshipper, who arrived unescorted, wrapped
in a sea cloak, with a felt hat pulled low on his brows. At
first, fearing that he might be 'no friend of the Flotilla',
they had been guarded in their replies to his many

questions. Their Emperor had himself, on one of these incognito rambles, helped them to arrest a spy, a tattered individual, panting and bathed in sweat, who pretended to be a harmless gatherer of camomile. By good fortune, a sharp-eyed fishwife had recognized the fellow as a *soi-disant* mussel picker whom she had once observed to vanish in a suspicious manner amongst the rocks of Le Portel. The spy, who spoke perfect French, had groaned in English, when rough hands tore a map traced on leather from his waistcoat lining, ' There's twenty guineas gone! ' and ' All right—the game's up!'

Two thousand shallops, bomb-ships, despatch boats, caïques, fishing sloops, transports, gunboats, praams and sailing packets awaited orders to sail. But the Flotilla was not intended to operate alone. French squadrons must protect it, and make a diversion at the correct moment. Fortunately for England, the French Navy was by no means up to the standard of the *Grande Armée*. The Revolution had performed devastating work in this service. The navy had always been officered by *aristos* of talent, and seamen accustomed to self-control and subordination. ' Real sailors, old sailors, are what I want! ' demanded the Emperor.

On a midsummer evening of 1804, while he waited for despatches from Paris to be brought up from Pont de Briques, the would-be invader opened the window of the apartment adjoining his bedroom, and directing his telescope in the direction of Dover, was heard to murmur in tones of complete conviction—' Yes—a favourable wind, and thirty-six hours. . . .'

The despatches received that night included one forwarded by the Minister of the Interior, signed by an

England Expects (I)

American citizen, Robert Fulton. The name was not strange to the Emperor, or for that matter, to the British Admiralty, although in Whitehall Mr. Fulton was known as Mr. Francis. He was Irish by descent, and had invented harmless machines for spinning flax, making ropes and sawing and polishing marble, but, very understandably, of recent years had been pressing the claims of his 'plunging boat', with apparatus containing combustibles to be discharged under-seas. Mr. Fulton believed that if his under-seas machines were let loose from his plunging-boats into Torbay or the harbours of Plymouth and Portsmouth, England must surrender. Three years ago, French experts had watched the daring inventor embark in a vessel of his own contrivance, called the *Nautilus*, which could not be cajoled to reverse. He had spent an hour in her, twenty-feet below water, in Brest Harbour, in total darkness, but without mishap. He had now got a new bee in his bonnet—'Steam Power'. 'I can remove the obstacles—wind and storm—which protect your enemies, and, notwithstanding his fleets, transport your armies to his territory at any time, and within a few hours!'

On the night of July 21st, 1804, the Emperor wrote to the Minister of the Interior with youthful eagerness, 'I have just read the proposition of the Citizen Fulton, engineer, which you have sent to me much too late, since it is one which may change the whole face of the world. Submit it instantly for examination to a special committee.'

In a Paris workshop, die-sinkers who had been working overtime, put away their tools and prepared to straggle home. M. Denon's employers were much too nervous of M. Fouché's police to explain to any irate relative what important business had detained them while dinner burnt. The trial pieces struck to-day were really very pretty. The obverse showed the Emperor's bust, laurel-crowned, the reverse, Hercules strangling a sea-monster. The inscription ran ' Invasion of England. Struck in London, 1804.'

VII

Nothing could have presented a greater contrast, or have been more characteristic of their owners, than the royal residences occupied during the summer of 1804 by the Emperor Napoleon, and George III.

While the Emperor made lightning journeys between his Parisian palaces, his Headquarters in the Château of Pont de Briques, and his pearl-grey Baraque on the Boulogne cliff top, George III prepared to leave the shaded seclusion of Dutch House, Kew, for Gloucester Lodge, Weymouth. The King had been ill again, sadly ill, but the doctors shared his belief that at his chosen watering-place, under wide and pacific skies, soothed by the sounds of waves breaking in a sickle bay, surrounded by beloved members of his family, and pursuing a regular routine of sea-bathing and little expeditions, his insomnia, his eye-strain, his shocking feelings of hurry and distress, would relax.

For the past six years the Royal Family had gone for the months of high summer to the little town of Weymouth in Dorset, where they lived in much the same style as most of their well-to-do subjects on holiday.

England Expects (I)

It was true that when His Majesty entered the water to take his morning dip, a brass band struck up the National Anthem, and that a crowd watched his embarkations for trips in his yacht, but at Gloucester Lodge the princesses and every royal attendant experienced many of the pleasures, novelties and discomforts of seaside lodgings. The red brick house on the Esplanade, built by the King's favourite brother, contained some fine reception rooms, and a few good bedrooms with noble prospects, but it was merely one of the best houses in the new quarter of the town. It was not nearly large enough for a royal suite.

Captain George Landmann, of the Royal Engineers, who had noted in his diary the scenes at Portsmouth on the outbreak of War, was agreeably surprised at the end of August, 1804, to find himself suddenly ordered on duty to Weymouth. Captain Landmann, who took himself seriously, had been entrusted in the hour of Britain's peril with a serious task. For some time past, naval and military authorities had been worried by the problem of protecting His Majesty during his summer holiday. The fate of the Duc d'Enghien was fresh in every mind. Weymouth was not fortified, and even the surrounding country had few defences. The awful possibility of the Royal Family being carried off by a *coup de main* could not be disregarded. Five or six frigates were continually in the roadstead, a large number of troops were stationed in the town and neighbourhood, a complete regiment mounted piquet every night. But in the late summer of 1804, somebody at Headquarters decided that this was not enough. Some Martello Towers would provide additional security. A spot called ' The Look

England Expects (I)

Out ' was locally believed to be suitable. It was with profound feelings of mingled awe and elation that Captain Landmann heard from his commanding officer at Gosport, that the Duke of Cumberland had written personally, desiring that an expert engineer should be sent without delay to report upon a scheme in which His Majesty himself took a considerable degree of interest. Captain Landmann, who had noted in his diary the occasion on which the aged Duke of Richmond had noticed him, saying most kindly, ' You must be a son of my old friend, the professor', and every occasion on which he had taken wine in the company of minor royalty, hastened to the royal watering-place. He believed that he had reached a turning-point in his career. Hitherto, when the inevitable question, ' What influence has he? ' had been asked in connection with his name, he had every reason to fear that the answer had been silence.

His first duty on arrival was to present himself before the Duke of Cumberland, whom he discovered after midday, attired in a dressing-gown and slippers, extended upon a sofa in a reception room of Gloucester Lodge, engaged in perusing a pamphlet. His Royal Highness directed him to wait upon General Garth for instruction, and the General passed him on to Sir Thomas Dyer.

Captain Landmann spent two days inspecting the possibilities of ' The Look Out'. The second morning after his arrival saw him abroad betimes. He had heard that the Queen and princesses were very fond of sea-bathing. They were called about five a.m. every morning, and unless the weather was very boisterous or wet, entered the water about six. Consequently Weymouth had taken to early hours. Shops opened regularly at five-thirty, and by six the Esplanade was as crowded by fashionables, and would-be fashionables, as Bond Street on a fine afternoon.

There was always a knot of amused spectators in front of a little printseller's shop near 'The Look Out'. It was known as 'The Caricature Shop', and displayed many typical cartoons, not particularly distinguished for delicacy of sentiment or even loyalty. There was a well-known plate entitled 'Affability', which showed George III bawling into the ear of a stone-deaf and scared husbandman. The matrimonial infelicities of the Prince of Wales were ferociously satirized. The majority of the caricatures were the work of a person called Gillray, resident above the St. James's Street shop of a Miss (by courtesy, Mrs.) Humphreys, who earned a well-deserved income by selling her lodger's work, and dissuading him from intemperance. A romantic story told that the couple had once been seen on their way to St. James's, Piccadilly, bent upon matrimony, but had returned home with their errand unfulfilled, deeming upon reflection that things were better as they were.

The Emperor Napoleon would never for a moment have tolerated within a few yards of his holiday home, on the route which he must pass every day to his morning bathe, pictures representing him and his circle in a ridiculous light, but there were well authenticated rumours that Mr. Gillray's efforts, wet from the press, were regularly delivered at the London residence of George III, and much enjoyed by the Royal Family.

England Expects (I)

English artists had learnt a little more about the personal appearance of the Corsican Conqueror, and a much-advertised cartoon of last winter drew attention to the fact that he was the smallest figure in his house. Bonaparte's relations, according to Mr. Gillray, were all against the Invasion of Britain. On the wall behind them, a map showing England divided for distribution amongst his followers, bore scrawls of 'Edinburgh, for Myself', 'Hull, for Talleyrand', 'York, for my brother Jerome', ' Bath, for my wife', 'London, for Myself'. Bonaparte's brothers, on bended knees, besought him to give up a mad idea. Joséphine removed his hat and sword. Mr. Gillray had heard that the Emperor's step-daughter was attractive, so she appeared as a coy brunette. The Empress, a lady in her later thirties, was most unjustly depicted as a leering hag of mountainous figure. Another recent plate known as ' The King of Brobdingnag and Gulliver', was far from civil to Lord Salisbury's nose. To represent the Emperor as of Lilliputian stature compared with the English Royal Family, and his famous fleet as 'nutshells', was a popular form of ridicule. A likeness of the eight-year-old Princess Charlotte of Wales showed a little giantess drowning Bonaparte in a punch-bowl, to cries of ' There! you impertinent, boasting, swaggering pigmy, take that! You attempt to take my Grandpap's Crown indeed, and plunder all his Subjects! I'll let you know that the Spirit of Indignation of every Girl in the Kingdom is roused at your Insolence!'

It seemed unbelievable to Captain Landmann that their gracious Majesties were not shocked or displeased by these vulgarities.

England Expects (I)

As he scanned the shop-window in growing horror, he heard some people murmuring 'The Queen . . .' In vain he searched the window for the latest caricature of a royal lady on whom he had never set eyes. In the end, hearing various clocks beginning to strike six, he moved away from the window, still looking at it, and collided so violently with a pedestrian that he nearly overset her. 'Hello, old lady!' he exclaimed, releasing her from the embrace that had saved both of them from a spill. 'I very nearly had you down!' To his surprise, the little old person, who was wearing a bonnet of the style affected by the aged poor, and a short plain scarlet cloth cloak, pushed him from her with energy and indignation. In the same moment he found himself seized from behind by many members of the crowd, while a tall footman, in splendid livery, striking the pavement with the heavy ferrule of his gold-headed cane, shouted, with flashing eyes, 'The Queen, sir! The Queen!'

'But where, where, where?' retorted Captain Landmann as loudly, staring about him.

'I am the Queen!' sharply exclaimed the old female.

The unhappy officer flung himself on his knees, and pressing the hem of her dress to his lips, German fashion, made what apologies he could muster. The Queen, although obviously much offended, said in broken English, 'No, no, no! You may kiss my hand. We forgiff; you must pee more careful. Fery rute! Fery rute indeed! We forgiff. There, you may go!'

The crowd, now greatly augmented, cheered as the royal lady scuttled on to her bathe, and so ended an incident of which Captain Landmann was thankful to

hear no more during his stay at Weymouth, and which
he was careful never to confide except to the pages of
his diary.

But before that summer's day was out, he made
another mistake of the same nature. Reconsidering the
event, he really could not blame himself for forcibly
arresting a suspicious-looking elderly fellow in dirty
clothes and dusty shoes, whom he found making a
stealthy advance towards his sovereign on the Esplanade. It afterwards appeared that Lord Hawkesbury
always walked like that, and was famous for his careless
dress. Many years later His Majesty still rejoiced in
reminding his Secretary of State for War that he had
once been mistaken for a King's Messenger.

Decidedly Captain Landmann's happiest day at Weymouth was that on which he went on board the royal
yacht by royal command, to discuss with His Majesty
the all-important question of sites for his Martello
Towers. He was not perfectly sure that he was correct
in presenting himself, for all the King had said, walking
and talking at a great pace, was, ' Well, well, I want
to talk to you a great deal more, yes, yes, a great deal
more about those towers. Yes, yes, that's true. You will
be on board the yacht to-morrow—that will do, that
will do. There will be plenty of time to-morrow, plenty
of time.' The Duke of Cumberland's elegant aide-de-
camp assured Captain Landmann that if the King had
said that, he must consider himself commanded in
attendance. The King appeared to know all about Martello Towers—particularly the original one on Martello
Point in Corsica, which had, with its single gun,
caused so much damage to British ships of war. He

kept on repeating, 'They are capital things, those Martello Towers, capital things. We must have some here'. But, looking back, the expert could not remember that during their twenty minutes' progress up and down the Esplanade—the cynosure of all eyes—he had ever been called upon to utter. His Majesty had such an obliging habit of answering all his questions himself, in the same breath.

The pleasure expedition which followed was for ever imprinted on Captain Landmann's memory. No sooner had their Majesties and two daughters come on board, than, as if by magic, the yacht spread her sails and shot out to sea, with streamers flying, the Royal Standard hoisted at the main, and a band playing. The populace on the wharves huzzaed, cannon from the shore thundered, and the protective frigates in the bay responded, raising echoes from the Portland cliffs. Gradually the loyal uproar faded, and the smoke of the cannon was blown away, giving place to an uninterrupted view of azure brightness. No sound broke the stillness but the murmur of Royal voices, and the rustle of waves against the sides of the little vessel, which carried so precious a freight.

Their guests had to gobble while the royalties dined in their cabin, for etiquette demanded that all should be drawn up on the deck, ready for their Majesties' reappearance. Captain Landmann had an interesting hour, discoursing on scientific subjects with a married lady-in-waiting, and a dazzling but shorter interview with a spinster Princess who, since the vessel had by now got out of the shelter of Portland and was pitching considerably, had the condescension to avail herself of the support of his arm during their promenade. He found that H.R.H., whom he had always been told was very proud, was all amiability, and he was struck by her adroitness in disguising the fact that on the subject of Martello Towers she was much less well informed than her father.

The only cloud in a brilliant day was that by four o'clock, when the yacht was directing her course home, the King had shown not the slightest recollection of his invitation, or the Towers. The dejected expert had raised to his eyes one of the numerous spy glasses provided for the use of guests on the yacht, when he heard an unmistakable voice close to his shoulder, and turning so hastily that he lost his hat, found his Majesty exclaiming, ' Well, what are you looking after? Ay, ay, I know. You are right! This is the best place whence to select the fittest position for the Martello Towers! ...'

It was while he was being marched up and down the quarter-deck, arm in arm with his voluble majesty, that the most exciting incident of this memorable day occurred. The officer on the look-out at the fore-topmast-head, announced a strange sail in the offing, and, after a momentary interval, five sail of vessel, all standing towards the Royal yacht with every inch of canvas they could spread. The vessels gained upon the yacht, and were distinguishable as large armed ships. ' Probably,' said the Captain, ' men of war.' Upon this, his Majesty strongly desired to put about and meet them; a suggestion evidently unwelcome to the Captain. They might, he added, be some of the Channel fleet, or ships returning from chasing the Brest fleet, or again—looking very serious—enemy ships, though that was not very likely. The King, on hearing of this last possibility, doubly desired to put about, stamping his foot and repeating with extraordinary vehemence that of all things in this world he would like to have a meeting with 'Boney'. 'I should like to fight Boney single-handed. I'm sure I should! I should give him a good thrashing! I'm sure I should! I'm sure of it!'

Everyone aboard, except the sovereign, was far from disappointed when the ships were discovered to be East Indiamen.

To his next expedition in royal company, ordered, in this week of constant strain and excitement, for the very next day, Captain Landmann looked forward with far less pleasurable feelings. The King had said before quitting the yacht, 'Well, well, to-morrow we shall consult on the spot about the Martello Towers for Portland. You must arrange with Garth'.

General Garth said he had no instructions from His Majesty, but most kindly offered to mount the expert, 'We shall start at nine o'clock'.

Shortly after eight, Captain Landmann presented himself at Gloucester Lodge, and was immediately ushered into a breakfast-room which he wrote down as 'magnificent', where at least thirty uniformed staff officers and members of the Royal Household were engaged in discussing a splendid morning meal. No one took any notice of him, except a remarkably tall, severe-looking officer called Campbell, who had been on yesterday's trip, and he considered his duty done when he had pointed in silence at an empty seat. Long before the new arrival had tasted half of the succulent baked meats whose aroma burdened the air of the richly decorated room, the company began to drift from the table. He was feeling very awkward and at a loss, when an aide-de-camp came up, and asked him to step to a window. General Garth's aide-de-camp pointed out a striking animal, held by a groom outside, mentioning silkily, ' He has not been out of stables for a few days, so you may perhaps find him rather impatient at first, but that will soon go off'.

The innocent engineer of Hanoverian extraction who had already in a week at Royal Weymouth succeeded in nearly felling Her Majesty and Lord Hawkesbury, and lost his hat at sea, still had no idea that a set of young puppies were preparing to amuse themselves at his expense. The horrid boys had decided, from his looks, that the Martello Tower from Gosport could not ride.

A groom, one or two footmen and an orderly dragoon got Captain Landmann into a saddle which long evaded him, and General Garth's horse, who evidently strongly objected to being lent, shot like a poisoned dart towards the shingle beach of Portland, on which a string of mounted ladies-in-waiting were gently cantering towards the spot where their Majesties would land from the yacht. A knot of spectators outside Gloucester Lodge made matters worse by cheering as Captain Landmann departed in a cloud of golden dust. He kept his seat by clinging with his long legs round his horse's body, in a manner which he strongly felt must be unscientific. Shouts and cheers from heartless townsfolk followed him to the end of the Esplanade. A little farther on, he noticed General Garth's aide-de-camp, with a select party, standing with folded arms, watching his progress. They looked a little disappointed.

The inevitable did not happen until His Majesty, riding along a narrow cliff path, returned the salute of a naval officer by swinging off his hat to the full extent of his arm. He struck General Garth's horse a smart slap in the face. It was not to be expected that so spirited an animal would patiently submit to such an insult. With a single bound, the fiery steed leapt over the cliff-side.

The last sound that Captain Landmann heard as he disappeared from view, was the piercing shrieks of many high-born females. When he came to himself, he was not at the bottom of the sea, as he had expected, or even at the bottom of the cliff. A narrow ledge, nine or ten feet from the top of the precipice, had arrested his fall, and the first object that he saw when he opened his eyes was the pink moon-face of His Majesty peering over the cliff-edge very cautiously, and crying—'He's not dead! No, no! He's not dead! I see, I see, he's not dead. He's moving, he's moving! That's right, that's right! We'll help you in a minute. Here! ' turning to those behind him, ' Help him! Save him! '

Captain Landmann never knew how he was raised to road level, for he soon began to feel too ill to notice much. He vaguely realized that many of the party expressed civil satisfaction at his escape, and that he was carefully carried in a chair to a landing place for transport by a man of war's boat to Weymouth.

His fears of mortal damage proved, to his surprise, to be groundless. In a couple of days he was able to go out, and complete his duty at the Royal watering-

place, and soon afterwards he returned to his regular
occupation at Gosport, whence he was presently ordered
to Gibraltar, and, after an interval, to the Spanish Peninsula, where he made valuable plans of fortifications
for Sir Arthur Wellesley. But horses were destined to
be fatal to his hopes of promotion, for in a fall on the
field of Castilejos he sustained an injury which meant
Home service and eventual retirement to the neighbourhood of Hackney, with the rank of Lieutenant-
Colonel.

He beguiled his leisure hours by writing his memoirs,
and devoted thirty pages, full of unconscious humour,
to his week at Royal Weymouth in 1804. After the
lapse of nearly half a century, he still vividly remembered the unfriendly uniforms in a splendid royal
breakfast-room, and a kindly sovereign stamping with
impatience to meet ' Boney ' single-handed, and the
rustle of silk dresses, and small talk and small waves
on a sun-bathed Esplanade, and a royal lady on his arm
while a royal yacht pitched considerably. But some sentiment withheld him from disclosing, except in a
chapter-heading, that the Royal Highness in question
had been the Princess Augusta-Sophia.

Chapter 7

England Expects (II)

❧

During the months whilst the invasion threat was at fever-heat, the Emperor's controlled Press printed some captured English correspondence calculated to give French readers a cheering impression of feeling in their promised land. The East-Indiaman *Admiral Aplin*, bound for Madras, had carried a mail-bag of over eighty private letters, including communi-cations from Lord Grenville for the Governor General. Lord Grenville, in far from confident vein, wrote to Marquess Wellesley, ' I hope nothing will prevent me from having the pleasure of seeing you next year—supposing at that period that you still have a country to re-visit! ' A female scribe's effort provoked from the *Moniteur* the comment, ' Mrs. —— seems to judge pretty well of the state of her country'. Mrs. —— had said, ' You will have learnt by the public prints the difficulties we are in—subscriptions asked for every-thing—all articles of absolute necessity dearer than ever! I fear lest the people, in their discontent, would join the French if they should attempt to land. The times are sad indeed!' A trembling Mr. Jones suffered from similar fears. ' I really think they will effect it, but God protect us! They would carry the whole country!' Another victim of war-nerves could not subdue his anxiety when he reflected upon the unprecedented good fortune of Bonaparte—everywhere victorious. A third defeatist sought to raise the spirits of a relative six months' passage distant, by confiding, ' No day passes without witnessing the ruin of another rich commercial house. Judge of the situation of those possessing less brilliant resources!' ' When this reaches you,' wrote an innocent, who had not foreseen that his words would blossom in the enemy press, ' the grand blow will have been struck! Two hundred thousand men upon the Calais coast wait only for orders from the conquering Bonaparte. My hope and my confidence are in the arms of God Almighty. Our coasts are lined by troops, and the greatest consternation prevails everywhere.' ' This terrible War, coming so suddenly upon us,' wailed another heavy loser, ' has given such a shock to the commercial world that no one dares trust his neighbour.'

A London agent reported that the gentlemen volunteers of the capital could do nothing without their morning tea. Certainly a vast number of Englishmen had volunteered for Home Defence, but their administration was in the utmost confusion. Lord Hobart was at a loss how best to utilize the zeal fostered by imminent Peril. Mr. Windham had told His Majesty's Ministers that in calling for volunteers for Home Defence, they had turned a stop-cock which had spurted in their faces. Of the three hundred and forty

England Expects (II)

thousand enrolled by the end of the first winter of renewed war, only one third had muskets. The Prime
Minister himself had warned colleagues that if the
enemy landed they would pass ' with the rapidity of a
torrent ' over the sixty miles to London, and Londoners
of authority seemed to regard the fall of the capital as
inevitable, should a landing be effected. The Exchequer,
Treasury and duplicate books of the Bank of England
were prepared for evacuation to Worcester Cathedral.
The contents of Woolwich Arsenal were destined for
transport inland by the Grand Junction Canal.

Could the Emperor have seen some more private
letters from English Ministers, he would have felt even
more encouraged. The Additional Force Act was proving a flat failure. Sufficient volunteers for Home Defence were forthcoming, but not for the Regular Army.

And yet, in the threatened isle, business and pleasure
appeared to be continuing much as usual.

On a March day of 1804, Mr. John Wedgwood, whose
father had left a cool half million, was to be seen making
his way down Piccadilly in spring sunshine. He had con-
vened, at the house of Mr. Hatchard, a meeting which
had as its object the foundation of a National Horticul-
tural Society. A future President said that such an institu-
tion had long been a national need, and his opinion was
evidently shared by many persons, for the Society
founded that day prospered so greatly that it soon had
an Experimental Garden in Kensington, a Nursery in
Ealing, and a London Headquarters office, purchased
for the sum of £4,200.

English gardens enjoyed a world-wide reputation.
Bonaparte's wife had ordered one at "Malmaison".

Her husband had said furiously, 'Why an English garden?' and insisted that her garden ought to be French. But the Empress, like most fashionable horticulturists, was tired of the geometric style brought to perfection by André le Nôtre, and wanted a pleasaunce in the modern ' English ' style, designed to bring out the undulating lines of the natural landscape. A nation of gardeners returned the compliment, and British naval officers, on active service, received Admiralty orders that when an enemy prize was found to contain seeds or plants addressed to Madame Bonaparte, the parcels were to be expedited. To a French botanist belonged the honour of having evolved a new variety of plant much admired by the owners of pedimented and pillared mansions of brick or stucco, set in English park or street. While the Empress of the French had her English garden, English gentry filled summer *parterres*, greenhouses, hanging baskets and window-boxes, with brilliant displays of strongly-scented plants, with velvety petals of deep rose, scarlet, powder-pink, salmon-pink, crimson and ivory; zonal, ivy-leaved, shrubby and climbing, all of which they termed 'geraniums'.

A Chapter of the Garter was held with undiminished splendour at Windsor in 1805, and the procession to St. George's Chapel displayed the usual profusion of blue velvet, silk and bullion embroideries and waving white plumes.

While the Emperor turned his telescope on the cliffs of Dover, entertainment in London proceeded. The stars of the stage continued to delight their devotees by nightly and sometimes daily performances. Lord Glenbervie, entering a drawing-room, noted with interest

England Expects (II)

Mrs. Siddons taking her leave, 'with great solemnity and buskined manner'. Nerves, upon the whole, were remarkably steady, and some people thought it their duty to let other countries appreciate this. A worthy merchant of Bristol, writing in a beautiful copper-plate hand to an American commercial house in March, 1804, devoted only four lines to business, before proceeding, 'The so long threatened Invasion of this Country has not yet been attempted, but we expect that in a few days it will be, and there seems to be no dread here about it. The whole Nation seems confident of being able to defeat the Attack whenever it is made. It is a very fortunate Circumstance that our good old King is so much recovered'.

II

Of course, during the years of acute tension there were invasion alarms and wild rumours. Keepers of Eastbourne lodging-houses reported the summer season of 1804 a total loss. A story that the French were to land in that neighbourhood had seemed to gain confirmation by the hasty erection on the beach of a barracks to hold ten thousand, and another of larger size in Pevensey Bay. Local farmers had received an order to fire their corn directly the enemy landed. Even householders had been warned that the demolition of their homes might be a military necessity.

The Rev. Thomas Twining, translator of Aristotle's *Poetics*, fled from Essex. 'I suppose you will not ask me why I leave Colchester. I leave it because I am afraid to stay in it. Many have left, more are preparing to leave it. Though I myself think there is very little danger, yet I should be very uneasy to stay here and run the risk. And if I stay here till the moment of the alarm upon the coast, I may not be able to get away at all, unless I walk away with a knapsack on my back.'

Mr. Fox, in a letter from St. Anne's Hill to his military brother in Ireland, though characteristically critical of Government preparations, added, ' We have begun our harvest here—as some suppose for Bonaparte, but I am as stout as a Lyon'.

The Emperor, according to popular belief, was perfectly prepared to sacrifice one hundred gunboats and ten thousand troops. A thrilling, but not well attested rumour, declared that he had under construction a monster bridge, by which his troops were to pass from Calais to Dover, directed by skilled officers in air balloons, and a Channel Tunnel, engineered by a mining expert. The most dramatic tale was that the Emperor, disguised as a British tar, was aboard a south coast fishing smack. He patrolled England's shores by night, and during the hours of daylight spied ashore.

A Mr. Neild, on holiday in Wales, was very nearly lodged in gaol by mistake for the Fiend of the Bottomless Pit. The townsfolk of Radnor believed that Bonaparte had escaped from a France hostile to his schemes, and was lurking disguised in Welsh mountains. Mr. Neild assured a crowd of Welsh ladies, ' buzzing ' in their native tongue, that he was old enough to be Bonaparte's father. One of them said that she believed he was not the Emperor. She had been observing his features from the moment he entered the town, and he did not squint. Bonaparte squinted horribly, as every

England Expects (II)

Welsh lady knew, since he had been born in the Principality and two of his brothers transported.

Dr. Johnson's old friend, Mrs. Piozzi, also a visitor to Wales, writing to London for an up-to-date Annual Register, took a detached intellectual view. ' I wish to be told likewise what Publications attract Notice, and how the World stands towards the new War. We have a strange Antagonist, it must be confessed, and his Conduct wholly *new* so far as I have been conversant in Historic Annals. But if Bonaparte shows more Sincerity than Discretion, our King certainly shews Europe a true Model of Dignity, Tempered with Moderation. There is a wide Door open yet for Peace.' Her only underlined paragraph disclosed 'WE HAVE NO COOK', a subject which occupied the principal place in her epistle.

In East Anglia, a peeress of less domestic tastes wished to raise an Amazon corps. Lady Jerningham thought that the women of threatened Norfolk should be allowed to enrol in the militia.

All able-bodied males, aged between fifteen and sixty, had been called upon to enrol in their parish for some form of national service. People living within fifteen miles of the coast had been provided with instructions for ' driving the Country ' as they retired inland, and routes were planned by which all livestock should be removed. Bodies of from twenty-five to thirty volunteers were ready to assist the regular military by ' desultory warfare', and Pioneer companies, of from twenty-five to seventy-five men, armed with axes, spades and bill-hooks, were detailed to clear or obstruct routes. Seventy-four Martello Towers, of uniform circular shape, thirty feet high had been erected at strategic points along the coast. Their construction was solid. Their brick walls were nine feet thick, facing the sea, six feet on the landward side. Their lower storeys contained powder magazines and warehouses. Each was armed with a swivel gun and a couple of howitzers.

In the event of Invasion, the Press was instructed to publish no accounts of the movements of troops, either friendly or enemy, except by authority of the Secretary of State, who engaged himself to issue an official bulletin twice a day.

Throughout the country the beacons were ready and manned. Open-mouthed school children watched the steady progress up to local view-points, of wagons loaded with cord-wood, tar barrels and faggots. By night, a fire of such material would be used. By day, wet hay was expected to produce the necessary column of thick smoke. On more than one occasion beacons were fired by mistake. On the night of February 2nd, 1804, some accidental fires in adjacent heights of Northumberland were sighted by a watcher at Home Castle, who promptly lighted his beacon. The signal was at once taken up and transmitted to the lovely valleys of the Border. If the beacon at St. Abb's Head had been lit, all Scotland would have sprung to arms. But the watchers at St. Abb's Head reasoned that if there had been a landing on the east coast, the alarm should have come along the shore, and not from inland.

Mr. Walter Scott, who had seriously commenced the business of author, was proud of the response of the men of Liddesdale, who, fearful of being the last at the *rendezvous*, seized all the horses upon which they could lay hands, and when they had reached their goal turned their borrowed steeds loose to find their own wise ways home through the winter mosses and hills. All reached their stables safely. Two members of the corps chanced to be in Edinburgh on private business. The bride of one and the widowed mother of the other, sent their uniforms and chargers to meet them at Dalkeith. Mr. Scott was much struck by the answer made to him by the widow, when he complimented her on her promptitude to equip her son to meet the invader. She might, he thought, have considered that he had a fair excuse for absence. ' Sir,' replied she, with the look of a Roman matron, ' none can know better than you that my son is the only prop by which, since his father's death, our family is supported. But I would rather see him dead on that hearth than hear that he had been a horse's length behind his companions in the defence of His King and Country.'

Mr. Scott's French lady was not romantic, but he had known that before his wedding-day. After seven years of marriage she was still also quite obviously not British. However, he had a promising brood of what he called ' prattlers ', with whom he sported on holiday at riverside resorts of lovely name—Lasswade, Ashestiel . . . The children came running in, disturbing him at his writing, to ask such innocencies as ' would there be daisies again next year? ' In his handsome son he hoped that he saw a future cavalry officer. His elder little girl was decidedly romantic. Lady Dalkeith, who dominated the Border landscape as unmistakably as her feudal residence, had suggested a local legend to Mr. Scott, as a subject for a narrative poem. National sen-

timent flowed from his pen as he obeyed the gracious
lady—

> *O, Caledonia ! stern and wild,*
> *Meet nurse for a poetic child !*
> *Breathes there a man, with soul so dead,*
> *Who never to himself has said,*
> *This is my own, my native land . . .*
> *Land of brown heath and shaggy wood,*
> *Land of the mountain and the flood,*
> *Land of my sires ! what mortal hand*
> *Can e'er untie the filial band*
> *That knits me to thy rugged strand . . .*

Mr. Scott never forgot the false alarm of invasion
which disturbed the first anniversary of the birth of his
daughter Anne. Fifteen years later, he introduced the
circumstances into one of his inimitable sketches of
Scottish country life. The elderly hero of his novel was
an Antiquary of a type familiar to him. He depicted
the old gentleman, ' his head wrapped warm in two
double nightcaps', woken by the screams of a sister, a
niece and two maidservants. Starting up in his bed, the
Antiquary exclaimed, ' Womenkind in my room at
this hour of night! Are ye all mad?'

' The beacon, uncle! ' said Miss McIntyre.

' The French coming to murder us! ' screamed Miss
Griselda.

' The beacon, the beacon! The French, the French!
Murder, murder! and waur than murder! ' cried the
two handmaidens like the chorus of an opera.

Armed with the sword which his father had worn in

England Expects (II)

the Rising of 1745, the agitated Antiquary proceeded to the marketplace of the little town of Fairport, and the final chapter of the novel included a fine crowd scene, with bells ringing, drums and fifes beating, yeomanry coming in under the command of aged noblemen, and fishwives with shawls over their heads, running down to the harbour where ship lights pierced the midnight blue, as men and guns were landed to assist in the defence. Every important character in the book obligingly rushed to the *rendezvous*, and showed himself in an heroic light. The curtain descended soon after a post-chaise drew up in the square, and amongst cheers from the inhabitants, the brave major come to lead the opposition to the invader proved to be the long-lost Lord Geraldin.

In quite another part of Great Britain, another author, on a visit to his birthplace, was startled by the midnight arrival in his bedroom of an undergraduate son, destined for Holy Orders, who kindly said, ' Do not be alarmed, but the French are landing. The drum on the quay is beating to arms'. After a moment's reflection, Mr. Crabbe, senior, answered with equal calm, ' Well, you and I can do no good, or we would be amongst them. We must wait the event'. He thereupon fell asleep again.

Britain's authors, in her hour of peril, were pronouncedly pro-British. Mr. Southey was noisily patriotic. Mr. Coleridge had personal reasons for anti-Bonapartist feeling. ' In 1803 I was a specified object of Bonaparte's resentment—during my residence in Italy —in consequence of essays in *The Morning Post* . . . I was warned by Humboldt, and, indirectly, by Cardinal

Fesch. An order for my arrest was sent from Paris, from which I was rescued by the kindness of a noble Benedictine, and the gracious connivance of that good old man, the present Pope. . . .' Cynical fellow writers said that Mr. Coleridge's imagination had, as usual, run away with him, but the poet remained darkly triumphant. As the War years dragged by, Mr. Wordsworth waxed more and more gloomily magnificent—

> *Another year, another deadly blow !*
> *Another mighty empire overthrown !*

Two members of the younger generation, both of aristocratic birth, were anti-Bonapartist for quite different reasons. Sir Timothy Shelley's problem child, who had been dismissed from Oxford University for his atheistical pamphlet, was against all existing institutions and contemporary politicians and war. Lord Byron, although like Mr. Scott, alive to the grandiose in the Napoleonic conception, loathed a despot.

The City of Oxford ranked high amongst the victims of war rumours during the years of the invasion threat. In Christmas week of 1805, the town was surprised by the sudden pealing of joy-bells. The Mayor had received a packet, bearing the official seal of the Treasury, which announced to him the defeat of the entire French Army, and the death of Bonaparte. But before ' more solid demonstrations of relief ' were ordered, someone drew the Mayor's attention to the fact that the despatch from London was not signed and that the seal had been ' curiously cut ' from some other envelope. There is no evidence that Town accused Gown of ' the very reprehensible hoax' played off at a date when most undergraduates could plead an alibi.

III

The Emperor's first notable attempt at pageantry, designed to fill the eye and stimulate the spirit of an obedient people, was really a rehearsal for others on a much larger scale which were to follow shortly.

His distribution of Stars of his newly-founded Legion of Honour, in the chapel of the Invalides, in July, 1804, did not arouse much interest in England. A few weeks later, a much more magnificent spectacle was staged in his camp at Boulogne. He had chosen his birthday, August 15th, for the fête at which he was to review the army for the Invasion of Britain, and personally present Crosses of the Legion. Full accounts of this day's happenings crossed the Channel, and Englishmen read with varied feelings the address of their Leader to eighty thousand men of the Army of England, and sycophantic descriptions of the colossal camp on the pale-coloured cliffs facing their island, the dazzling weather of the historic morning, and the grace and elegance added to the occasion by the arrival of the Empress and her ladies. The Corsican Conqueror had sat upon the antique chair of Dagobert, raised by twelve steps above his saluting base. The helm of Du Guesclin, the shield of Bayard, had been forwarded from Paris to deck his throne, which was backed by a curtain of two hundred standards and banners, bullet-ridden, tattered, and stained with the blood of the heroes of Arcola, Lodi, Marengo and other victories.

England Expects (II)

In the middle distance, however, British ships had been persistently visible, and it was some satisfaction to English readers to learn that the dénouement of the ceremony had been marred by an accident to a French Fleet, designed to make a dramatic appearance towards the close of the proceedings, and that punctually at six p.m. torrents of rain had descended upon the tents in which the soldiers of the Army of England had just seated themselves to a banquet. The fireworks had to be postponed, but ladies slippered through mud and gale to a Ball. On November 6th the Emperor laid the foundation stone of a colossal Column of the Grand Army, destined to be topped by a figure of himself in classic costume, visible to every Englishman approaching Boulogne by sea. On December 2nd he passed to his Coronation by the Pope in the Cathedral of Notre Dame.

The mushroom Potentate's pompous coronation was naturally the subject of much criticism and rumour in England. He had succeeded in getting the saintly Pius VII to travel from Rome to Paris to deck his triumph. Not above a dozen of the performers in the thoroughly theatrical performance planned by him had previous knowledge of court etiquette. He was paying the husband of a well-known actress 2,400 francs for performing the duties of stage-manager. At the last moment he had decided that the Empress too must be crowned. No queen consort of France had been so honoured for centuries. The coronation of Marie de Medici had been an unhappy exception. At the last moment, also, Madame Bonaparte had tearfully confessed to the Holy Father that she was no more than the legalized concu-

England Expects (II)

bine of the Conqueror. Only a revolutionary civil ceremony united them. A hasty and private religious marriage had taken place at the Tuileries on the eve of the Coronation. Joséphine had been very clever. The Emperor had been trapped. Alternatively the Emperor had been willing. The Pope had been the victim. Or again, the Pope had stood firm, and the Imperial couple cut a ridiculous figure. It was difficult, in England, to judge, since French papers often took twelve days to penetrate winter weather and war conditions, and Dutch news outstripped them by only two or three days.

English caricaturists waxed ribald at the expense of *L'Impératrice* (*l'impure actrice*). Little was known in England, or for that matter in France, of her adventures before the Revolution. She had been married very young, and separated from her husband. After 1788, however, her situation as financial dependant of several well-known men had been notorious. The Pope, ' poor weak old man! ' had known so little about her, that he had addressed his thanks for a magnificent gift to his dear daughter 'Victoire, Empress of the French'. Joséphine, who was no needlewoman, had not put a stitch into the *rochet* of lace sent to Rome in her name. Her husband had paid Messrs. Vanderbocht, Keith and Co., 7,111 francs for its creation.

The Emperor had settled the matter of his partner's coronation by declaring that he would perform it himself. Many English believed that in his heart he considered the whole ceremony mere mummery. He had a low opinion of the Paris crowd, and had said that it needed to be amused and awed. Other readers insisted that Bonaparte set great store on the mystical rites of his consecration as a sovereign by the supreme Catholic Pontiff. He thought that henceforward he would rank as the equal of every crowned head in Europe.

He had sent to Aix la Chapelle for the insignia used at coronations of Holy Roman Emperors. The greater part of them were unavailable. They were kept at Nuremberg. Only a plain sword was forwarded. The Abbey of St. Denis should have been in possession of the crown, sword, sceptre, Hand of Justice and spurs of Charlemagne, but authorities there had to report losses. The crown and sword had disappeared during the Revolution. The appearance of the sceptre and Hand of Justice, preserved in the *Cabinet des Antiques* of the Capital, disappointed the Emperor. He saw at a glance that goldsmiths of the reign of Charlemagne had not known their business. He had no fancy for flawed stones deep sunk in faded gold. He ordered a new shaft for the Hand of Justice, and the plain sword from Aix. Almost at once, two further swords of Charlemagne were presented for his inspection—one a hiltless blade, the other entire. He chose the finished article, regardless of the pronouncements of antiquaries, whose pebble-eyes softened at the sight of a piece of fine metalwork at least eight centuries old. Charlemagne's reputed spurs were inadmissible. The *fleur de lys* were too plain upon them. Eventually the Emperor ordered a complete new set of regal ornaments from his Court jewellers, Messieurs Biennais, at the sign of The Violet Monkey, Rue St. Honoré.

A new dynasty called for new insignia. His embroiderers were commanded to deck many yards of Tyrian purple velvet with golden Bees, and crowned initials N. and J. Nobody exactly knew whether he was influenced by the antiquaries' report that the Bee had been a favourite emblem of Chilperic and Louis XII. The Grand Master of the Ceremonies objected to the Bees. He styled them 'ludicrous', but Bonaparte continued to order them. He sat in solemn council as to whether the cock, the elephant, the lion or the eagle should be adopted as his heraldic emblem. He chose the spread eagle; and for the Imperial liveries, green, a colour hitherto deemed unfortunate.

The Pope's arrival was delayed. The Coronation was postponed from November 9th to November 29th—to December 2nd. The Emperor sent word that unless the Pope arrived by the third date, the Coronation would take place without him. On November 25th the much harassed Pontiff reached Fontainebleau. At last the scene was set, and the actors as ready as they were ever likely to be.

The royal procession had been cut down to thirty carriages, so that its progress should not occupy more than an hour. Notre Dame and neighbourhood had endured considerable reconstruction, so that over twenty thousand official spectators could be accommodated. The chapel of the Ancient Chapter had to go, a number of private houses and the choirboys' schools. The Clerk of the Works regretted that only time prevented his demolition of the complete *Hospice* of the Rue du Parvis.

The work went on by torchlight, as well as daylight. Two altars and a screen were removed from the interior of the cathedral, and its dark-blue gloom echoed to the sound of carpenters erecting tier upon tier of timber platforms and galleries, from many of which no view whatever of Imperial figures would be obtainable. Gradually in English newspapers para-graphs about the impending pageant were headed simply *The Coronation*.

December 2nd, 1804, dawned fine in Paris, but with a biting wind and heavy skies. From dusk on the pre-vious evening, hourly salvoes of artillery and discharges of coloured Bengal lights had kept the city awake. Theatres had been open free, and military bands had paraded the streets. Thirty-seven cartloads of river sand had been cast upon mirey portions of the route. Before six a.m. ticket-holders had been trying to reach their seats in the cathedral. Snow had fallen during the night, and had not thawed. Workmen were still hammering. Several streets leading to Notre Dame were blocked by sightseers. Windows to view the procession only had been let for three or four pounds, a balcony cost five hundred francs. The Prefect of the Police had closed the Place du Parvis to all carriages except those of the Imperial, Papal, and Arch-Chancellor's processions. Many shivering ladies, attired in low-necked, high-waisted satin gowns with elbow sleeves, had to dis-mount from their equipages and finish their journey on foot. Many gentlemen in skin-tight breeches, silk stockings and coats glittering with embroidery and orders, looked pinched as they picked their way through narrow and odorous alleys, in which wits of the slums waxed merry at their expense. At nine a.m. the Pope, in a gilded and painted coach, formerly the property of the Empress, but appropriately refur-bished, left the Carrousel. His procession gained no applause in the streets. Few heads were uncovered. No-body knelt on the frozen cobbles. But the crowd had been kept off large portions of the route by strong detachments of military. The Emperor's Chief of Police was determined that no ' incident ' should occur to-day. Pius VII performed his journey, and was reverentially conducted to his appointed throne, but ten o'clock had sounded before artillery announced the departure of their Imperial majesties from the Tuileries, and not until after eleven did the ceremony begin.

Mr. Gillray's caricature of what followed had a great success in England. He depicted M. Talleyrand limping at the head of the cortège, borne down by the weight of the documents attesting his master's lineage. The Pope was followed by Cardinal Fesch, waving incense before the Emperor, garbed as a jester, and an Empress, well-stricken in years. Ladies of court were labelled 'former fish-fags', and deposed kings carried the Imperial trains, followed by armies of Generals.

During that afternoon the sound of gun-fire was heard in southern England, and watchers on the coast and family parties drowsy after Sunday dinner, told one another that Bonaparte's coronation had taken place. For the first newspaper accounts they had to wait patiently, and the official *Moniteur* eventually published no details of what had happened from the moment their Imperial Majesties arrived in the Cathedral. The issue of the day following the Coronation stated that feelings of reverence and deep thankfulness were as yet too profound, and time too short, to admit of an adequate description. Presumably the Emperor himself must have forbidden its appearance.

But other papers, received in England, supplied the deficiency, and the reports of anonymous eye-witnesses were presently forthcoming. English critics learnt that the 'Spanish' court dresses, of light-coloured satins and velvet, worn by the Emperor's brothers, had given them the appearance of mountebanks. Joséphine, very well made up, had looked not more than five and twenty as she passed to her scene of triumph in her fairy-tale coach drawn by eight dapple-greys. Her sisters-in-law had objected violently to carrying the train of a woman whom they had always hoped to see dismissed with ignominy. The Emperor had been obliged to threaten the ladies of his family with banishment, and as a concession allow each an officer attendant to carry her train. The effect had been ridiculous, and the unwilling Imperial princesses had performed their duties so ill that the Empress had nearly fallen backwards when ascending to receive her crown, but perhaps the ladies had not been to blame, for the Emperor too had staggered when mounting the same steps. He had crowned himself with a brand-new gold wreath of laurel and oak leaves, from the 'Purple Monkey'. It was not true that at the crucial moment he had snatched the garland from the trembling fingers of the astonished Pope. All such details had been settled beforehand by correspondence —the Pope giving way on nearly every point. It was useless to deny that picturesque shafts of sunshine had penetrated snow-heavy clouds during the journeys to and from the candle-lit Cathedral, and at intervals throughout the long ceremony. Two orchestras had discoursed interminably. Tradesmen had slipped into the building to sell lemonade, marrons glacés and sausage rolls to hungry and chilled spectators, who were seeing scarcely anything except velvet and tinsel hangings.

England Expects (II)

The winter's afternoon had been closing in before the return procession set out for the Tuileries. The Emperor had been amiability itself after the ceremony had gone off without a single hitch, indeed with a certain dignified austerity. Only one official, whose report did not reach England for many years, saw His Imperial Majesty, wishful to attract the attention of his uncle, Cardinal Fesch, give that dignitary a prod in the back with his sceptre. The illuminations after dark had been beautiful—double rows of orange trees in all the principal streets, linked by rows of stars. There had been cheering, but by people whose faces were distorted by cold. People offered free fowls and fountains of wine in December streets do cheer.

The Emperor had been obliged to insert a note in the *Moniteur* to the effect that the Coronation had cost, not sixty millions, as was asserted, but four and a half.

The Emperor's Painter in Chief had been very difficult. He had said that his employer had promised him a box in Notre Dame, from which he could watch the ceremony, undisturbed by Philistines. The Grand Master of the Ceremonies had sent him two tickets for a stand which the artist returned, demanding a whole stand above the High Altar, for himself and impedimenta. According to M. David, a duel had very nearly resulted. He must have obtained a good view, judging by the result, with which the Emperor was delighted—every portrait judiciously idealized—the whole glossy, colourful composition leading up to the central figure. The Emperor, after a prolonged silent scrutiny, had removed his hat. ' David, I salute you! ' ' In the shade of my hero,' responded the Court Painter emulatively,

' I shall glide to Posterity.' But neither the Emperor nor his chief artist realized that to posterity a crude pencil sketch of Capet's widow on her way to the guillotine, set down in a hurry by a hungry young Revolutionary, would be far more interesting than any of his glowing canvases of Imperial splendour.

Londoners awoke on December 7th to the thickest fog known for fifteen years and read, ' We presented our readers yesterday with a description of that compound of absurdity and impiety the Coronation of Bonaparte. The puerile vanity of these details is excessive. But Bonaparte is fond of parade, and the French, a light and frivolous nation, no doubt take amusement in it'. The close print, difficult to decipher by candlelight, ran on . . . ' Mad pranks of a band of slaves, made drunk by their Tyrant and suffered to dance in chains.' Bored *élégantes*, in London, who had been over to Paris during the Peace, laid aside with a shrug and a sigh accounts of panoply created at establishments which they had patronized. Picot, of the Rue St. Thomas de Louvre, had supplied the embroideries, Veuve Toulet, the innumerable Russian ermine skins and astrakhan lambskins required for the Imperial mantles, and the leopard and bearskins for officers' uniforms. Chevallin had made the tunics. L'Olive and Beuvry and Demoiselle Fournet had produced the laces and gloves, Jacques, the boots and slippers, Poupard, the plumes and hats. Description of some gowns ordered by the Empress from Leroy and Raimbaud for the week of the festivities, showed that a once-lovely brunette, who thoroughly understood the art of dress, had made the most of a great opportunity. Three of her evening *toilettes* had a sumptuous sound—' an under-robe of silver satin and tulle with train of lilac velvet embroidered with silver convolvulus '—' an under-robe of silver net, with a train of rose velvet'—'an under-robe of gold net, very richly embroidered in gold, with a train of white velvet powdered with knots of violets and emeralds.'

Suddenly ' The Coronation ' faded from the English Press, and ' The Boy Betty ' took its place, occupying three and even four principal columns in leading organs. Master Betty might even claim the distinction of having pushed Bonaparte out of the newspapers altogether on the very day of his triumph.

IV

William Henry West Betty came of respectable stock. His paternal grandfather had been a successful physician, his mother, Miss Staunton of Hopton Court, Shropshire. His father (who combined the professions of gentleman-farmer and linen-manufacturer) had instructed him at his mother's knee in declamation. Mr. Betty taught the infant ' Farewell, a long farewell to all my greatness! ' and Mrs. Betty ' My name is Norval! '

When William Henry was ten, the family made a pilgrimage from Ballynahinch, County Down, to Belfast, to witness Mrs. Siddons as Elvira. On his return from the playhouse Master Betty announced that if he were not allowed to become an actor he would die. Two years later he made a brilliant first appearance in the same theatre. Triumphs in Dublin, Cork, Waterford,

Glasgow and Edinburgh followed. By way of Liverpool, Sheffield and Birmingham he reached London, where he was engaged for twelve performances at Covent Garden, at the rate of fifty guineas a night, and a clear benefit.

The arrival of an Infant Prodigy in the Metropolis had been well-advertised. Mr. Home, author of that popular play, *Douglas*, had told the manager of the Edinburgh Theatre during a long conversation on the windy North Bridge, that seeing Master Betty in the name-part of his tragedy, he had realized for the first time his own imaginings. ' He is a Wonderful Being. His endowments are great beyond conception. . . . He will soon be one of the first actors on the British Stage.' Another Scottish admirer declared that the boy already totally eclipsed John Kemble. As Prince Arthur, and—which was more difficult to believe—Romeo, he had drawn tears from spectators of both sexes. He had committed the part of Hamlet to memory in three hours.

Saturday, December 1st, 1804, the eve of Bonaparte's coronation in Paris, was the day chosen for Master Betty's début as 'Achmet', in Dr. Brown's tragedy *Barbarossa*, at Covent Garden. The Prince of Wales had signified his intention of being present. As early as noon, all avenues leading to the theatre were nearly full, and between one and two o'clock they became unpleasantly crowded. Some enthusiasts, found concealed in the playhouse since Friday night's performance, were ejected. The management had taken ostentatious precautions to preserve law and order, but the presence of a large number of Bow Street officers and constables proved insufficient. Shortly before the arrival of the Prince's carriage, the Guards had to be summoned from their Barracks, to prevent further disaster. Already seemingly lifeless bodies of ladies in gala attire had been handed over the heads of the struggling mob to the ministrations of doctors. The moment that the Bow Street door of the theatre was opened—an hour early—a tide of struggling humanity had surged in, and taken possession of the space between the outer door and the bar in the lobby where money was usually received. Gentlemen who were prepared to pay almost anything to behold Master Betty, continued to elbow their way through a stout-hearted throng intent on standing-room. Inside the house a great many spectators, prostrated by the heat and emotion, desired only to leave. The crowd broke all the windows on either side of the entrance. At six o'clock a notice was put up, saying that all boxes were full, yet the rush continued. It was calculated that at least half of those who had suffered so much fatigue and discomfort were obliged to return home unsatisfied. The pit, when the play began, presented a novel appearance. There was scarcely a female in it, and the pressure was so great that during the course of the first Act several men, overcome by faintness, had to be lifted into the boxes, whence they were carried out of the building.

At the end of the second Act, Master Betty presented himself, ' amidst the convulsed and tumultuous acclamations of the house. He received the animated expressions and greetings of the admiring audience with a prepossessing modesty, and through the whole of his performance experienced as loud, as liberal and as just applause as was ever given or received within the walls of a theatre. . . . The Prince of Wales, from his box, applauded Master Betty loudly and frequently.' A command to Carlton House followed.

For the guidance of those who had not yet had the privilege of seeing Master Betty as 'Achmet', Monday's newspapers were explicit. The boy had natural grace of movement, an extremely sympathetic voice and features of a frank and lofty cast, ' capable of expressing all the wildness of joy, the enthusiasm of filial love, tempered by reverential awe, the triumphant consciousness of noble descent, and the nobler dignity of inborn worth'. 'Never did we see these feelings more chastely conceived, more beautifully blended or more powerfully expressed. . . . The readings, deportment, conception and whole manner of this boy are entirely his own. He is, so far as we can judge, entirely ORIGINAL. He has no artificial pauses, no affected modulations, no statue-like attitudes.'

Night after night during December 1804, ' this astonishing Star of the first magnitude ' filled Covent Garden, and presently Drury Lane. On the morning that Londoners woke to the thickest fog for fifteen years, copies of Master Betty's portrait, on view for the first time at the print-seller's, passed into wide circulation. Mr. Opie was painting him in the act of drawing inspiration from the tomb of Shakespeare. Mr. Fox had included him amongst a select company, invited to a reading of *Zanga*. The boy was considering adding *Zanga*, *Richard III* and *Macbeth* to his repertoire. Mr. Pitt had received him at an early morning hour. Mr. Pitt had shed tears when viewing Master Betty's

England Expects (II)

Douglas. Finally, the Prime Minister adjourned the House, so that members might have the opportunity of seeing Master Betty as Hamlet.

Before long, the familiar and beloved figure of His Majesty, escorting his wife and daughters, was seen to arrive at the playhouse. The first Paterfamilias in Great Britain sent for Mr. Sheridan to the Royal Box, and beamingly announced, ' We want to see the Young Actor.' At the audience which followed, the young actor gave universal satisfaction. His manners were just right, neither too assured nor obsequious. To an ardent student of Shakespeare's historical plays, aged thirteen, there probably seemed nothing unusual in the fact that his Sovereign addressed him kindly while Life Guards repelled mobs anxious to witness his acting.

By the New Year, Bonaparte's Coronation had quite ceased to be News in London. London had discovered ' The Young Roscius '.

Master Betty, between his two first seasons in London, appeared with equal success at Stourbridge, Worcester and Wolverhampton. The provinces were faithful to him long after the capital had proved fickle.

For it presently occurred to a number of thoughtful people as demonstrably absurd that a child of thirteen should so affect them by expressing major passions, which he could not possibly have experienced. Master Betty's love, hate, agony, etc., must all be pinchbeck. The bringing out of a female infant prodigy, a young Roscia, completed public disillusionment.

Master Betty appeared for the last time as a boy actor in 1808, at Bath, after which he went up to Cambridge. His father's decease was the reason given for his failure to graduate. He had a large fortune to control. Now came the moment for which hungry critics, snubbed veterans of the boards, jealous neophytes and accomplished members of the great theatrical families had long been waiting. But Master Betty, who had been behind the scenes at an observant age, did not proceed to waste his substance in riotous living. He returned to the profession, aged twenty-one, and prepared to work hard.

Every effort was made to ensure a repetition of his success of 1804. The same part and the same play at the same house were carefully chosen for his first adult appearance in London. Bursts of laughter came from the heartless audience at the most moving moments of the tragedy.

Master Betty struggled on for twelve years before deciding to retire into private life. He survived for another half century, to enjoy the profits amassed by him as a minor. He became possessor of a handsome house in a London square, and a son who went on the stage, but was never prominent. Well-mannered to the last, Master Betty, aged eighty-three, sometimes told inquisitive guests that he really thought the public had been mistaken in forming so high an opinion of his childish efforts. The public, who had long been convinced of this, and sheepishly conscious of very ridiculous behaviour in 1804, never reconsidered their second judgment. Apparently it never occurred to anyone that a great many children are born mimes, with dry-plate memories, and that until dismayed by adolescence, possess the complete assurance and gusto necessary for the profession of actor. Only a few out of this joyous

company continue, in after life, to develop painstakingly
a natural talent, which has survived adult preoccupa-
tions. If Mr. Sheridan, who was a good judge, thought
that Master Betty could act, the boy probably could act.
It is unlikely that Mr. Fox and Mr. Pitt were entirely
mistaken, and that all the proprietors of British newspapers desired nothing else than to distract attention
from Bonaparte's performance in Paris.

Over a century passed before British audiences pronounced another curly-headed mother's darling, of even
tenderer age, separated from them by the Atlantic, their
favourite performer.

v

Sir Arthur Wellesley, just landed from India, after
a six months' passage and nine years' absence, found
Town, in early September, 1805, very thin. The House
was not in session. The Royal Family were at Weymouth. The death, after a long and painful illness, of
His Majesty's regretted but undistinguished brother,
had taken place on August 25th, but not until September 4th had his funeral procession set off for Windsor. An enormous hatchment still decorated his house
in Grosvenor Street. Any fashionables in London were
wearing court mourning, but in spite of the Invasion
Threat, most people of means were still in the country,
or at watering-places, and although the renewed war
had now lasted over two years, Paris fashions were still
illustrated and described in London magazines.

Pearl grey silk robes under ' Mameluke ' jackets of
taffeta had been much seen in Paris this summer. Nut-
brown was popular for day wear, lapis-lazuli, jonquil

and a new shade, *feuille morte*. The Empress and her
ladies had not spent the season in their capital. With
such a train of trunks and band-boxes that the Emperor
had declared he would sooner set an army in motion,
they had followed their master, in spring weather,
through lovely scenes. By way of Bourg, Lyons and
Chambéry—a holiday resort already beloved by French
ladies for its muslins, its chocolate truffles and its wild
cyclamen—they had passed over the snowy Mont
Cenis to sunlit castles of Italy. Naturally, attendance at
many court functions staged in strange towns had
created a demand for fresh gowns and fashions. Young
ladies of France, in the evening this summer, wore
their curls in a bunch on the top of the head, and
floral knots of moss-rosebuds, ranunculus, heliotrope
and hortensia. Their ball dresses, adorned with bou-
quets to match, were all made of the most diaphanous
materials, and slit at the sides to allow freedom of
movement and the display of ' Diana ' silver kid bus-
kins—so that in every way their costume resembled
that of performers at the opera. There was a new
Turkish undress *costume de Seraglio*, and for country
wear printed linens had been sold, but nearly all well-
dressed women chose pure white—cambric or muslin,
with short puffed sleeves, and aprons and fichus ex-
quisitely lace-trimmed and embroidered. Straw hats,
white or yellow, trimmed with country sheaves of corn-
stalks, and corded silk shawls, completed French
fashionable walking dress. There seemed no doubt
that London missed Paris taste. London had merely
seen the large ' Roxborough ' and ' Caravan ' hats,
ornamented with swansdown and roses, ' British ' lace,

and for evening headdresses, ' Installation ' plumes, grapes in the hair and velvet turbans. Costumes *à la militaire* included heavily frogged jackets of rifleman green. At court, before the mourning order came out, gowns and trains of oriental *lamé*, heavily trimmed with velvet geraniums, had been admired.

The Invasion Threat was just as real as it had been last year—rather more so. Bonaparte had returned safely from his Ascension Day coronation as King of Italy, in Milan Cathedral. He continued to travel between Paris and the Iron Coast. Last month he had attended embarkation rehearsals at Boulogne. As far as most people in London knew, he was at the moment on the coast.

There had, for some time, been rumours that the Army of England was not, after all, going to be used in that direction, but against Austria. Already a great part of it was on the march to the Rhine. Such rumours might be set about by Bonaparte himself to throw England off her guard. His Toulon Fleet, designed in conjunction with his Brest Fleet, to escort his flotilla across the Channel, had escaped Lord Nelson's blockade. Admiral Villeneuve had been pursued and attacked, but had succeeded in putting into Corunna. He had sailed again, but south, to Cadiz.

In England, parades and evacuation plans continued. An address 'To Country Gentlemen and Others commanding Volunteer Corps', published to-day in the *Courier*, opened, 'There never was a period at which the individual exertions of the British Country Gentleman was of such value and importance.' Advertisement columns called for skilled smiths and wheelwrights for the Woolwich workshops. In coastal villages, reverend gentlemen were ascertaining from the inhabitants of cottages that they perfectly understood what they were to do, and where they were to meet him, when the alarm sounded. Sons of toil, who would themselves have to muster with the volunteers, proudly displayed home-made go-carts, ready to receive the forms of bed-ridden granny and the baby. Women and children knew that they were not to block the main roads. Their parish priest would lead them to safety by devious paths.

Early in the year, flushed with the success of his first coronation, and well satisfied by Spain's declaration of war against England, the Emperor Napoleon had sent to his ' brother ' George III, peace proposals. Their tone had not been conciliatory. ' Peace is my most earnest endeavour, but War has not proved adverse to me.' His Britannic Majesty's Ministers had sent a refusal with a sting in its tail. His Majesty had found it quite impossible to make a particular reply to the suggestions made to him by the Head of the French Government until he had communicated with the Continental powers with whom he was engaged in diplomatic relations and alliances—especially with the Emperor of Russia. . . . Disappointed but not surprised, the Emperor Napoleon, who could not afford to let his laurels gather dust, had turned his face forthwith towards his spectacular Italian triumph.

Lord Nelson's long chase of Villeneuve was the leading topic in the London of early September, 1805. A few people knew that the Admiral was now in town.

England Expects (II)

Otherwise, except for an ugly outbreak of jail fever, and a satisfactory harvest, the English gentleman at home did not seem to have much to report to the returned traveller.

Sir Arthur Wellesley, tall, spare and erect, further distinguished by that straightness of glance and buoyant gait often noticeable in the man who has just landed from a long sea voyage, passed through emptyish streets towards the Colonial Office. The morning had been showery, but now the sun was saluting pavement and park. Arrived in Downing Street, he stated his mission, and was ushered into a small waiting room on the right side of the vestibule.

Only one other person was waiting to see the Secretary of State this afternoon, but although he had been out of the country for nine years, the General at once realized that this naval officer of slight stature, with worn irregular features, a shock of white hair and an empty right sleeve, could be none other than Viscount Nelson. Without any introduction, the Victor of the Nile began to talk, and Sir Arthur got one of the surprises of his lifetime. He had heard before that Britain's first Admiral numbered amongst his amiable failings a childlike vanity. As their conversation proceeded—if indeed Lord Nelson's bombastic recitative could be so described—Sir Arthur struggled with feelings of dismay and even disgust. Beyond doubt, it gave Lord Nelson genuine pleasure to recount to a total stranger that on his last visit to Mr. Pitt, the Prime Minister had himself seen the Victor of the Nile to his carriage. ' I do not think that he would have done such a thing for a Prince of the Blood.' Lord Nelson had been carried to the Colonial Office to-day by the Duke of Queensberry. Since about one o'clock the Cabinet had been sitting, to decide upon the instructions to be issued to Lord Nelson.

Sir Arthur was never skilful at concealing his emotions. Presently his companion left the room. A second glance at the high nose and cold light eye of the curt military officer whom he had carelessly dismissed as another tedious aristocratic man, had evidently aroused suspicions in the breast of Lord Nelson. Sir Arthur guessed him gone to make some enquiries from the office keeper. On the Admiral's return, Sir Arthur received his second shock of this morning. The Victor of the Nile had now adapted his manner to suit the Victor of Assaye. As far as social graces went, nothing could make him appear other than he was—a trustworthy member of the professional class—but all Sir Arthur had noted as ' the charlatan style ' in his address had vanished. Quarter past two sounded, half past, while Lord Nelson questioned, wondered, stated his belief. . . . He much desired to hear Sir Arthur's impressions of their country, after nine years distinguished foreign service. He discussed the next probable enemy move, the preparations of Austria, the true value of the Russian alliance. His information was good, his deductions were highly interesting. In fact, he talked like an officer and a statesman.

An hour passed, but Sir Arthur, completely spellbound, felt no impatience. Sir Arthur had responded to the vibrant and unmistakable 'Nelson touch'. At last the inevitable happened, and a quiet-voiced official announced Lord Mulgrave at liberty to see Viscount

England Expects (II)

Nelson. Sir Arthur was left alone, staring at London house fronts through the windows of a room which seemed suddenly not only void, but strongly marked with the dinginess characteristic of the outer chambers of public departments. . . .

In English country-house halls, and, later, passages, engravings of a couple of elongated crowd paintings, representing crucial moments in the careers of Lord Nelson and the Duke of Wellington, gave succeeding generations the impression that these great contemporaries must often have met. In fact that chance meeting in the Downing Street waiting-room on Thursday, September 12th, 1805, was the only occasion.

Lord Nelson sailed again in the *Victory* from Portsmouth three days later, and as he passed to his barge the people of England knelt on the cobbles and cried blessings on his name, and afterwards stood long staring out to sea, as if they guessed that the little Admiral had gone on his last cruise.

Sir Arthur Wellesley, however, never forgot their sole encounter, and in after years would urbanely confide, with all the *empressement* of a keen though not gifted psychologist, ' Now, if the Secretary of State had been punctual, and admitted Lord Nelson in the first quarter of an hour, I should have had the same impression of a light and trivial character that other people have had. Luckily I saw enough to be satisfied that he was really a very superior man. But certainly a more sudden and complete metamorphosis I never saw. . . .'

England Expects (II)

H.M.S. *Victory* fitted with a new rudder, was at sea again, and the sounds of canvas straining, and gulls crying, and rushing waters, and light footsteps at the double were audible in Lord Nelson's cabin.

The Admiral had desired the presence of Captains Hardy and Blackwood to witness his signature to a document. Such a request was far from unfamiliar to these brothers in arms. His lordship, whose domestic affairs were entangled, was always adding codicils to his Will. This would be the eighth in eighteen months. Like many great men of action, he was made anxious by minor ailments. He had explained in detail to his medical adviser, Dr. Beatty, heart symptoms which that gentleman diagnosed as typical of nervous indigestion. This morning, however, every man in the Fleet had the best of reasons for wishing to leave his affairs in order. Dr. Beatty was engaged, mercifully not in full view of his future patients, testing tools of his trade, which he must expect to use before dusk. Ship's surgeons were provided with a stout lad to carry their paraphernalia, and ghastly stories were told of angry medicos shouting above the clamour of an action, ' Name of goodness, where's that boy? ' while the irrepressible imp lay silent at last, shivered to atoms. Almost more to be feared than the ship's doctor with his knife and pitch, employed by the light of swaying lanterns amidst shifting timbers, was the well-meaning amateur, liable to record in his memoirs such anecdotes as ' hearing a marine with a head wound calling repeatedly for water, at last

236

England Expects (II)

I procured a bottle of Porter, which he drank off with grateful avidity. He died within the hour.'

Yesterday the unmistakable shape of Gibraltar had faded from view, whilst last conferences were held on board the *Victory*. The great naval battle, desired by Bonaparte five weeks past, was about to take place, but under circumstances not of the Emperor's choosing. Bonaparte, who must move, had turned his Army for the Invasion of England away from the shining Picardy coast line. ' Brave Soldiers of the Boulogne Camp, you are not going to England! The Emperor of Austria, bribed with English gold, has declared War on us. His army has crossed prohibited frontiers. Bavaria is invaded! Soldiers! new laurels await you beyond the Rhine.'

Reliable sources declared that the Emperor's rage on hearing of Admiral Villeneuve's retirement to Cadiz, at the moment when the presence of his fleet was essential to escort the flotilla to England, had been startling to witness. ' We were ready everywhere! His appearance for twenty-four hours would have sufficed. What a Navy! What an Admiral—not fit to command a frigate! ' He had postponed the Invasion of England, but the naval engagement necessary before it could take place was about to occur, and Lord Nelson, weary of waiting and chasing, was determined not on a victory, but on annihilation. The hour of Admiral Villeneuve—who now knew himself to have been superseded in his command—had come, and for that vacillating officer it was an evil hour. Two days ago, obeying the orders of his terrible master, but too late, he had put out from Cadiz to form a junction with his allies at Cartagena.

England Expects (II)

At noon yesterday he had turned and steered south, closely watched by British frigates. After nightfall, blue signal lights from the English fleet had lit the western horizon. At six-thirty on the morning of October 21st, 1805, Lord Nelson had made signal to form line of battle in two divisions. The British Fleet mustered twenty-seven sail of the line with a broadside of 29,000 lbs., the combined French and Spaniards thirty-three ships, with a broadside of 30,000 lbs. But the allied vessels were undermanned, and their crews, in consequence of the blockade, ill fed and ill satisfied, while the British, according to their own commander, 'in the most perfect health', were very ready to engage in the greatest sea-fight of history.

The morning skies were heavy with cloud. Varying shades of grey light filled cabin windows. No reflections of dancing waters warmed with Mediterranean sun flickered above the Admiral's white head, as he sat at his little desk re-reading his last Will and Testament. A light wind was blowing from the North-West, and a swell was booming in upon a cape rising out of mist to the eastward, named on globes and maps Trafalgar.

The French Admiral, seeing the British approach, had at last found the courage he had long lacked, and stood north, so that if fight he must, it should be with a friendly port under his lee. At the head of the approaching British columns sailed Admiral Viscount Nelson in his flagship, *Victory*, and Vice-Admiral Collingwood in his flagship, *Royal Sovereign*. Their slow approach towards action was awful. During the necessary period of waiting, Lord Nelson had gone quietly to his cabin and written down a prayer before

England Expects (II)

he ordered the attendance of Captains Hardy and Blackwood.

The hour was by now about eleven a.m., and signs of bad weather were not lacking. The formal wording of the document in front of the engrossed Admiral suited the solemn scene. Only persons who had listened to London gossip of the past five years—but their name was legion—would be able to read something startling between its lines. All well-informed and many simple admirers at home had heard that before he left England in 1801, the Admiral had written to his wife, announcing a handsome allowance and his intention not to revisit her. Little surprise had been felt by the few who had sat in heated continental drawing-rooms, watching with mixed feelings the crumpled figure of the little Admiral, dropping asleep at the Faro table, while Lady Hamilton, in high spirits, won and lost large sums. Loyal officers, if they ever approached the subject, admitted that the Admiral's attachment to Sir William Hamilton's lady—now widow—was very great, ' to the injury of that to Viscountess Nelson'. Wedded wives, eager to hear the truth of a low-born charmer, learnt with satisfaction from less reserved eye-witnesses, that the Ambassador's wife whom Queen Charlotte would not receive, was extremely vulgar, bold and unguarded in her talk, no longer the gorgeous girl whose perfection of peach-tinted tresses and skin had enslaved more than one famous painter. Few of her physical features now did more than remind old admirers of ' Lady Hamilton at the Spinning Wheel', ' Lady Hamilton as Diana', as Circe, as Joan of Arc, as a saint. . . . She had acquired accomplishments, but her ease of manner was that of the bar-maid. She had been odiously rude to the small and somewhat bird-like Lady Nelson, and the resentful Captain Nisbet, whom she dubbed ' Tomtit and her cub'. She was at least four-and-forty, and fourteen stone. At a date when brides of sixteen abounded, pillars of the British home refused to believe in the possibility of an idealistic *grande passion* for so unsuitable an object. They could not conceive why their favourite hero should prefer to his lawful, if somewhat faded spouse, Lady Hamilton, who had grown fat, and drank freely, and was—although unknown to them as yet—bearing him a child, his first child, hers too, he believed.

The future of his daughter, carried undiscovered, born in secrecy, baptised by the name of Thompson in the Parish church of St. Mary le Bonne, on a May morning of 1801, had long disturbed the Admiral's peace of mind. In his Will he had left an ample sum to Lady Hamilton, ' knowing she will educate my adopted child in the paths of religion and virtue, and give her those accomplishments which so much adorn herself'. Until she reached the age of eighteen, Horatia Nelson Thompson was to remain in the care of her guardian. After that, if her ladyship judged the boy grown a worthy mate for such a treasure, it was the Admiral's wish that a marriage should take place between his nephew and heir-presumptive and his adopted daughter.

Codicil after codicil followed—an annual sum to be paid to the widow of a younger brother, a bequest to Lady Hamilton of all the hay on his estate at dear, dear Merton, the country home in which Emma and he and old Sir William had lived so happily and peacefully. To-day's codicil expressed the Admiral's desire that Horatia should not wait until her marriage to adop Nelson as her sole surname.[1]

About an hour later, Lieutenant Pasco, signal officer suggested that the words ' Nelson confides ' necessitated the hoisting of six and eight flags. ' England expects', would only require two. The Admiral accepted the correction, and a round of ringing cheers greeted the message ' England expects that every man will do his duty', quickly followed by, 'Engage more closely'.

In the bellying sails of the inevitably approaching fleet the wind had died. The advance was extremely slow and nerve-racking. Bands struck up aboard the British men-of-war. With midday the sound of gunfire began to startle the cloudy autumnal landscape.

VII

Autumn lingered long in England in October, 1805. Mr. Joseph Farington, R.A., on a sketching tour in Norfolk, found the effects of sun and mist on the morning of October 7th ideal from the point of view of the landscape artist. ' A beautiful morning—rays among

---

[1] Horatio Nelson, eldest nephew of the Admiral, died five years after Trafalgar, before reaching his majority. Horatia, daughter of the Admiral and Lady Hamilton, married, at the age of twenty-one, the Rev. Philip Ward, Vicar of Tenterden, Kent, and died in 1881, leaving issue. A fourth daughter of Lady Hamilton, her second child by the Admiral, born in the year before Trafalgar, survived only a few weeks. When Lord Nelson's Will was published, Lady Nelson ' did not know who the girl is, that was so particularly mentioned'.

the trees—grass most dewy—objects under the sun, massed in successive gradations—light fleecy clouds, shadows very tender while the fog was thick, and gradually becoming stronger as the exhalation cleared. . . .'

Five days before the naval engagement off Cape Trafalgar, the Prime Minister, attended by a distinguished staff, emerged on to the terrace of Walmer Castle after dinner, to witness a marine experiment. Mr. Fulton, engineer, of Pennsylvania, disappointed in his reception by Bonaparte's advisers, had turned to England, where his name as an inventor was not unknown. In years of peace English patrons had encouraged him to devote his attention to canal locks.

The Prime Minister and Lord Melville, after granting him a private interview, had agreed with the Emperor Napoleon that the American gentleman had 'something in his brain'. They were inclined to believe that his sub-marine combustible machines were worth a trial. Lord Castlereagh, Secretary for War and for Foreign Affairs, had also been favourably impressed. A couple of experiments upon the French flotilla in Boulogne roads, in October and December, 1804, had been expensive, and not very effective. Bonaparte had scornfully described the result as ' breaking the windows of the good Boulonnais with English guineas '.

Mr. Fulton's sub-marine combustible machines, officially classed as 'catamarans', and by their unwilling employers as 'infernals', were coffers, over twenty feet long and three feet wide, covered with planks, lined with lead, caulked and tarred. Their appearance suggested to ingenuous observers, handsome mahogany logs. They contained one hundred and seventy pounds of gunpowder apiece, and fired by clockwork. One of Lord Keith's officers, reporting after their use, said that had an enemy shell fallen on his vessel and hit an ' infernal ', 'there would have been an end of us '. A number of the wretched objects had drifted ashore near Boulogne without exploding, and a crowd of thousands assembled on the beaches to gloat over them. For his part, this officer would not draw an easy breath until he had returned the unused remainder into store, ' from which, as a true friend of the Service, I heartily wish we had never taken them '.

Mr. Fulton explained to the Navy Board that the failures at Boulogne might be attributed to a slight constructional defect. And unfortunately, the secret that Britain was about to use a new weapon had not been well kept. A week before the first attempt, the President of the Royal Academy had been telling friends, in deepest confidence, that ' within ten days they would hear of something extraordinary'. When pressed, he had gone so far as to explain that the French Invasion flotilla was to be destroyed in harbour ' by some extraordinary means which the enemy could not prevent'. 'You began blabbing out at supper last night,' wrote a newly-appointed Ambassador to his mistress, 'what I had been telling you just before, about 'the Means made use of to surprise the Boulogne ships. I hope you have not told anyone of the attempt that is to be made upon the pier at C——.'

An old sloop of three hundred tons was due to be broken up. She was towed to the Downs, anchored in full view of Walmer, and on October 16th the inventor was empowered to do his worst to her.

England Expects (II)

The day was cold, the news from the Continent depressing. The tread of the giant Russia's troops sounded largely in every English leading article, but there seemed no doubt that the Emperor Napoleon had, so far, proceeded according to his plans. Yesterday, a boat launched from Boulogne inner harbour and taken up by a British frigate, had contained a small packet saying— ' Ulm has surrendered to French Arms ; the Austrian Army is annihilated '. It did not seem probable that an army of one hundred thousand could have dispersed as if by magic, and press commentators suggested that even Bonaparte's warmest admirers could hardly have been prepared for such a claim.

The Prime Minister was in weak health, his doctors were urging a visit to Bath. Lord Mulgrave's brother, General Phipps, thought Mr. Pitt's cough was a gout cough. There was general relief amongst the staff on the terrace when at length the American inventor's machine performed its duty. Three galleys had placed the ' infernals ' across the cable of the *Dorothea*, under which, by the running of the tide, they had soon been fixed about the centre of her keel. No deafening reports startled wheeling birds, or shook the windows of Walmer. Only a cloud of smoke appeared. The vapour dispersed, and the mob on the beach below exhaled admiring sighs. From the terrace it was soon obvious that Mr. Fulton's ' infernals ' had secured a success of the first order. The poor old *Dorothea* was completely shattered.

Telescopes were collapsed and slipped into the pockets of civilian greatcoats or taken under-arm by

England Expects (II)

gentlemen in naval and military uniforms. The party adjourned indoors gratefully to discuss further action. Lord Castlereagh prepared an account for Lord Nelson, with a view to attacking Villeneuve's fleet in Cadiz.

But already the Prime Minister had presentiments that to-day's success would do little to soften the hearts of the Navy Board. Sir Evan Nepean, formerly Secretary to the Admiralty, had always deposed that if Britain began to use 'infernals' sooner or later the enemy must retaliate, and Britain had much more to lose than France by the perfection of such an invention. Old Lord St. Vincent, at his most violent, saw in his mind's eye the Channel littered with stately and beloved three-deckers reduced to the pitiable state of the poor *Dorothea*. He held that Mr. Fulton, whom he somewhat illogically described as 'a gimcrack', was laying the foundations for doing away with the British Navy on which depended the safety and prosperity of our island. He even went so far, though not on this occasion, as to call the Prime Minister the greatest fool that ever existed, to encourage the use of a weapon which those who commanded the sea did not want, and which, if successful, would deprive them of their command.

While Mr. Fulton was still awaiting the decision of those who had witnessed his experiment on the *Dorothea*, news arrived which made his invention no longer of pressing importance to England. For several months he lingered on in his Vere Street hotel, or at a Dover inn, writing long letters to Sir Sidney Smith and Lord Castlereagh, about an attack to be made next spring, on Brest or Ferrol. Eventually he sailed again for the

New World, and devoted his talents to further investigation of Steam power.

An unexpected sequel to the story of his vain attempts to impress England or France took place on October 17th, 1815, when H.M.S. *Northumberland*, with the captive General Bonaparte on board, bound for St. Helena, came in sight of a long trail of dense smoke pouring from an approaching vessel which appeared to be provided with 'a sort of chimney'. The Emperor asked an attendant British naval lieutenant, 'What is that?' and received the answer 'A steam boat'. In great agitation the Emperor repeated, 'A steam boat?' upon which the young officer, regarding her through his telescope, added kindly, 'Yes, sir, the *Fulton*, of thirty-eight tons, the World's first Steam War-ship'.

With a strangled groan of '*Mon Dieu!*' the would-be Invader of Britain covered his brow, and retiring to the farther end of the deck, sat silent for a considerable period.

Chapter 8

The Map of Europe

~~~~~~~

Shockerwick House, some five miles outside Bath on the London road, seemed in appointments and situation exactly designed to provide the object of a short winter's day expedition for an eminent politician in weak health. A History of the County of Somerset, published fourteen years past, and adorned with many steel-plate engravings of religious edifices and gentlemen's seats, told that the hamlet had given its name to a family in the days of the first Plantagenet. The manor had since changed hands three times only. The new-built mansion of Mr. Walter Wiltshire, present owner of the estate, had been erected in a warm and pleasant situation and possessed good gardens.

Of the gardens the Prime Minister could not hope to see much, for he was on sticks. The Bath waters had quickly produced the effect desired by his physicians, and brought on an attack of gout in his right foot, described as 'pretty smart'. On his daily visits to the Pump Room, General Phipps supported him to and from his carriage. Ghoulish whispers told that anyone grasping Mr. Pitt by the sleeve these days, would feel no arm within. He had always been thin. He was now only the ghost of a man. So great had been the anxiety of local worthies to see the famous statesman, that he had been obliged to alter his hours of attendance at the springs. One loyal Tory had come one hundred and thirty-nine miles by coach to catch a a glimpse, and having been gratified, immediately returned home.

The report of the warm house, of moderate size, so easily accessible, so picturesquely set, had decided the Prime Minister to break his rule, and accept the invitation of a local landowner while taking the cure. During the morning of December 30th, his carriage drew up at the doors of his Bath lodgings. The sharp frost which had set in a week before was still holding. In London, people were skating on the Serpentine and the lake of St. James's Park, and the daily performances on the ice of two popular ballerinas—with French names— had gained much applause.

London had recovered well from the bad news of the surrender of Ulm, for four days later Lieutenant Lapinotière of the *Pickle* schooner, had arrived at the Admiralty between one and two a.m., and a typical newspaper heading of November 6th ran—

GLORIOUS VICTORY

OVER THE
COMBINED FLEETS

DEATH OF LORD NELSON

The Map of Europe

It had been noticeable on that memorable morning that friends, and even strangers, meeting in the streets, had stopped to exclaim, ' We have lost Nelson! ' before proceeding to congratulate one another on the result of the greatest sea-battle in naval history; and throughout the foggy days which followed, Trafalgar and Nelson had ousted almost every other topic from the Press and conversation. A suggestion that National Mourning should be ordered, as for a member of the reigning House, had not been adopted, but every eye was turned towards the wild and wintry waters through which the frail body of the hero was being brought home to a worthy resting-place. On December 4th the *Victory* with her precious cargo came in sight of Spithead. Plans of the funeral procession, anecdotes of the action filled every paper and magazine. Captain Hardy, who had vainly implored the Admiral before the action of October 21st, not to expose himself wearing his orders, was to occupy a leading position in the *cortège* carrying the fatal decorations on a black velvet cushion. Preparations for so great a pageant could not be made in a hurry. The second week of January was announced as the most probable date for the interment, and the interior of St. Paul's Cathedral was stated to resemble already a scene from the Arabian Nights.

Few people were rash enough to predict that Trafalgar had saved England for ever from fear of invasion. The possibility that the Emperor Napoleon would built another fleet could not be disregarded. But it was certain that no invasion need be feared for many months. For the first time in nine years—including the uneasy winter of the Experimental Peace—Englishmen would be able to enjoy Christmas festivities without the slightest fear of interruption by beacon or bugle-call. In Bath, many bow-fronted shops were gay with suggestions for seasonable gifts, especially for children. The words ' improving ' and ' young reader ' loomed large in advertisements of juvenile literature, but *The Life of Lord Nelson*, *The Memoirs of Dick the Pony*, a new *Robinson Crusoe* (illustrated) and puzzles and dissections of all sorts, had a less intimidating sound. For London children, the Panorama of that departed bogey, the Invasion Port of Boulogne, soon to be on view in Spring Gardens, promised an agreeable Christmas holiday outing.

The attendance of several peers and many country gentlemen at Smithfield Fat Stock Show was chronicled. The Marquis of Abercorn was entertaining a large house-party at his Middlesex villa, the Priory, Stanmore. In their relief and preoccupation, the general public failed to notice editors beginning to admit strong anxiety for news from the Continent. The weather at sea was very foul. By December 16th, nine Gothenberg mails were overdue, and five from Hamburg. Nobody exactly knew what had happened, round about December 2nd, at a place called Olmütz, in Moravia, once the strongest fortress of Austria. Rejoicings were said to have been heard from Boulogne, always a bad sign. On the 19th, the glad tidings BRILLIANT VICTORY OVER THE FRENCH was announced by the *Courier* in heavy type. A Captain Hudson, of the *Triton*, who had reached Hull *via* Hamburg, said that not half an hour before he sailed on the 13th, an agent had come into Lilburn's

well-known coffee house, having travelled express from
Olmütz. This person, who showed signs of great fatigue
and was suffering much from swelled legs, had declared
that when he had left Olmütz on the 6th, Russians and
Austrians had been driving the French in confusion
towards the Danube. Bonaparte's claim to have destroyed half the Russian army and routed the other half,
might therefore be discounted. The editor who printed
Captain Hudson's good news on Christmas Eve,
begged his public not to forget that this paper had
never varied from its assertion that the battle of the
2nd of December had been continued on the 3rd and
4th. On the 2nd, it now seemed probable that the
enemy had succeeded, after heavy fighting, in defeating
the Allied centre. The independent *Times* continued to
discuss a French victory of the 2nd. Opposition papers
said that it was scandalous that His Majesty's Ministers
had no official advice, and expressed great desire to see
the next mail. In London, the Prince of Wales was
explaining to interested cronies exactly how and why
Bonaparte had been beaten. In Bath, on Christmas
Day, the Prime Minister took his first extended drive,
and was noticed to be looking so much better that his
return to the capital, early in the new year, was predicted. Boxing Day brought another impressive announcement of Most Important News. The *Argus* of
December 17th had a wonderful tale of an Armistice
concluded between France and Austria, and a significant meeting during the battle of the 2nd, in a
mill, between Bonaparte and the Austrian Emperor.
' This,' commented the *Courier* blightingly, ' is a
most improbable story. Both His Imperial Majesty

and Bonaparte would have something else to do, during a battle, than to be conferring together in a mill.'

The morning of the 30th brought no more certain intelligence, and the Prime Minister's carriage duly left Laura Place for Batheaston. On such a brilliant winter's morning, when dazzling sun lit the uniform terraces hanging on her hills, Bath suggested somewhat in colour and perfection of design, an exhibition cluster of Muscatel grapes. There was a sprinkling of snow on the round top of Salisbury Hill, and frost was still sharp on leaf and grass, but since the county was Somerset, the colouring of the scene was not cold. Further hills were of the *matte* blue shade which formed so popular a background for white classic figures, in Mr. Wedgwood's ware. Hedges of rustling beech and ploughed fields resembled in hue the tan of the riding-school.

The Prime Minister never had much taste for general conversation. Strangers had remarked that when he graced a large gathering of supporters, his fellow guests, and even host, developed the air of schoolboys attending their master. He much preferred an expedition of this morning's pattern—a gentle drive over a fine road into country renowned for its effects of wild rock, stone quarries, irregular patches of wood and serpentine waters. Connoisseurs agreed that Bath, and the twenty miles surrounding it, possessed scenery superior to any in the world. Take away Tivoli, and even Rome could not compare. Only one village lay on the Prime Minister's route. His coachman had no difficulty in finding his direction. Every London visitor to Bath must have remarked, on his incoming journey, those park gates giving directly off the high road.

The Prime Minister's carriage passed through Mr. Wiltshire's gates and proceeded through parkland, diversified by tall bare elms, scattered on either side of the long drive. On the right hand, links of the Avon sparkled. Presently came a sideways view of the promised warm house, its southern façade of golden Bath stone bathed in mid-winter sunshine, its gardens looking somewhat emaciated as gardens will in December. The approaching guest obtained a fleeting glimpse of stately pillars, glinting panes and a pediment with a laurel wreath. To a University man, the house was reminiscent of the residence of the Provost or Master of an historic college. The drive took a sharp bend, and rounded hills came into sight, and a north entrance, shadowy and further shadowed by flanking wings, containing perhaps an orangery or a breakfast-room, on which were trained non-deciduous shrubs. The carriage drew up with a scatter of gravel, and watchers at windows of Shockerwick House saw a tall bent gentleman with a wasted look, hobbling towards shelter, and the expectant guest perceived sculptured reliefs of classic design above doorways and passage heads, and an ample staircase and hall, with plaster washes of pale sea-shades, and the certain promise of fireplaces adorned with cold marble faces, and proportionate rooms with noble prospects of park land and tree tops and winter-bound pleasure gardens.

II

During the fine and frosty night of December 29th-30th, the proprietors of posting-houses on the Great West Road received hurried warning of the approach of an important traveller. Viscount Castlereagh, Secretary of State for War and the Colonies, was taking up fresh horses at every post between the capital and Bath. A picturesque scene, familiar in the annals of eighteenth-century travel, was repeated that night against varying backcloths. It opened with the arrival of an imperious groom who knocked and halloed until a nightcapped figure thrust a head from an upper window. Unbarrings and unlockings followed, the lighting of candles and shakings into consciousness of tousle-headed stable boys, asleep in lofts amongst hay, or under odorous sinks and trestles. By the time that a nobleman's carriage rumbled into sight, bare-armed ostlers in leather aprons were at their posts. The handsome, but not spotless, equipage shattered to a halt, and postilions, agile as monkeys, leapt from their seats to assist with practised ease the business of unharnessing. Mired buckles and warm leather were separated, the incoming horses were led drooping into darkness, and fresh ones backed into the shafts. There was no undue delay, though plenty of noise and bustle. Within a few minutes the change had been effected, the postilions scrambled to their seats, two ostlers released their hold on the heads of the leaders, and the carriage shot off again on its hurried journey. The chance ray of a stable lantern revealed to those left gaping, the outlines of a tumbled but fine neckcloth, the collar of a fur-trimmed pelisse, and the immobile profile of one of the handsomest men in Europe.

The Secretary for War was naturally weary. At ten a.m. this morning he had arrived with his admired lady at the Priory, Stanmore, where, as to-morrow's newspapers would announce, the Yule-tide party already assembled included the Duchess of Devonshire, Earls and Countesses of Bessborough and Essex, Countess Cowper, Lady E. Foster, and a score of younger notabilities. Amateur theatricals were taking place nearly every night, under Lord Abercorn's hospitable roof. In *The Rivals*, on Christmas Day, Lord Aberdeen had been striking as Falkland, the Hon. William Lamb an adequate Captain Absolute, the Hon. Miss Butler a most unconvincing lady's maid. The further large company invited to witness the theatricals, supped every night in brilliant saloons, where small tables were laid with covers for ten or fourteen. The revelries commonly lasted till two a.m. But almost before the Secretary for War had made his entrance, the unwelcome sound of despatches from his office had disturbed his serenity. There were apologies, and orders for fresh horses and re-packing. Lord Castlereagh stepped back into his carriage, re-entered an unsuspecting London, and after a snatched meal with Lord Clancarty in Spring Gardens, settled himself to travel through the night on the Bath road.

Dawn saw his carriage toiling up frost-bound heights in good hunting country. In the garish sunshine of a particularly fine noon he bowled past a lodge of the warm house in which the Prime Minister was enjoying bucolic hospitality for the last time. For in the leather-covered boxes facing his seat, the uneasily drowsing Minister for War carried news which was to bring to the features of Mr. Pitt a change described as ' the Austerlitz look', but which was in truth the look of Death.

French accounts of the battle of December 2nd had been justified. Near Austerlitz, a place only a seventh the size of Olmütz, and nearer to Brno, the Emperor Napoleon had achieved the most spectacular victory of his career. There had been no successful Allied counter-attack on the 3rd and 4th, no despairing flight of French troops from avenging Russians and Austrians, followed by frightful carnage—exactly the reverse. The Tsar, staggered by his losses, had withdrawn northwards. The Emperor Francis was preparing to sign away to the Conqueror his fair provinces of Venice, Istria and Dalmatia, and historic possessions of the house of Hapsburg in south-west Germany. The fate of Prussia, to anyone who knew the King of Prussia, seemed inevitable. The small British Expeditionary Force recently despatched to the Elbe must be recalled at once. Trafalgar might have saved England from the threat of invasion, but to-day's news meant that the Continent lay at the feet of the Emperor Napoleon.

On his arrival at Laura Place, Lord Castlereagh learnt that the Prime Minister was gone into the country for the day, and a groom was sent at the gallop with the despatch, which caused a stricken man to call for a map of Europe, and when he had looked upon it, say in accents of despair, ' Roll up that map. It will not be wanted these ten years.'

The Map of Europe

The Conqueror of Europe had reached the banks of the Niemen, and invited the Tsar to a conference on a raft. There were historic precedents for such a meeting-place between great sovereigns; moreover, to a Muscovite, the selection of a council chamber to which no eavesdropper could possibly penetrate, should commend itself. The raft ordered by the Emperor Napoleon for his first encounter with the Tsar of all the Russias, was no ordinary affair. The Niemen was navigable a short distance above the little town of Tilsit, seventy-two miles north of the important city of Königsberg. The raft, moored as nearly as possible in midstream of the broad frontier river, was of impressive size and finely constructed. On its timber floor, raised by two steps above the lipping waters, stood two pavilions, in shape slightly reminiscent of Noah's Ark, but amply provided with sash-windows. The smaller pavilion was designed to accommodate the Imperial staffs during the forthcoming interview. The larger, surrounded by a wooden railing, over which hung richly coloured carpets, had two entrances. Its primitive roof was hidden by festive draperies, and its six windows revealed looped curtains which would have been admirable in any Paris drawing-room. Over the entrance on the southern side of the principal pavilion a large gilded initial N was encircled by a laurel wreath. Triumphal swags of greenery surrounded it. The entrance facing Russian territory had exactly similar decoration, except that the initial encircled by laurels was an A. Everything possible had been done to strike the fancy and spare the feelings of a young and enthusiastic, but so far unsuccessful, brother ruler.

At one hour after noon, discharges of cannon announced the departure from the Prussian shore, in an ornamental barge, of the Emperor of the French. The Russian, surprisingly, was not late. Crowds of military and civilians on both banks got a good view of a well-staged historic meeting.

The Grand Duke of Berg, the Prince of Neufchâtel and three Marshals of the French Empire withdrew to the smaller pavilion, escorting the Grand-Duke Constantine, Prince Labanoff and Generals Benningsen, Ouvaroff and Lieven. The Tsar, a splendid figure of a man, not yet thirty, with sparkling eyes, broad shoulders, a neat waist and fair hair thinning on rounded temples, expressed his sincere pleasure in to-day's occasion. If the Tsar's smile looked a trifle fixed, he could not be blamed. Two of his staff had been present in the death chamber of Paul I, and also at recent Russian reverses in the field. As his barge neared the raft, an unidentifiable voice had purred, ' Sire, let me humbly beg you not to forget your father's fate.'

The smiling potentates disappeared from view, and light rain began to fall. The expensive hangings of the pavilion fluttered in a chilly breeze. On the Prussian shore, where spectators were drawing towards the shelter of some groups of trees, loaded with leaf, a church spire and some roofs stood out in dark blue silhouette against a lowering sky. Under one of those humble roofs, the King of Prussia, the man for whom no one in Europe at the moment had a good word, was waiting like a lacquey while the fate of his country was decided. On the Russian shore, mile upon mile of sand and scrub and lake and marsh and forest stretched to the Courland border. That the afternoon should have turned out wet was a disappointment, for up here, the day after Midsummer might reasonably be expected to provide uninterrupted sunshine. But even in sunlight, the Tilsit district was ultimately boring.

Mr. Colin Alexander Mackenzie, British secret agent, nodding over his oar in the Imperial Russian barge, kept his ears open. He was a genuine Seaforth Mackenzie, descended from the branch of Torridon in Ross-shire, a place which sounded a far cry from this obscure spot on the Baltic shore. Of course, like most successful agents, he was not of a single nationality. His mother had been a Dutch lady. Mr. Mackenzie could make himself understood equally well in various dialects of England, Holland, France, Germany, Poland and Russia. He had served in the Russian army of the Caucasus, and being very anxious for news of home towards the close of 1805, had managed to get himself sent to St. Petersburg, where the Tsar had been unaffectedly glad to see him, since the Caucasian army had been cut off and no despatches from it had reached the capital for many weeks. Mr. Mackenzie, having delivered his despatches and made his arrangements with his English employers, had departed for the disastrous Eylau-Friedland campaign, after which he had resigned his Russian commission and become attached to Lord Hutchinson's military staff at Russian Headquarters. He had not much fear that the Tsar, who had sufficient worries to-day, would recognize him. The only other British subject at present in Tilsit, Dr. James Wylie, President of the St. Petersburg and Moscow Medical Academy, was a fellow Scot. The Tsar's Cossack head boatman had not been proof against a heavy bribe. Mr. Mackenzie, drowsing in the shade of a damp sail, attired in regrettably scented borrowed garments, had every hope of sending to Mr. Canning, Secretary of State for Foreign Affairs, a first rate eye-witness's impression of the meeting between the Tsar and Bonaparte. Four nights ago, he had dined as quietly and comfortably as possible in Tilsit, with General Benningsen, an officer whose hand had, at least, lain heavy on the shoulder of the late Tsar a few seconds before that unhappy despot had died of official apoplexy. Mr. Mackenzie was in a position to reassure Downing Street that a number of the Russian nobility cherished no friendly feelings for the present Head of the French Government, and that few Russian merchants would consider with equanimity the breaking off of trade relations with Great Britain. The Tsar, of course, had been piqued by England's opposition to his designs upon Turkey, and refusals to grant him a loan of six millions, or send an Expeditionary Force to the North German coast. He had nothing to gain by continuing to make war, and in spite of a romantic *penchant* for the heroic Queen of Prussia, was unlikely to run further risks on her behalf.

The interview between the Tsar and Bonaparte lasted three hours. It was impossible for anyone to know exactly what agreement had been reached, but it was obvious that on parting both sovereigns looked satisfied. Tilsit gossip of that evening told that Bonaparte had pronounced Alexander I a very handsome prince, with more brain than usually credited. The Tsar confided easily to his suspicious staff that the Emperor Napoleon, with all his genius, had his weak spot—vanity. Rumour added that he had found this weak spot by saying with youthful impetuosity, ' I loathe England as much as you do! ' to which Bonaparte had replied, ' Then why are we fighting? '

Ten weeks later, when Admiral Gambier's Fleet carrying an Expeditionary Force of twenty-seven thousand, under Lord Cathcart, seized the Danish Fleet in Copenhagen, voices in both London and Paris declared that M. Talleyrand must have betrayed his master. From no other source could Mr. Canning have learnt so correctly the details of the secret articles of the Peace concluded on the raft at Tilsit.

By the public treaty Prussia lost nearly half her area and population, and was required to assist France and Russia against Great Britain. Two new tributary states were called into being, a Kingdom of Westphalia for Jerome Bonaparte, and a Grand Duchy of Warsaw under the King of Saxony. The Emperor Napoleon would mediate between the Tsar and Turkey, and the Tsar between France and his late ally, Britain. Mr. Canning, who did not know of the secret articles, but had long foreseen a French occupation of the Danish mainland, and believed that Denmark, Sweden, Portugal and Austria were to be called in immediately to blockade Britain, had not hesitated to act strongly. He had heard from Lisbon . . . He had heard from Talleyrand . . . He had heard directly from a Russian source at Tilsit . . . How and what exactly he had heard, no member of the general public knew. In fact, he had heard more than the truth, for the Danish fleet had not been prepared for action against Scotland or Ireland or any other part of the United Kingdom, and the secret articles provided that the coercion of the Baltic Powers was only to be undertaken if Britain refused the Tsar's mediation.

Mr. Mackenzie followed his Tilsit despatch to London after four weeks. He had been up to Memel to see Lord Granville Leveson-Gower, British Ambassador to Russia, a representative selected, according to spiteful tongues, for no other reason than to continue the tradition, which had existed since Tudor days, of sending into Muscovy the most personable Englishman available.

Great Britain was violently criticized as a result of the Copenhagen action, and gained solid advantages. Mr. Mackenzie was employed again.

IV

During the black thirty months after Austerlitz, when the action in Trafalgar Bay had paralysed the invasion threat, but the Emperor Napoleon marched from strength to strength upon the Continent, a solitary success in arms was greeted in England with enthusiasm, and several babies, and at least one famous dog, received the name of Maida, in celebration of Sir John Stuart's victory. His defeat of five thousand French troops stimulated the natives of Calabria, but could not be followed up.

The people of England faced an unwholesome situation characteristically. Even on the subject of Napoleon

The Map of Europe

Bonaparte British opinion varied. Some persons of culture who had studied the *Code Napoléon* loudly proclaimed that the organizing capacity and vision of the most remarkable man of their age must excite universal admiration. In the Press, and political circles, party feeling continued to be violent. The conduct of the Royal Family, the privileged and the unprivileged classes, was as usual freely criticized. On one point only opinion appeared unanimous. England was not going to submit to Bonaparte.

On the death of Mr. Pitt, the King had sent for Lord Grenville, who had said that he must ask permission to include Mr. Fox and some of Mr. Fox's party in any new administration. The purblind King had replied resignedly that such had been his intention. In the new government, nicknamed 'All the Talents', Mr. Fox was Foreign Minister, Mr. Windham Secretary for the Colonies. Mr. Addington, who had been raised to the peerage as Lord Sidmouth, on joining Mr. Pitt's last administration, became Lord Privy Seal. Mr. Canning said that he supposed Addington was like the smallpox. Everyone must have him once in his life. The King soon discovered that if a dislike is to be kept in good condition, the enemies must never meet. He was surprised to find Mr. Fox so agreeable. His opponents beheld with malicious satisfaction, Mr. Fox urging with all his old eloquence the necessity for a strong Army and a strong Navy to continue the War against France. His friends hoped that he gained some satisfaction, during the last months of his life, from the fact that his motion for the abolition of the Slave Trade passed through the House after slight opposition. For his enlargement had come too late. Untiring attendance in a London office did not suit the constitution of a man of eight and fifty who, of recent years at any rate, had lived a regular life of leisure in fine air. While the Emperor Napoleon was winning the campaign which ended in the Treaty of the Raft, stories that Mr. Fox was breaking up were repeated, and bets laid as to his chances of lasting five years. He outlived his greatest political rival by less than eight months, and the government of which he had been the leading figure was dismissed six months later. The Tory Anti-Catholics who came into power early in 1807 remained in office for close on quarter of a century.

The fall of the Grenville ministry was not occasioned by any complaints that it had failed to prosecute the war with sufficient vigour. When the Emperor Napoleon issued his Berlin Decrees, forbidding France and her dependent countries to trade or communicate with Britain, the Grenville Ministry retaliated by the first of a series of Orders in Council, forbidding vessels to trade between any ports in the possession of France or her allies. In fact, it was impossible even for Bonaparte to do without the goods he pretended to exclude. The smuggling profession received many new recruits, and the Emperor Napoleon's troops marched in Northampton boots and Leeds overcoats, while the ladies of his court went in India muslins. But although he failed to destroy British industry, British trade was hard hit. The commercial campaign destined to drag on for eight years, aroused in Prussia impotent wrath against France, and in America bitter anti-English feeling, doomed to culminate in a declaration of War.

The Map of Europe

Amongst the new sovereigns created by Bonaparte during his re-division of Europe, was the only son-in-law of George III. The prodigiously stout little Duke of Würtemberg had trimmed his sails so successfully that in his senescence he found himself one of Bonaparte's puppet kings. Londoners heard with feelings of amused irritation that their Princess Royal had ordered a large gold crown for the roof of her palace at Stuttgart, and sent her mother a letter beginning, ' Très chère Mère et Soeur'. Queen Charlotte had been revolted by her married daughter's description of Bonaparte as a much misrepresented character, ' he has so bewitching a smile'. No doubt Bonaparte had smiled to find himself the cherished guest of the eldest daughter of His Britannic Majesty. Lady Uxbridge confessed to having been flung into a raging fever on hearing of the civilities paid to the Monster by ' our poor Princess Royal', who was said to have grown so shapeless that she reminded children of a snowman.

On a May evening, after the Exhibition had closed for the day, a royal carriage drew up outside the Royal Academy. A gawky, fair-haired school-child, a harassed-looking lady of middle age and two clergymen dismounted. The Princess Charlotte of Wales was becoming of increasing importance, since even if her father succeeded in divorcing her mother, he was unlikely to marry again. The Press had been much exercised by the problem of providing a suitable establishment for the heiress-presumptive, and great hopes had been held out of the results likely to be obtained by the appointments of the Lady de Clifford, Governess, the Bishop of Exeter, Preceptor, and, as assistant to the

Bishop, a young Fellow of All Souls College. Dr. Fisher had noticed with regret that the Princess Charlotte evinced no taste whatsoever for the Fine Arts. He had intimated to the President of the Royal Academy that he would like to bring H.R.H. after hours, to view a collection of the works of Britain's first contemporary artists. The Princess, a well-disposed young person, whose education had been sadly neglected, could be led, though not driven. To-day's expedition would form an inspiring introduction to drawing lessons.

The Princess, a child of fine physique, rather full in the cheeks at present, fixed the same light blue stare of uncomprehending hate upon the Picture of the Year, Mr. Lawrence's portrait of Sir F. Baring, Mr. Westall's 'Sleeping Nymph', Mr. Wilkie's 'Blind Fiddler'. . . . In their more exhausted moments all her preceptors were assailed by unspoken fears that H.R.H. seemed to have inherited her father's figure and her mother's understanding. The ladies of her household were appointed by her mother, the gentlemen by her grandfather. The Prince and Queen Charlotte must also be placated. Nobody guessed, as the pathetic procession passed slowly through the famous gallery, that the Bishop was furiously considering the terms of his resignation. Lady de Clifford, who carried tales to the Prince, and left the child of the broken home to the care of maid-servants, must go. ' Either the Bishop must give up his situation or the Women must give way! '

Mr. James Boswell, son of the biographer, on his summer visit to London, told Mr. Farington that affairs looked so ill, he was afraid to ask acquaintances ' What news? ' Yet for the very night on which Mr.

The Map of Europe

Mackenzie waited in the Tsar's barge below the raft at Tilsit, a Superb Gala was advertised to take place at Vauxhall, under the patronage of H.R.H. the Prince of Wales—the concert to include a new Grand Symphony by Beethoven, and two full pieces of Haydn and Mozart, followed by a Grand Arcadian Finale, National Airs, and fireworks—price for admission 3s. Petitions were arriving in London from Leeds, Bolton and other manufacturing towns which were feeling the effects of Bonaparte's blockade, but guests entertained to dinner by Mr. Angerstein, of St. Petersburg and London, sat down at six-fifteen at 'Woolands', Blackheath, to a war-time two-course meal served off plate and gilded porcelain, of two soups, mackerel and turbot, Madeira, Hock, Burgundy, and, with the ices and pines, claret and port. Tea was served at nine-fifteen.

The Prince, who was beginning to despair of a Regency, was running up vast bills by his improvements at Carlton House. Lord Stafford's additions to his London residence were on so large a scale that one good result was inevitable. Since everyone in his saloons appeared Lilliputian, nobody would seem of any consequence. Mr. John Kemble and Mr. Lawrence held earnest converse long after the curtain had fallen at Drury Lane. Their subject was nothing artistic. The famous actor was explaining to the fashionable painter that the late Lord Nelson had once told him that Britain would never have a secure and honourable Peace until she had been at War with all the powers under Bonaparte's control, and made him and them feel the invincible power of this country by sea.

267

The Map of Europe

The bombardment of Copenhagen and seizure of the Danish fleet provoked much hostile comment, even at home. That a weak neutral should have been attacked without warning seemed an imitation of Bonaparte's methods. Bonaparte, hoist with his own petard, had, according to Paris sources, never raged so furiously against perfidious Albion since he learnt the news of the assassination of Paul I. He had a scheme for an expedition against Egypt, a new plan for an attack on India. . . .

In rural England, while Bonaparte remorselessly proceeded to invade the Spanish Peninsula, and Russia declared War on Great Britain, people who no longer feared ' raft-weather,' gathered in their thousands on Clapham Common and Newmarket Heath, in early autumn sunshine, to watch Curley, the Brighton Shepherd, break the record for the mile, and Barclay of Urie outwalk Wood of Lancashire. At Badminton, poor Lord Granville Leveson-Gower confessed himself overcome by the noise made by the children of the house—'no less than ten come to dessert. It quite stuns me.'

The Vicar of Hoddesdon continued to empty his church of influential parishioners by opening his sermons, ' Fellow Worms! ' The Prince of Wales set a bad example, when staying self-invited in country houses. His looks and behaviour had horrified towns of the West Country, where the teachings of John Wesley had brought light into many humble homes. Religious observances were beginning to be regarded in castles as well as cottages. At Berkeley, when asked on a Sunday morning by his hostess if he would like to go to church, H.R.H. had replied that he would go to oblige her ladyship, if she desired it. She had made no answer, and he had not gone. To watch him take snuff was in itself a lesson in deportment; he was graciousness itself, singing with the ladies after dinner in the drawing-room, but he was late for every meal, and his suite were intolerable. The servant sent ahead to historic Berkeley, when shown the Gothic chamber prepared for his master, had ejaculated, ' This the room! A gloomy room like this will never do!' Lord Berkeley's *major domo* had quietly instructed the flunkey of Carlton House that 'this was an ancient, not a modern building', and the chamber in which they stood was considered the best. The Prince's flunkey himself had slept in it, after selecting another for his master.

In many well-appointed but unfashionable dining-rooms the toasts of ' The Prince of Wales—for ever!' and ' O King, live for ever!' were drunk with fervour. The usual stream of pleasant anecdotes of his homely majesty filtered to shop and cottage. ' I should not think,' said the half-blind old monarch to Lord Thomond, aged eighty-two, as they ambled quietly side by side in Taplow Woods, ' that any two gentlemen in England ride more than you and I.'

The appearance of a Comet, visible with the naked eye at nine p.m. on October 24th, distracted public attention from the flight of the ruined Portuguese Royal Family to Brazil, and the arrival at Yarmouth of Louis XVIII, travelling as the Comte de Lille, attended by many members of his family. In English country mansions of suitable dimensions, many exiled foreign royalties were beginning to comprehend what English cold and damp could mean. In Manchester, mobs of distressed weavers were being forcibly dispersed by cavalry. The unrest of the commercial world was spreading to the agricultural. Cattle-maiming and rick burning were becoming common. Bells rang in London to celebrate the re-taking of Cape Colony from the Dutch, but Bonaparte had trapped the Spanish royal house, and put in his brother Joseph as King of Spain.

Rather suddenly, in May, 1808, stories of a general insurrection in Spain reached London. At last a warlike people, whose decadent rulers had feebly capitulated to the tyrant, had risen united by national wrath.

In his thin grey house in Harley Street, Sir Arthur Wellesley was explaining to a person who had called by appointment, that he wished a secret message delivered as soon as possible to the Commander of the valuable Spanish Army, recently lured by Bonaparte into the north of Germany, and there detained. Mr. Mackenzie, British secret agent in Heligoland, would supply Mr. Robertson with funds and further him on his dark and dangerous journey. 'They tell me, Mr. Robertson, that you are a man of courage.' Mr. Robertson, who was by birth a native of Galloway, and by profession a Benedictine monk from the Scottish Monastery in Ratisbon, learnt his password, which related to a certain picture in a palace at Toledo, and his message, which was that a British fleet only awaited the Spanish commander's signal to rescue the Spanish army from the Usurper's thrall. England, ready to help revolting Spain by every means in her power, had an Expeditionary Force lying at Cork, ready to embark for the Spanish Peninsula.

The Map of Europe

The black thirty months, after Trafalgar had shattered the invasion threat, but before a single Continental nation had dared to oppose the Emperor Napoleon, were at an end. A new campaign was about to begin. Sir Arthur Wellesley, who affirmed that his Expeditionary Force was ready to the last button, and Britain's soldiers of every rank were only longing for the chance to measure themselves against the troops of France, hoped that in a campaign of the Spanish Peninsula Bonaparte might find ' a running sore '.

Chapter 9

Roly-Poly Square

O n a stormy July morning of 1808, an overcoated
gentleman with neat side-whiskers, and the
type of erect profile which looks well against a
seascape, lay gasping in the confines of a British government lugger, straining his eyes for the appearance of
land on the eastern horizon. The passage of the *Black
Joke* (Captain Alt) bound from Falmouth for Corunna,
had been rough and even dangerous. 'H.C.R.'s'
cronies of Printing House Square would hardly have
recognized, in the pitiable figure who had for ten days
been doggedly attempting to learn Spanish, while sea-
sick, their most hilarious *raconteur*.

The Times newspaper was sending a special correspondent to the Peninsula. The idea of despatching a
literary man to report on the progress of a British Expeditionary Force, was new in the annals of journalism,
but Mr. John Walter II, chief proprietor of *The Times*,
had never allowed such a consideration to dissuade him
from a project. He had long held, and acted upon the

belief, that if a paper could be relied upon to offer impartial opinions and accurate early information, its sales would increase. Naturally his independence had involved him in serious consequences. His tussle with the managers of the theatres alone, would have filled the eight volumes of a contemporary novel. He was continually at war with the minions of the Post Office, and complaining to the Home Office. Foreign captains at Gravesend reported that they were asked if they carried anything for *The Times*, and that if they admitted this, such packages were seized, while those for the ministerial journals passed on.

Mr. Walter's correspondence with his continental agents either arrived late at Printing House Square, often bearing signs of having been re-sealed, or did not arrive at all. He had instructed his Emden correspondent to address all copy under cover to a mercantile house in the City of London. Messrs. Buller's clerks found that the letters containing enclosures for Mr. Walter of *The Times* were delivered after the remainder of their mail, with excuses of mis-direction and illegible handwriting.

Now that Bonaparte's blockade was beginning to close the Dutch and Baltic ports, Mr. Walter was being reduced to depend for foreign intelligence upon persons accustomed to carrying contraband—in plain English, smugglers. He was in touch with a French officer near a certain north French port, ready to forward regular packets to Deal; another of the same sort had been engaged by him to supply Harwich. He had represented that he would not employ such persons unless they abandoned illicit traffic. He had offered that

papers so obtained should be at the disposal of the
Government. Even his Deal and Harwich packets were
closely watched, and sometimes delayed or missing.
Nevertheless, by August, 1808, a large section of the
public were reading the official gazettes for confirma-
tory details, *The Times* for the first news. For, in spite
of all difficulties, *The Times* often outstripped government couriers, and the day was not distant when Viscount Castlereagh would present his compliments, and
beg Mr. Walter to have the goodness to tell him if he
had any intelligence of a recent French defeat; and
foreign diplomats would send elaborate thanks for information not yet available to them through official
channels.

Mr. Henry Crabb Robinson, Britain's first special
correspondent, was not one of *The Times*' 'supercilious
lads'. At the age of twenty-two, a timely legacy had released him from uncongenial toil in an attorney's office.
He had always wanted to travel. He was now thirty-
three, and had conversed with Goethe and Schiller and
Madame de Staël, and gained a Jena degree, and
reached his native shores after long absence, in the
same vessel which had brought to *The Times* the sad
news of Austerlitz. Mr. Fox had not been able to
employ his talents in the diplomatic service, but Mr.
Walter had engaged him, and sent him abroad again—
to Altona.

Mr. Robinson's letters, describing the fall of Dant-
zig, the Battle of Friedland and the Peace of Tilsit, had
given British readers the fullest information available
of these events, but the Emperor Napoleon's occupation of Denmark had obliged him to beat a retreat

home, by way of Stockholm, ignominiously disguised
as a German. While Bonaparte continued to carve up
Europe undisturbed, he had spent an enjoyable six
months in London, as 'a sort of foreign editor', noting
the amiabilities and peculiarities of Mr. Wordsworth
and Mr. Coleridge, and the Lambs and Mr. Southey;
for he was an excellent mixer, and although a good
talker, could also listen. Rumours of a national Spanish
insurrection and the despatch of a British Expeditionary Force to the Peninsula, had suggested to Mr.
Walter that his foreign editor could be sent abroad
again. For this astute and far-seeing man had early
recognized in his new *employé* ideal journalistic qualities. Mr. Robinson's graphic descriptions of Lord
Erskine conducting a case at the Assizes, and Mr.
John Wesley preaching at Colchester, must be based
on the observations of a schoolboy. At a performance
by Mrs. Siddons, according to fellow students, the
youthful 'H.C.R.' had so interrupted a pathetic speech
of the favourite, that he had narrowly escaped ejection
from the Pit. In fact, his hollow laugh had been provoked by deepest emotion. It appeared, therefore,
that he had, in addition to the quick eye, tenacious
memory, strong digestion and balanced affability
essential to success in his new profession, some
sensibility.

The British rank and file, and even the British officer
of public school education, would lack the time and
capacity, during the forthcoming campaign, to communicate to those at home vivid impressions of the
Peninsula. A few officers, who could draw, might
commit to paper neat little pen and wash studies of

attentive rustics and engrossed, scarlet-coated military. Only when a man came on leave could the family circle hope to hear of bare-footed, golden-skinned water carriers, and ladies with their heads veiled in black lace, and women in bright shawls edged with jingling coins, riding pillion on mules, behind patriot peasants with knives in their hose—all on the move through the crazy, dirty, intensely romantic alleys and streets of sea ports and mountain towns—and catch an echo of the tread of British soldiers marching under cold, light-blue skies, through scenery in which oranges and lemons hung on the trees, while the streets of Falmouth were still covered with black ice.

Mr. Robinson landed at Corunna on the evening of Sunday, July 31st, and found the town in joyous disorder. ' I put myself in immediate connection with the editor of the miserable little daily newspaper '. A number of resident British merchants, and the officers of H.M.S. *Defiance*, proved valuable and interesting acquaintances.

The disembarkation of Sir Arthur Wellesley's Expeditionary Force at Mondego Bay was completed by August 5th, 1808, and on August 9th *The Times* published the first of a series of letters, headed ' Shores of the Bay of Biscay'.

II

The campaign in the Peninsula opened auspiciously. The French force under General Dupont, which had invaded Andalusia, capitulated to the Spanish patriots a few days before Sir Arthur Wellesley's small army landed. On August 23rd General Junot's Army of

Roly-Poly Square

Portugal was driven by Sir Arthur from the field of Vimiero.

The news of a shock to Bonaparte's arms—even though the Emperor himself was absent from the scene —heartened the country. An English lady of fashion, dallying away the last days of a heat-wave summer, surrounded by her sunburnt family, amongst the red fishing nets and blue isles of Loch Fyne below Inverary, wrote to London in triumph. ' Now we shall be no more told, I hope, that whatever we may do by sea, our land troops are inferior to every other nation—that we are always worsted, and that it is ridiculous for us to attempt to cope with the French. How I should like to be near some of the croakers! ' But English triumph was short-lived, and the croakers soon had unlimited material for grim speculation.

The mails brought stories of trouble in India, and discontent in Canada. That the Victor of Vimiero should be coming home to face a Court of Enquiry at Chelsea could not, whatever the circumstances, be interpreted as a reassuring symptom. Sir Arthur Wellesley, who had not been allowed to follow up his victory, left the court satisfied, but a general impression remained in the public mind that Britain's commanders would be well advised to cease fighting one another and concentrate upon Bonaparte. Early in the New Year grumblings that all was not well at the War Office culminated in the exposure of an abuse in high military circles calculated to stagger a country fighting for existence.

His Majesty's second son, the Commander-in-Chief, had an expensive mistress called Mary Anne Clarke, who had long been augmenting her irregularly paid allowance by promising commissions in the Army. The unedifying scene of witty, pretty Mrs. Clarke's long examination at the Bar of the House of Commons was attended by the wives of many leading officers and politicians. A snowstorm of pamphlets pelted upon the freezing country. Mrs. Clarke published her opinions of the Dukes of York and Kent, and the leaders of the party who had called for the investigation. She was narrowly prevented from publishing the love-letters of her sterling but slow-witted royal admirer. After many weeks, the Commander-in-Chief was acquitted of having connived at, or profited by, Mrs. Clarke's efforts, but in deference to public opinion, sadly resigned his commission and the lady.

The squalid scandal was at its height, when London learnt that Sir John Moore had advanced from Lisbon to attack Marshal Soult, but that the Emperor Napoleon, coming from Madrid with an overwhelming force, had obliged him to retire. Until the full story was known, Sir John, who had died a hero's death, after fighting a masterly retreat, was gloomily accused of having been 'Bonaparte-struck'. The landing, in stormy weather, of the wreck of his army, and exaggerated reports that the Spanish patriots had collapsed, further lowered spirits at home. Unluckily, only a small circle could know that Sir Arthur Wellesley pronounced himself not at all 'Bonaparte-struck'. When his victory, though after heavy losses, at Talavera, was announced in September, expectations were so modest that some chroniclers thought the action had better be styled a repulse. The Whig opposition had done their best to minimize the exploit of a general whom they considered a Tory nominee.

Lord Castlereagh arrived for a sitting to Mr. Lawrence, so silent, so strange in his air, that the painter took alarm, and refrained from commemorating a perfect figure of woe. More evil tidings from central Europe had shaken the aristocratic composure of the Minister for War. The Austrians, who had been inspired by Spain's example to make one more effort against Napoleon, had been forced to sue for peace after one more defeat. The name of Wagram was added to the list of the invincible Emperor's victories. Worse was to come. A British Expeditionary Force sent to Antwerp, where Bonaparte was building a fleet, was evacuated after losing half its numbers in the marshes of Walcheren. Indignant cries were raised that the expedition had been ill-conceived and ill-equipped, especially with regard to medical supplies. At the very awkward Parliamentary investigation, a young Scottish officer, the future head of Lord Wellington's Medical Staff, was so overcome by the atmosphere that he succumbed to aphasia. He could not, for the life of him, find words to explain what he perfectly well knew— that the Peruvian bark essential for the treatment of his patients, had been supplied by philanthropic American adventurer craft. A first-class War rumour declared that Lord Castlereagh had been sent to the Tower, convicted of collusion with the Emperor Napoleon. Lord Castlereagh and Mr. Canning met on Putney Heath, and Mr. Canning received a ball in the thigh. Both ministers resigned; the Prime Minister followed suit.

Roly-Poly Square

The Duke of Portland's successor exhibited painstaking mediocrity of the most unmistakable description. When a deputation from the City of London petitioned that the English force remaining in the Peninsula, withdrawn behind the Tagus, and reputedly decimated by fever, should be recalled, Mr. Spencer Perceval threw upon Sir Arthur Wellesley—now Baron Douro of Wellesley in the County of Somerset, and Viscount Wellington of Talavera, and Wellington in the same county—the responsibility of making the choice. Lord Wellington chose to stay.

'*Il paraît que c'est un homme, ce Wellington,*' said the Emperor Napoleon, in Vienna. But the official *Moniteur* was instructed to hope that a British general who essayed grand catastrophes might ever remain in command.

III

Bonaparte had become a legendary figure during his lifetime. English grass-widows, troubled by nightmare, saw that travelling carriage rattling across Europe. At every frontier, a French sentry sprang to the salute. The stillness of the night was broken by the cry of '*Vive l'Empereur !*' On the box, his dusky countenance greenish in the moonlight, his arms folded, sat the Emperor's Mameluke, Roustam. There were fine green liveries, and fine horses. Bonaparte's saddle horses were always greys—flea-bitten, dapple, trout, slate, mouse-coloured, ash . . . He wore under his famous '*redingote grise*' the green, piped scarlet, uniform of a Mounted *Chasseur* of the Guard. His travelling *berline* had been made large enough for him to sleep in. It contained a silk couch which let up and down, and in day-time accommodated six persons. At nights he exchanged his traditional black felt hat for a fur-lined nightcap, and wore scarlet morocco slippers. Morocco and shagreen valises, with silver-gilt furniture, plentifully sprinkled with Bees and crowned laureated letters N. were amongst the splendid fittings of the fatal equipage. A bottle of wine, a cold capon, fresh rolls, were always in their accustomed place, lest the Emperor should not choose to dismount to dine. So far, he had been over the Pyrenees but once, and was leaving the campaign of the Peninsula to various marshals. But the day would come when some British success would determine him to take the command in person, and roll up the map of Spain and Portugal as he had rolled up that of every other country of the Continent. A horrible cartoon depicted him dragging all the nations of Europe in the wake of Death, a skeleton figure playing frenziedly on a violin. Ladies with invaluable relatives in Lord Wellington's army sometimes slept ill during dank winter months when transports were bringing in the ghostly men who had fought their way through the snowy mountains of Galicia to Corunna, and the Paris news was that the Emperor was free to found a dynasty. He had divorced his wife.

The last event, long expected, was no surprise to those who had noted in the Paris Press the arrival of a large assemblage of vassal sovereigns, clearly called as witnesses to some important occasion. The English reader was presented with a *fait accompli*, on December 27th 1809. 'BONAPARTE HAS DISSOLVED HIS MARRIAGE'. ' He wishes to get rid of an old woman and marry a

young one. As usual, he has made his sacrifice at the call
of France!' The only surprising factor was that there
had been no scandal. Her infidelities had not been the
declared cause of his putting away the fading but
vehement Joséphine. Indeed, for years past, the un-
faithful partner in that unsound marriage had been
Bonaparte himself, and a dark tale which had filtered
to royal Windsor, accused him of having sired the
eldest son of the fair Queen of Holland, a young lady
who was at once his step-daughter and the wife of his
younger brother. George III credited the Monster
with believing, or wishing the world to believe, that
this adopted child was an actual son. The death of this
boy, and the pregnancy of a young and aristocratic
Polish mistress, whose fidelity he could not doubt, had
sealed the fate of Joséphine, who confessed to forty-
three, but was probably forty-six. The Emperor, aged
forty, required, and at last had reason to believe that
he could produce, a legitimate heir to his great and
growing possessions.

Extracts from smuggled copies of the *Moniteur* were
languidly scanned for descriptions of the ceremony of
the divorce, which had been quite a quiet and formal
affair. The English Press made an unabashed *volte face*
and Joséphine was suddenly recognized as essential to
Bonaparte's career, his Lucky Star. It was remembered
that she had attempted to dissuade him from the invasion of England and the murder of the Duc d'Enghien.
Her generosity had been unbounded, although at some
audiences it had taken such unpractical shapes as presenting to the hungry orphan of a fallen soldier a
mechanical toy valued at many pounds. There would

be no more pleasant informal country-house dinner parties on hot summer nights at 'La Malmaison', where the graceful *châtelaine* had raised so many new varieties of rose and carnation, and French sunshine slanting into wainscoted rooms, all painted light green, from parkland filled with glimmering Belvederes and ornamental water, woke answering brilliances in many mirrors, and furniture of shining mahogany, upholstered in gold and green leathers and brocades, adorned with gilt metal wreaths. . . .

All her frailties were forgotten when the 'old' Empress drove out of Paris, and as far as the eye could see, out of history, in a carriage of surpassing elegance, built for the occasion, and named 'L'Opal'. She was to retain her rank, and had been handsomely pensioned. Who would succeed her, was a far more interesting subject for speculation.

A Princess of Saxony was mentioned by English newsmongers, or, since his inclination towards his brother's wife was marked, perhaps after another divorce in the Imperial family, Queen Hortense would take her mother's place. A story welcome in England declared that the haughty Empress-mother of Russia had told her 'Bonaparte-struck' son that sooner than give a Romanovna to the upstart, she would drown both her unmarried daughters in the Neva. The Grand Duchess Catherine had been hastily married off to an unspectacular mate. Court physicians smoothly averred that the Grand Duchess Anna was not yet marriageable. A breach between France and Russia was predicted by wishful thinkers.

The Emperor Napoleon showed himself perfectly

undismayed by Russian lethargy. Only a few weeks
elapsed between his dismissal of Joséphine and the
announcement that the eldest daughter of the Emperor
of Austria was the chosen victim. The Archduchess
Maria-Louisa, who was just eighteen, had a step-
mother who would gladly part with her, and a particularly invertebrate father. She was not a *belle* or a wit,
and though good-humoured, fair and fresh-looking,
was slightly marked by the smallpox. However represented, the fact remained that Bonaparte had succeeded
in allying himself with the oldest and proudest dynasty
in Europe. His children would be half Hapsburg.
Authors of English posters and handbills, much addicted to the rhetorical question, and accustomed to
reply to ' WHO IS BONAPARTE? ' by the scornful explanation, ' Why, an obscure Corsican, that began his
Murderous Career in Turning Artillery on the Citizens
of Paris', were faced by the realization that Bonaparte
was about to become the relation by marriage of most
European royalties. ' The Vagrant Common Disturber,
known by the name of Napoleon Bonaparte, alias Jaffa
Bonaparte, alias Opium Bonaparte', dealt a shrewd
blow at British equanimity when he decided to become
the son-in-law of the Austrian Emperor.

The French Press excelled itself in accounts of the
trousseau being prepared for the lucky bride. The prices
of the scores of pairs of silk hose, court dresses and
shawls ordered for her by an indulgent bridegroom old
enough to be her parent, were much advertized. The
Emperor had himself shown the Queen of Westphalia
a bathroom furnished and hung with Indian cashmeres
at a cost of 400,000 francs. The jewellery awaiting the

gauche girl beggared description. The list of her future
household included some of the noblest names of
France. *Faute de mieux* many returned *émigrés* were falling into line, had obeyed the nod of the conqueror.
They could salve their consciences by assuring themselves that they were called upon to serve a royal lady
of unblemished reputation. A few people pitied the
blonde and blushing Archduchess led as a lamb to the
slaughter, and in fashionable classical style alluded to
her as 'Iphigenia' and 'Andromeda'. Lord Castlereagh supposed that a Virgin must occasionally be
sacrificed to the Minotaur. As the day of her departure
drew near, a romantic legend asserted that she had fled
to convent shade. But, as English editors pointed out,
no convent of Europe could protect an Unwilling Fair
from the ravening grasp of Bonaparte. Neither did
they believe that a peace-offer to England was to grace
Bonaparte's nuptials. Such a move would be against his
interests.

The proxy wedding which transformed the Arch-
duchess Maria Louisa into Marie-Louise, Empress of
the French, took place on a showery March day, in the
dark Augustine church of Vienna. She was set on her
road to Paris, attended by a bickering cavalcade. England was reduced to ridicule of Bonaparte's family and
entourage.

His mother, a Spartan dame, was the type of old lady
who, under less favourable conditions, would have hidden her savings in a stocking, not trusting the Banks.
Madame Mère, installed by her pretentious son in a
spacious Parisian *hôtel*, infuriated him by living as fru-
gally as possible, in preparation for the inevitable crash.

Roly-Poly Square

Visitors to her marble halls fell over the shrouded furniture illuminated by a single gaslamp. *Madame Mère* would have liked to invest some of her easy-come money in safe British stocks. She had been prolific. Bonaparte had four brothers and three sisters, all of whom were unable to adapt themselves with dignity to improved circumstances. Everything was false about the ladies, even their fashionable Christian names. Queen Caroline had been baptized Maria-Annunziata; the Grand Duchess Elisa had begun life in Corsica as Maria-Anna. Bonaparte affected much fondness for their offspring. It was part of his propaganda to have himself depicted on the terrace of St. Cloud, the centre of an enchanting nursery party. Of his brothers, the King of Spain was a laughing-stock, the King of Holland, a decadent. Two brothers had incurred his wrath by stealing love-matches. One had obediently abandoned his lively American, and received a Princess and a Kingdom in recompense. The other, proving adamant, had been cut out of Bonaparte's will, and was expected in England. More thoughtful, but not more charitable observers said that, with the exception of the Princess Borghese, who was simply a fashion-plate, all Bonaparte's brothers and sisters had unusual ability and were amusing caricatures of the successful member of their family, exhibiting his unscrupulousness and narrow egotism in exaggerated form.

The characters of the Emperor's celebrated Marshals were fairly well appreciated in English military circles, and their portraits were familiar in many homes. Bernadotte, heir-presumptive to the throne of Sweden, the son of a Gascon market-gardener, was an efficient officer, but a born and unscrupulous intriguer. With his astounding nose, black curls and glaring eye, he looked mad, but was far from being so. Masséna, Duke of Rivoli, Prince of Essling, had Genoese Jew written all over his dark-lined countenance. He was the greediest for money of the whole precious lot, more even for money than for power. He was universally disliked. Murat, King of Naples, owed his position to his marriage with Bonaparte's most ambitious sister. Of all the Emperor's Marshals, English officers decided that Murat pleased them best. He was the most complete vulgarian and poseur. To see the King of Naples taking the lead in any action, attired in the gorgeous uniform of an Imperial hussar, lavishly trimmed with lace and sables, was to see something unforgettable. Soult, Duke of Dalmatia, was bourgeois by birth, selfish and cold, a great collector of plunder—greater even than Masséna —but a fine commander. Ney, Duke of Elchingen, son of an Alsatian cooper of means, red-headed, frank, impulsive, was loved by all his officers and men. He was insubordinate when placed under others, but recovered esteem by his brilliant tactical skill and courage. . . . Any officer might be glad to serve under Mortier, the Duke of Treviso, a most gentlemanly person, or Lannes, Duke of Montebello, who had begun his life in a livery stable and died of wounds after the battle of Essling—reproaching his Emperor for reckless bloodshed, said a story popular in English dining-rooms. Poor Junot, the Duke of Abrantés, one of those who had not yet found the *bâton* in his knapsack, did not look mad, but seemed likely to become so. . . .

While the new Empress was drawing towards the

French frontier, a number of English ladies who had been detained in France for nine years, landed at Plymouth. They reported that their unfortunate compatriots were as well as might be expected. In France living was cheap, but all articles of dress were inordinately dear. French authorities had attempted to dissuade them from attempting to return to England, a country in which there was no food.

Some astonishing anomalies existed in the belligerent countries during the darkest of the war years. Parisian ladies who led an exacting social life, had discovered that beloved children delivered to an English ' miss ' had better health, and were more amenable to discipline than their contemporaries under native control. The wife of more than one Bonapartist Marshal kept in her household, throughout the Peninsular struggle, a rigidly correct English governess.

A young English lawyer of pro-Bonapartist tendencies, received permission to visit Paris in December, 1810, in order to collect materials for a history and description of the French capital. His admission was a mistake from the French point of view, for he returned quite disillusioned, to tell London acquaintances that theatres were silent when the Despot entered the royal box. Bonaparte, a little fat man, with a greasy complexion, and active eyes, always playing about, had so much deteriorated in looks that he had ordered court painters to copy old portraits, and declined to give further sittings. The people of Paris, and indeed of France, were being kept in a state of ignorance of all political proceedings abroad, and in a subjection scarcely credible. Bonaparte had in reality no Ministers.

Roly-Poly Square

He appropriated all business of importance, and nothing but the fears of a revolutionary war in case of his disappearance, kept him where he was. Sooner or later his generals must rise against him. But generals do not rise against a leader who is still providing them with opportunities for conquest.

At Lord Lonsdale's London residence, on June 20th, 1810, a distinguished company sat down to dinner at seven-twenty. 'Bonaparte was mentioned.' One distinguished guest believed that if Bonaparte could have foreseen the resistance with which he would meet in Spain, he would never have attempted the subjugation of that country. His design to invade England was dismissed as impracticable. Though he had all the ports of the Continent, and might build ships, yet he could not make sailors. The many failures in the City were distressing. . . . The King's health was most unsatisfactory. His fondly-loved youngest child, the Princess Amelia, was unmistakably succumbing to phthisis and heart-break. . . . The prospect of a Regency under the Prince was not a cheerful prospect. H.R.H. was developing a growing resemblance to his ancestor, Henry VIII. He was said to be an affectionate brother to his spinster sisters—poor old cats, a dead weight upon him and upon the nation. The words were a quotation from a letter of the Princess Sophia.

With such agreeable subjects for conversation, served by nine footmen, on a profusion of massy gold and silver plate, Lord Lonsdale's guests sat at table till nine-ten.

The audacious Mr. Mackenzie found himself in a Paris beflagged for the entry of Marie-Louise. Mr.

Mackenzie who had, since his return from Tilsit, been acting as a post-box in Heligoland, in touch with every redoubtable smuggler and British secret agent of the Baltic, had reason to be satisfied with his new employment. Father Robertson of Ratisbon had been forwarded by him to the captive Spanish army in Denmark with complete success. The escape of La Romana's force, in a British fleet, had earned Bernadotte a severe reprimand. Mr. Mackenzie, who had well-founded suspicions that the Paris police had a full *dossier* of his activities, was now official British representative, accredited to make arrangements for the exchange of Prisoners of War. Already, authorities in the districts haunted by him for the purpose of visiting British prisoners, complained of his wolf-hunting expeditions, entailing long friendly talks with peasants of coastal and frontier villages. Mr. Mackenzie, who was the most cautious as well as one of the cleverest of agents, and destined to die in harness as an affluent Consul-General at Lisbon, found much to interest him in the appearance of Bonaparte's capital prepared for his second nuptials.

The new Empress was to be left in no doubt as to her future duties. The decorations of the triumphal arch of the *Étoile* announced, ' She will charm the leisure hours of the hero', and ' She will be to France a tender mother'.

The *Moniteur* of March 30th, 1810, quoted in London nine days later, announced that the Emperor and Empress had arrived together at the château of Compiègne between eight and nine p.m. on the night of the 28th. They had been visible in Soissons for an instant only. Her Imperial Majesty was in the best of health. The *Moniteur* had not received permission to recount details known to many readers. An elaborate pavilion had been erected at Soissons for the ceremony of the reception of the bride. At the last moment the bride-groom of forty, whose first wish was to secure the suc-cession, who knew that Nature could be coy, had decided against a first meeting witnessed by eager thousands. The proxy wedding was valid. Attended by the egregious Murat only, he had hurried through driving rain to Courçelles, stopped the Empress's coach, introduced himself, and given orders for an uninterrupted progress to Compiègne.

The virgin habit in which Marie-Louise had pro-ceeded to the altar six days later was a hollow mockery. Although the *Moniteur* was discreet, of course anec-dotes of an occurrence to which many people could attest, reached England. Four years later, when her desertion of a fallen man was desired, interested advisers of Marie-Louise did not hesitate to draw her attention to the appalling affront offered to an Arch-duchess of Austria, and the ductile Marie-Louise did not remember that Bonaparte had proved the most indulgent and generous of husbands.

The *Moniteur* continued, during the early summer of 1810, to describe the many happy public appearances of the bridal pair. English critics heard that the young Empress was an automaton, and her court, severely regulated by etiquette, much inferior in attractions to that of Joséphine. Bonaparte's sisters and sisters-in-law were spitefully inclined towards a genuine princess, whose child would supersede their children. Unlike her husband, Marie-Louise did not feel cold much, and enjoyed long meals. She was always unpunctual. The ill-matched couple departed for a holiday tour of the Netherlands, and refreshing sea-breezes. At a reception at Antwerp, Marie-Louise swooned, but the incident signified nothing. Six months passed before the *Moniteur* was empowered to announce the good news for which all France was hungrily waiting.

An interesting event, affecting all Europe, was the subject of unblushing publicity. Engravings of this winter represented a Marie-Louise, matronly in figure, cosily regarding a mountain of fine baby-linen, and practising a *berceuse*. The silver-gilt and mother-of-pearl cradle prepared by the City of Paris for the most important child in the world, occupied the foreground of the picture. Lesser cradles of mahogany, with quilted velvet and satin linings and curtains of silk and gauze, all presided over by crowned Victories and powdered with gold bees, were described and drawn. Long columns of mercers' bills detailed the *layette*, valued at £120,000. An army of goldsmiths and artists created an avalanche of toys suitable for the son of a Conqueror. Even his coral and bells was shaped in the likeness of a veteran of the Guard. The Emperor was prepared, should the first arrival in his nursery be a girl. ' My daughter cannot be allowed to leave France.' He had promised Queen Hortense that her infant son should marry the princess.

English families knew of the Empress's confinement within a few hours of the event. Throughout England's struggle against Napoleon, no tidings passed so quickly from Paris to London. Everyone had read in the paper that twenty-one rounds would be fired if the child were a girl, a hundred for a son and heir. When, on the morning of Wednesday, March 20th, 1811, fishermen off Dover heard the guns of the enemy coast speak, they knew enough to bring in with their catch the news that Boney, successful in everything, had got his boy.

For a few days, ill-disposed English journalists circulated stories that the infant had been still-born, that the Empress could never bear again; that the Empress had succumbed, and that the child was so delicate that its christening had been performed within twelve hours. Gradually it appeared undeniable that Marie-Louise, after a difficult first experience of child-birth, had made an exemplary recovery, and that a finer infant could not be found than 'young Napoleon'.

English propagandists had to devote their attention to the grave aspect of French disagreements with Russia. The regrettable truth was that the Emperor Napoleon seemed as firm as a rock.

IV

Roly-Poly Square was not to be found on any map, or plan of the city of Lisbon. It was one of the principal squares of the Portuguese capital, but its official native name was O Rocio. British tars, fascinated by its pavement of white and black marble, arranged in a curious pattern of waves, had long ago nicknamed it after a leading British pudding. When British soldiers arrived in the Peninsula, they never doubted that ' Roly-Poly ' was the name. Nor, while ministers in London quar-

relled, and indignant citizens, and even officers of his
staff, awaited an explanation from Lord Wellington,
and Paris rang joy-bells for the birth of the young
Napoleon, and the news from home was the old King
had run mad again, and the Prince Regent was giving
showy parties, and the people of Lancashire were breaking up their machinery, did the British Expeditionary
Force ever seriously doubt that from the men who had
known and loved Roly-Poly Square must come the
eventual answer to Bonaparte.

Officers' wives, attended by their ladies' maids, a
groom, and sometimes many infants, set up their sketching stools in its corners. They dashed off impressions of
a street given up to the cloth-merchants, and another
famous for its goldsmiths' and silversmiths' shops, and
houses with windows which were also doors, and bal-
conies everywhere, and cloaked beggars, and cloudless
skies and flourishing exotics. They found the climate of
the Peninsula very agreeable, except during a few weeks
of high summer. Seven o'clock in the evening was the
hour when the town became most crowded, and everyone who wished to meet friends drove, rode or walked
in the neighbourhood of the square. An ancient suburb,
in the extreme west of the city, was military headquarters. Belem was noticeable for its antique tower on
the foreshore, its Royal Palace, and a white limestone
convent, with beautiful cloisters, built to commemorate
the sailing of Vasco de Gama, to discover the sea-road
to India. Some supposed remains of the explorer had
been recently re-interred in the convent church, and
above de Gama's tomb stared a figurehead from a
mediaeval bark which had probably looked down

as serenely and sightlessly on thirsty men becalmed.

Lord Wellington was said to be irritated by the growing tendency of officers and men to make lengthy descents for medical attention, supplies—and, of course, news—upon Lisbon. The chief of his Medical Staff was pressing upon him a scheme for mobile hospitals. But his lordship was decidedly against the addition of any further impedimenta to his army. Already, when on the march, it was an extraordinary sight. Many officers' wives, in travelling carriages or on horseback, followed their husbands, and naturally, being English ladies, they had brought their pets, and were collecting more daily—Spanish greyhounds, attractive mongrels, parrots, canaries, monkeys, etc. Wives and dependants of the rank and file, scores of amazing and homely figures on donkeys, brought up the rear of every regiment. Lord Wellington would dearly have liked to send the whole lot packing, but had no power to do so. The guns must come first. The great depôt at Lisbon would have to stay. Roly-Poly Square would remain the *rendezvous* and clearing-house, and in the opinion of its *habitués*, the focal point, of Europe's struggle against the Emperor Napoleon.

English housewives wrote home that the Portuguese were tractable and friendly, and the Spaniards a very fine people, their lower classes deeply religious, vigorous and gay, without French frivolity. The Spanish aristocracy appeared either pro-French at heart, or impenetrable. A few personages announced that their palace was the English officers' home, but if any English ever got within its forbidding walls, all the fare produced was a glass of chocolate, followed by a pint of cold water and a few preserved fruits. The only excellent meat in the Peninsula was the ham, sugar-cured, though some *gourmets* belauded the *olla podrida*, a medley something in the line of Yorkshire pie.

Spirits at home, and to some extent in the Peninsula, touched their lowest point in the War during the days whilst Lord Wellington was retreating to the lines of Torres Vedras. He had kept his intentions so dark, that even some of his officers had believed that when they reached Lisbon they would embark. In England, the general public only understood that a Ministry strongly assaulted by the Opposition was not at one with itself; that whilst Bonaparte was founding a dynasty, their Royal Family presented a pathetic spectacle; and that one more Expeditionary Force seemed likely to require evacuation. The voices of Nelson, Fox and Pitt were still. The thrill of preparing to meet an invasion which never came, had subsided. Bonaparte was not succeeding in starving England, but he was succeeding in every other direction.

For another eight months, from October, 1810, to June, 1811, for those in England, no lasting ray of light pierced a situation of which the gloom was only equalled by the boredom and cost. A few privileged Londoners heard of a private letter from Lord Wellington, in which his lordship stated that he was so well satisfied with his position near Lisbon, that he wished for nothing better than that Marshal Masséna should attack with a hundred and fifty thousand men.

In February, 1811, General Stewart, Adjutant-General, brother to Lord Castlereagh, home on six weeks' leave, appeared in good health and spirits. He explained that military operations in Portugal were necessarily suspended by the weather, and that if he were Marshal Masséna he would do nothing more than stay where he was, obliging Lord Wellington to remain covering Lisbon, while expensively and erratically supplied from home. Contrary to wishful stories, Masséna's army was not starving. At any rate, recent prisoners had said that, through the winter months, they had been getting one pound of bread and one pound of meat a head per day.

When at last the news of Marshal Masséna's retreat reached England, many persons, and especially politicians of the Opposition, loudly voiced surprise. The troops of the Peninsula, who had been engaged in fortifying the lines of Torres Vedras during the black months, and had not reached so low an ebb of spirits, except perhaps for a few days during the retreat, thenceforward trusted their Commander-in-Chief implicitly; but at home his actions continued to be criticized, even after the battles of Salamanca and Vittoria, and only after the last triumph was he allowed to send home incompetent brigadiers, and refuse officers who possessed more influence than capacity.

England settled down to the realization that successes were being won in the Peninsula, but only a limited number of people took an intelligent interest in the distant and expensive campaign. Their homes were no longer threatened. Marriageable young ladies now existed who had never known what it was not to be at war with France. The War, to many of them, meant little more than the possibility of meeting officers if they went for a shopping expedition into Meryton, and the prospect of partners in uniform at country balls. From such thrilling companions they might gather that the lines of Torres Vedras were a chain of defences occupying a fine site on high ground in the neighbourhood of Lisbon, and perhaps form some hazy picture of the shining waters of the Tagus and the wrinkled sheet of the Atlantic, and a thin red line waiting for the attack of many blue columns.

Judging by the number of articles on this subject in ladies' magazines, large tracts of moorland in Portugal abounded in wild flowers, especially the sweet-scented cistus. English schoolrooms learnt that the landscape of Portugal lacked the grandeur of Spain. It had no vast plains, no inland seas or high mountains, but its Flora, the richest in Europe, combined with its continual sunshine, the vivid costumes of its peasantry and the white, or pastel-tinted, houses of its towns and villages, to give it a fascination quite distinctive.

Officers' wives and mothers read with fast-beating hearts that British troops had been successful after a sanguinary struggle at a place with a grim-sounding name—Albuera. Gentlemen, passing the port, confided in one another that sad scenes of intemperance had followed the capture of Badajoz.

The Marquis of Wellington entered Madrid in triumph, and editors hurried out special editions, lyrically describing Spanish rapture on the arrival of the deliverer. They scornfully quoted Bonaparte's claim of four years past, that by Christmas he would have driven the English into the sea, and that there would not be an insurrectionary village in Spain. The Marquis of Wellington left Madrid after a visit of nineteen days, and three weeks later the French reoccupied it, which was hard on the editors, and Madrid. . . .

A number of sightseers of means and leisure embarked for Lisbon. Mr. Walter Scott, whose narrative poems had taken Great Britain by storm, and had occasioned such a rush of tourists to Loch Katrine that the Scottish post-duty was rising, had been much bitten with the idea of a trip to see ' Lord Wellington and his merry men '. But Mrs. Scott, who had a large young family and a new house to consider, thought that the author would be better employed at home, writing more and more popular verse. He had bought a meadow on the Tweed, one hundred acres of rough land and a small farm-house, which he was going to rebuild. He had designs for a museum of local antiquities and the most attractive country-house library in the kingdom. In earshot of the murmuring waters he loved best, Mr. Scott achieved his nearest possible touch with the War by entertaining at dinner captured officers of Bonaparte's army.

As the Peninsular campaign slowly drew to a successful conclusion, only a few people at home, perhaps planning a history, or accustomed to note their impressions of contemporary high-lights, retired to study or library to jot, in a marbled notebook, such details as the following—

' Vimiero—our line tactics can beat French column tactics.

' Corunna—a British army, even dilapidated, will fight to the end.

' Busaco—the Portuguese can fight, which has been doubted.

' Albuera—as at Vimiero—line can beat column, even when directed by a second-rate commander.

' Salamanca—a complete smash—showing Ld. Wellington as a consummate tactician, beating 40,000 men in 40 minutes.

' Vittoria—a strategical rather than a tactical victory. We recovered half Spain before the French could concentrate.'

Chapter 10

'He's Falling! He's Falling!'

～～～

The Emperor Napoleon's scheme to bring Britain to her knees by the destruction of her commerce was not progressing with the necessary speed. A small British Expeditionary Force was winning victories in the Peninsula. Early in 1812 the Emperor decided not to re-visit Spain, but to turn his whole attention to tightening up the Continental blockade. Lord Wellington would cease to compose terse despatches announcing successes, when his supplies from home were cut off at the source. The annihilation of his little army would be effected at leisure. The Emperor's uneasy alliance with the Tsar was dying a natural death. At heart he had always realized that the Russian was an Oriental. His annexation of the Duchy of Oldenburg had entailed the dethronement of Alexander's brother-in-law. A peremptory demand that Russia should combine with France in severer repressive measures against British and American trade had been met by a cool suggestion that France should evacuate ruined Prussia.

' He's Falling! He's Falling! '

Russia was feeling the effects of the blockade sufficiently already. The Emperor left Paris on May 9th for Dresden, and by June 24th had crossed the Niemen on his road to Moscow. The French public were not informed of the war with Russia until it had been in progress ten days. The English Press was preoccupied by an event which it rightly described as ' unparalleled in the history of our country '—the assassination of the Prime Minister in the lobby of the House of Commons at five p.m. Mr. Perceval's assailant was a person of disordered mind; he was hanged, nevertheless. Many eulogies of a statesman who had excelled in his domestic capacity filled the London papers for several days. After the funeral had taken place with suitable ceremony, public attention was re-directed to the Emperor Napoleon.

At forty-two, an age at which, after so hard a life, he might reasonably have been expected to settle, to rest on his laurels, his plans were vast, and so was the army which he was about to lead East. He reckoned on a three years' campaign, at the end of which time he would be Master of the Universe. In the first year he would defeat the Russians in Lithuania, and in the second, after dictating a peace from Moscow, advance on India. He spoke of the Russian adventure as merely the first stage of a grand new triumphal progress.

The prospects from the French point of view were encouraging, for although in July Russia concluded a treaty with England and Spain, so as to leave her hands free for the ensuing struggle, her army could not compare in numbers with the *Grande Armée* of over half a

million highly trained men, which had already crossed
her frontiers; and she lacked a first-class commander.

At a London dinner table, a party of merchants of
Russian extraction murmured to one another that the
decision for peace or war had never lain with the Tsar,
who had long known that if he moved for further
alliance with Bonaparte he would die or disappear.
They admired the methods of Lord Wellington, who
avoided unnecessary battles and wasted the strength of
his enemy by protracted war. The English General's
system of eternal evasion commended itself strongly to
these Russian gentlemen of the City of London. A
clergyman lately arrived from Stockholm had told Mr.
John Julius Angerstein that Bonaparte had sent Bernadotte to rule in Sweden for reasons of jealousy, and
that now Bernadotte was determinedly hostile to his old
master. If the Russians were well advised they would
imitate Lord Wellington's strategy.

The Tsar's position was very difficult. Of his
generals, Benningsen was a German, an intriguer, and
had suffered much in reputation by previous defeats at
the hands of Bonaparte. The reverses preceding the
Treaty of Tilsit had struck a deadly blow at the care-
fully-nourished old legend of Russia's illimitable resources and weight in arms. The Tsar did not like
General Kutusoff, who was sixty-seven, and who had,
by his independence, delayed the peace with Turkey.
General Barclay de Tolly was disliked by his troops as
a foreigner, and by his staff as an obscure tactician.
The Tsar himself undertook the Supreme Command.
In mid-August, interested English learnt that the Tsar
had retired to Moscow, whence he had issued a flaming

proclamation, declaring that this War was a National War, and that no peace should come with Bonaparte while a single hostile soldier remained on Russian soil. The appointment of the patriot General Kutusoff to the Supreme Command was popular in Russia, but in England people commented unhopefully on the usual results of changing horses in mid-stream, and the confusion and discord which must have made such a change necessary at such an hour.

The Emperor Napoleon, meanwhile, appeared to be carrying all before him. The weight of sheer numbers in open country must tell. The Russians were retiring in good order before a force three times their number. Bonaparte had left a shattered Smolensk, and was following the line of the Russian retirement towards Moscow. English ministerial organs, and *The Times*, claimed the Battle of Mojaisk, fought on September 7th, as a Russian victory. It was difficult, at such a distance, to obtain a clear picture of what was happening. As the conflict proceeded farther east, the period of time which must elapse before a French or Russian bulletin could be printed in English papers lengthened from three to four weeks. To add to the difficulties of editors, Russian bulletins still adhered to Old Style dates. Certainly the losses on both sides in the recent battle had been tremendous. The engagement, which had lasted for ten hours, had been broken off owing to sheer exhaustion on both sides. Russia had lost half her troops of the line, France about twenty-eight thousand men. English Opposition papers discounted Russian bulletins, and said that the French were more valuable. Borodino had been another costly victory for Bonaparte.

' He's Falling ! He's Falling ! '

The Russian army had retreated through Moscow, followed by the greater part of the population of that city. Only about fifteen hundred natives had sullenly watched the triumphal entry of French troops into their old capital. By September 14th the Tsar was in despair. Bonaparte was seated in the Kremlin.

The remainder of a nightmarish story reached England in disjointed fragments, *via* Berlin, Gothenberg and Stockholm. At the country seat of Sir George Beaumont, artist and patron of the arts, the London papers came in about five p.m. Just before dinner on October 16th, the Cole-Orton house-party were informed by their host that it was now certain the gallant Russians had themselves burnt their city, sooner than let it become the winter headquarters of the invader. The house-party, who had for two or three days past been disturbed by rumours of the burning of Moscow—though not sufficiently disturbed to prevent their admiration of the wild rocks and autumnal tints of Charlewood Forest, three miles distant—was relieved to hear so satisfactory an explanation.

Some reports had asserted that Bonaparte's troops had fired the city by his orders, or by mistake when indulging in orgies. *The Times* had been convinced that the Corsican attorney's son had commanded a horrible act of French incendiarism. Bonaparte, however, it now appeared, had been anxious to preserve Moscow. In his despicable ignorance of the human heart, he had not foreseen a patriotic Russian counter-stroke which must incommode him extremely. He had been forced to pick his way from an inferno, where flames roared like the waves of the sea, and take up his residence in a palace without the walls, whence he could obtain an inimitable view of ancient domes and towers of uncouth but noble design, silhouetted against a sheet of living flame. He had returned to the Kremlin after some days, and now sat couched amongst blackened ruins, surrounded by streets impeded by depressing wreckage, awaiting peace proposals from the Tsar.

For nearly two months, from October 16th to December 8th, no further reliable news out of Russia reached England. On October 27th a Riga message dated October 9th said that the Emperor of the French had left Moscow and a great battle was expected. A French bulletin, received a fortnight later, stated that he was still in Moscow.

In England Russia's dramatic counter-stroke was not universally commended. Mr. Cobbett thought the conduct of the Tsar in ordering the destruction of his ancient capital, the home of thousands of poor subjects, an act of atrocious tyranny. Lord Holland said darkly that he did not believe that either the Governor of Moscow or Bonaparte had given any order. The deed had been ' done by robbers '. As days shortened, persons who had travelled in Russia, and appreciated the length of the Emperor's communications, and the difficulty of the journey from the frontier, even under favourable conditions, could not believe that he was still sitting in the Kremlin, waiting for Russians to reply. This seemed madness.

November 6th was a most beautiful day in London. Mr. Farington, who had heard much of Wordsworth's sonnets at Cole-Orton, spent the morning studying the effects of light upon the scenery of the River Thames. He walked over Blackfriars Bridge and proceeded along the river bank to London Bridge, noting the haze and colour upon St. Paul's and the buildings of the Middlesex side. He then walked along the bank above Blackfriars Bridge for the same purpose. In Russia, on the road from Moscow to Smolensk, the first snowflakes of the coming winter—unusually late this year—had begun to descend, three days past.

On December 8th, a long despatch from Lord Cathcart, British Ambassador to Russia, dated November 11th, announced that the Emperor Napoleon had left Moscow on October 19th, riding in a coach. December 16th was a dark and cheerless day in London, but when the Tower and Park guns fired to celebrate the total discomfiture of Bonaparte's army, after a disastrous battle near Smolensk, the whole town was exhilarated. Lord Grey, who had not believed the Russian bulletins received last week through Sweden, said, ' Now I see Bonaparte is in a scrape.' Sir Charles Blagden, another inveterate admirer, who had throughout the long pause never ceased to predict that the world's greatest General had some scheme to extricate himself from a situation of extreme danger, now admitted that his hero's escape seemed unlikely.

Two days before Christmas, Mr. Lawrence, on his way home from the General Meeting of the Royal Academy, enlivened fellow artists by the story that Bonaparte had arrived in Paris, and himself published a bulletin acknowledging the destruction of his army. He had escaped in a sledge, through the snows, travelling incognito, and shocked his young wife and sleeping child by a sudden appearance at the Tuileries at eleven-thirty p.m. last Friday.

'He's Falling! He's Falling!'

On Christmas Eve, the twenty-ninth bulletin of the French Army, dated Molodetchno, December 3rd, stated the great distress of the army, but made no mention of any battle. Inhabitants of comfortable English homes, in seasonable weather, warmed by ample fare told one another that they had always said, should Boney ever get into a real difficulty with an army, he would run away from it.

Slowly the first notes of a tremendous funeral march trembled across the wintry wastes to English fields and streets. Full details of the disastrous retreat from Moscow were not known for many months, but by late January, inhabitants of Prussian villages were reporting the arrival of scores of strange men, clothed in rags, missing ears and noses, wandering distraught in the woods of the frontier. By no means all of them were French. The vassal states had all been called upon to furnish their best troops for the *Grande Armée* for the invasion of Russia. Amongst the five hundred thousand soldiers who had simply disappeared had been Poles, Bavarians, Saxons, Illyrians, Italians, Rhinelanders, Westphalians. . . .

There were ghastly whispers that a large number of French females, stars of the Opera and ballet, had followed dashing officers of the Imperial Guard to a country where they had been promised unlimited diamonds, palaces, serfs and furs. Whole coachloads of such persons were still sitting, immobile for ever, in their finery, amongst the Russian whiteness, with a dead coachman on the box, and between the snow-clogged fallen shafts, the skeletons of horses. For days the retreating army had existed on horseflesh. Many men, women and children had been drowned, attempting to cross half-frozen waters. A strange sickness had broken out amongst the deserted army. Men would suddenly stagger, as if they were drunk, and then fall writhing, to rise no more. Their frozen hair and beards clanked like the lustres of chandeliers as they walked with bowed heads into the blinding snowfall. At intervals, as light faded, out of the bare woods would steal sounds which caused men who had been the best soldiers in the world to scream with terror. Now that their master had left them to their fate, they could not face the Cossacks and the wolves.

II

In England, in 1813, *The Times* led the cry of ' He's falling! He's falling! '

Mr. Scott, busy early as usual at his desk at Abbotsford, on a fresh January morning, thought the foreign news, ' By the Lord, sir! most famous! I had no hope, in my time, of seeing the dry bones of the Continent so warm with life again.'

A young Prussian nobleman told London acquaintances that he, and a number of friends, were preparing to set off for their native land. They had been privately advised from home that, if the British Government would lend support, a great effort would be made to throw off the intolerable yoke of French domination. The whole population of warlike Prussia might be counted upon. A War of Liberation was about to begin.

The Emperor had announced that he was raising a new Army. During his absence in Russia, posters saying

'He's Falling!   He's Falling!'

'No Conscription!' had been visible on the walls of Paris. There were signs that he was deteriorating in health and decision. However, the effort he intended was probably not beyond his powers. He attributed his late colossal failure solely to the severity of the season, and he knew that Prussia and Russia were not good companions in the field.

His first two victories against the combined Prussian and Russian armies were dearly bought, and barren of result. In June he concluded an armistice of two months. When the struggle began again, Austria and Sweden had joined his enemies. In England it had been feared that the Emperor of Austria would be loath to despoil his daughter's husband. Such doubts did Francis II great injustice. Never in his life did he consider his daughter's well-being before his own.

After the French defeat at Leipzig, on October 16th, all Germany rose against Napoleon Bonaparte. Holland announced her return to allegiance to the House of Orange-Nassau; Naples concluded a treaty with Austria. Lord Wellington had driven Marshal Soult over the Pyrenees, and was ready to invade France. In the English press the Emperor Napoleon's preparations for the campaign of 1814 were described as those of 'the condemned gladiator, sullenly re-entering the arena amidst hostile silence'. Prophets who had foretold that, once he suffered a serious reverse, the rot would spread quickly, congratulated themselves; but the Empire which had taken twelve years to build did not fall utterly to pieces for another six months, and Lord Wellington's opinion of the Emperor's strategy in 1814 was, 'Excellent! quite excellent!'

' He's Falling! He's Falling! '

In London, as every bulletin brought better news, there was much ringing of bells and firing of guns. While the Allies advanced from Alsace-Lorraine on Paris, the army of the Peninsula was drawing near Toulouse, through flat rich country, which reminded a Somersetshire diarist of the Bridgwater district. In the background of the scene arose white-capped Pyrenees. A young British officer, arrayed in the full uniform of a crack cavalry regiment, splendid in side-whiskers and shako, wrote home that, when he rode over the draw-bridge of the mediæval château in which he was bil-leted, he regretted his appearance as a sordid anachro-nism.

At home, Tory enthusiasts said that in spite of the efforts of the Whigs, England seemed likely to win the War. Princess Charlotte of Wales, the unhappiest *débutante* in England, drummed with impatient fingers on a London window, wishing that her parents were like other girls' parents, wishing that her father did not open and stop her letters to her one girl-friend; wishing that her mother did not wear such youthful dresses, and say and do things that made everyone look uncomfortable.

The lovely word Peace was much heard in the coun-cil-chambers and homes of England, but the Peace of Amiens was not forgotten, and all sober folk feared a premature and unsatisfactory settlement. They be-lieved that Bonaparte was still insatiable, and incapable of keeping any Treaty, except by necessity.

In the end, the hurry of events took the whole world by surprise. On April 4th, London papers printed wild tales of a great battle in which the Emperor Napoleon

had been mortally wounded. A second edition of the
Courier, on the following evening, held arresting head-
lines—' PRUSSIANS UNDER THE WALLS OF PARIS.
FLIGHT OF THE EMPRESS AND THE KING OF ROME.
PEACE PROPOSALS BY JOSEPH BONAPARTE TO THE PARI-
SIANS.'

Five days passed without further mention of the
Emperor's supposed wound, though the fact that he
had suffered another defeat was insisted upon. Special
late editions of April 9th contained an announcement
so welcome as to be widely disbelieved. A Gazette Extraordinary, published at eight p.m., and dated ' Foreign
Office ', ran—

' Despatches have been this day received at this
Office from General Lord Viscount Cathcart, K.T., announcing the abdication of the crowns of France and
Italy by Napoleon Buonaparte, in terms of which the
following is a translation—

' The Allied Powers having proclaimed that the
Emperor Napoleon was the only obstacle to the re-
establishment of the Peace of Europe, the Emperor
Napoleon, faithful to his oath, declares that He
renounces for Himself and His Heirs the Thrones of
France and Italy, and that there is no personal sacrifice,
even that of life, which he is not ready to make to the
interests of France.

' Done at the Palace of Fontainebleau the ——
April, 1814.'

The editions had been so hurriedly produced that
the date of the abdication was left a blank.

Extraordinary scenes took place in the streets of London on Easter Sunday, 1814. Congregations emerging

from church could hardly believe their eyes and ears.
They shook hands solemnly, agreeing that the Almighty had granted the prayers of all Christian folk.
' The sway of the most malignant and remorseless
tyrant ever known, has been, by Divine Grace, abruptly
terminated.' The shops of editors were beset by *queues*
of well-dressed persons, demanding the sheet in which
they might read, in cold print, the words DETHRONE-
MENT OF BONAPARTE. For the first time, when the news
was good, the city did not resound to the horn of the
newsvendor. The supply of papers ran out early in the
day, and would-be purchasers were reduced to ordering
their carriages, and driving to the houses of acquaintances who might possess a copy. Journalists searched
their files for descriptions of the Isle of Elba, Bonaparte's reported place of exile. The Lord Mayor drew
up orders to all public offices to prepare illuminations
for to-morrow night. No event of the whole war caused
such a complete sensation in England as the first abdication of the Emperor Napoleon.

III

The news of Bonaparte's abdication reached Toulouse at dinner time on April 12th. Lord Wellington,
who had just made a triumphant entry into the city,
after defeating Marshal Soult, was at table with about
forty officers, when the Paris despatches were brought
in to him. Champagne was at once ordered, and his
lordship gave the toast 'Louis XVIII', which was very
cordially received. A Spanish General then proposed
'Lord Wellington, *Liberador de España*', and all the

foreign guests present, leaping to their feet, echoed
that toast in their various native tongues for nearly ten
minutes. His lordship bowed, confused, and immediately called for coffee. The party went on to the
theatre, where ' God Save the King ' was played as they
entered, and the keepers of the box office smilingly
refused to accept any money from the English. White
cockades were everywhere visible, and *fleur de lys* had
replaced the Imperial eagles on the drop-scene. A ball
at the *Préfecture* followed. The only drawback to complete enjoyment was that carriages passing from the
Play to the Ball, met in the streets the many carts and
spring wagons, bringing wounded into the town. The
ball-goers comforted themselves with the knowledge
that the Toulouse hospitals were excellent.

In Toulouse, as in Paris, during the days that succeeded Bonaparte's downfall, busts of the Emperor
were smashed, and capital N's and B's hastily effaced
from furniture and buildings. In the streets of Toulouse, sheets, tablecloths and towels, decorated with
green paper lilies, hung out of every window. Women
pressed to their lips the coat-tails of a highly-embar-
rassed British Commander.

Not until June 4th did Wellington's army of the
Peninsula begin to march homewards. The old legend
of ' *Milord anglois* ' had revived, and all officers found
themselves ' *Mon Commandant*' or ' *Mon Général*', and
charged accordingly. Scarlet coats were seen in the
rose-red cloisters of Moissac. The Life Guards entered
Montauban with laurels. In the market-place of Auch,
ancient capital of Gascony, the victors of Vittoria gazed
at a market-place filled with milk white oxen, and

officers interested in architecture admired choir stalls
which reminded them of Winchester Cathedral. From
mediæval houses with over-hanging upper stories, as
the red line wound its way north, laughing Gascon
girls called out, ' How do you do? How do you do? '

IV

His Majesty, Louis XVIII, was prostrated with gout
when a travel-stained carriage, containing French deputies wearing Bourbon favours, drew up at the doors of
Hartwell House, near Aylesbury, Buckinghamshire.
His Majesty had been in exile for upwards of twenty-
three years, passed on like a marked card from Belgium
to Germany, to Courland, to Poland . . . After the
Treaty of Tilsit he had been obliged to seek English
hospitality. He was now nearly sixty, and a childless
widower, very stout and indolent, decidedly clever,
unmistakably a royalty, but not personally attractive.
Happiness proved such a good medicine, that within
ten days he was ready to leave the English country
home, in which he had lived with a large and quarrel-
some *suite* for six hopeless seasons.

For the last time French voices sounded in the handsome ground floor saloons of Hartwell, filled with
twinkling chandeliers and massive gilt and brocade
furniture, in which the mimic court had spent endless
quiet evenings, staring at green fields. Luggage was
carried down from large light first-floor bedrooms,
with brass plates on their doors, announcing that the
occupant was the Duc de Berri or the Bishop of Beau-
vais. The maids of honour had looked their last on a

Chinese wallpaper, and in the attics His Majesty's first physician had strapped valises containing many lotions and unguents. Now the fine great staircase might be restored to its ancient glory. It had, on the arrival of the French, been decorated by figures of helmeted heroes, shouldering weapons. But the sight of even a wooden man carrying a pike had evoked hysteric memories in the breast of her late Majesty, sister-in-law of Louis XVI and Marie Antoinette. At night, by candlelight, shadows of the spears and swords carried by the wooden warriors wavered uncannily on the staircase walls.

The King mounted into a cumbrous equipage, followed by an austere-looking lady of middle age, the Duchess of Angoulême, the Orphan of the Temple. The only surviving child of Louis Capet and Marie Antoinette had a frozen look. The experiences of her adolescence had left an indelible mark on her character. She was the new ruler's niece by blood, and again by marriage, but unfortunately, like her uncle, childless.

The French royalties saw for the last time, doorposts adorned two centuries past, by a happy chance, with *fleur de lys*. The procession moved off from a view of smooth lawns, a hazy lake and a magnificent cedar. They passed under an echoing gatehouse and beneath the tower of a grey village church. A rather grim street on their road into the adjacent market town had been renamed ' Bourbon Street ' in their honour. In the village of Stanmore, the Prince Regent, attended by cavalry, met Bonaparte's successor and escorted him in triumph to London. Many carriages filled with gentry sporting Bourbon cockades, drew aside to let the cavalcade pass. Cheering British families lined the route from the fields

of Paddington to Portman Square. Even butchers' boys
and farm labourers had bought white ribbons, and the
windows of houses in St. James's were filled by parties
of smiling and bowing notables. At length the exhausted exiles reached their first resting-place, Grillon's
Hotel, Albemarle Street, where, according to newspapers of April 21st, the King of France, taking from
his shoulders the Order of St. Esprit, threw it over the
neck of the Prince Regent, crying, ' To you, sir, I have
owed my all! I have nothing to give, but this. Keep it to
remind you of Louis XVIII! '

Two very corpulent royal gentlemen parted at a late
hour with many expressions of mutual esteem and con-
gratulation.

V

Londoners had a free entertainment nearly every day
during the summer of 1814. From May onwards, more
and more distinguished guests arrived in the capital. A
young lady, with dark almond-shaped eyes, clad in
mourning, was ceremoniously conducted around the
Bank of England by the Governor. The Tsar's widowed
sister, the Grand Duchess Catherine, Duchess of
Oldenburg, told her flattered escort that the emancipation of Europe was entirely due to the steady and per-
severing conduct of his great and happy country. In her
few weeks in England she had learnt more than in the
whole of the rest of her life. The Russian princess, who
had hastily married elsewhere when Bonaparte came
a-wooing, was a popular figure with the crowd during a
visit, which she evidently thoroughly enjoyed, but the
Russian Ambassadress suffered agonies in giving place

to a royal lady who could be remarkably capricious and unreasonable.

The Tsar and the King of Prussia disappointed crowds, on June 7th, by taking a short cut to Piccadilly by way of Peckham Gap and Battersea Bridge; but on his arrival at the Pulteney Hotel, the greatest sovereign of Europe showed himself on a balcony, leading his sister by the hand. Two plain carriages which drove into London during dinner on the same evening, contained the sons of the King of Prussia, and Marshal Blücher. The princes, fine upright lads with smooth flaxen hair and bright complexions, displayed no hauteur when intrusive citizens rushed forward and insisted on shaking hands with them. The horses were taken out of the Marshal's carriage, and he was drawn through the Horse Guards to sounds of continuous cheering. He stood up in his equipage with his grizzled head uncovered, and expressed his acknowledgments by a series of stiff bows. He was said to have a perfect passion for gaming.

London print-shops displayed the likeness of a fair royal lady with an expression of childlike innocence, and a star in her hair, stepping down a marble staircase in a high wind. The King of Prussia had never recovered from the loss of his wife, who had died of a broken heart after having humbled herself in vain to the Emperor Napoleon. Queen Louise had been the strong partner in an ideally happy marriage. Her widower kept a sitting-room in his house of exile exactly as she had left it, with a half-finished letter in her hand still on the writing table. He often retired to this apartment for hours of silent reflection. Before the

much-advertised, but select, ball at White's, he sent a
private request to the Regent that tickets might be sent
to a certain English *débutante* and her aunt. A person
acquainted with the court of Prussia explained, ' I can
at once account for His Majesty's attentions to this
young lady. She is remarkably like his late queen.'
Londoners were edified by these evidences that sincere
affection may exist in the highest ranks of life, and
anecdotes of this summer were far more favourable to
the King than the Tsar. A gentleman who had been at
the fêtes at Blenheim told that, on descending the steps
in front of the palace, the King had stopped, rapt, to
express admiration of a truly magnificent vista of park
and woodland, bathed in summer sunshine. The Tsar,
either accustomed from infancy to enormous prospects,
or deficient in artistic perception, had walked out into
the heat, without seeming to notice anything. Although
much the larger and more handsome potentate, the
Russian had something cat-like in his features and gait.
His dress indicated a love of display. The Prussian,
with his high cheek-bones and weather-beaten countenance, reminded sympathetic English observers of a
Highlander.

A royal escort clattered up Piccadilly, and mounted
guard outside the Pulteney. The waiting crowd gave
three huzzas for the Tsar and his sister, leaving in a
state coach, sent by the Regent to carry them to a state
dinner at Carlton House. The Regent himself did not
meet with such an enthusiastic welcome when he drove
abroad. On several occasions his carriage was both
hissed and stoned. The London mob still took the part
of the Princess of Wales, and there were stories that

the Regent was persecuting his daughter who, at the age of eighteen, undismayed by the spectacle of her many spinster aunts, had broken off her engagement to the Prince of Orange, for the laudable reason that she did not wish to leave Old England.

Mr. Lawrence was in some difficulty, for the Regent had commissioned him to paint a sort of family group of all Britain's distinguished visitors. As the artist had never undertaken such a composition, he staved off the evil hour by asking everyone to sit to him first for separate portraits. In his full-length of the rough old Prussian Marshal, by representing him apparently issuing contradictory orders during a thunderstorm, with a fresh horse in the offing, he managed to distract attention from the facts that his sitter had a nut-cracker profile and very short legs. Lord Stewart, Ambassador to Vienna, had suggested to the Regent that before England's most fashionable painter left for the forth-coming Congress in Vienna, he should be knighted. The title of *Chevalier* was useful when travelling abroad.

On a July day of this fine summer of festive events, a high-nosed gentleman, who arrived at Mr. Lawrence's studio on horseback, wearing a plain blue coat and a round hat, and attended by a single elderly groom, attracted no attention. The Ladies of Britain, headed by the Duchess of York, were getting up a subscription to erect a monument to Lord Wellington, now Marquis of Douro and Duke of Wellington. It was to be formed of cannon taken by him in his various engagements, and occupy a prominent site in Hyde Park. Opinion at present inclined towards a group of classic steeds, but the eventual expression of the regard of the Duke's

countrywomen was to be a colossal bronze nude, known
as ' Achilles ', but actually a modified copy of one of the
' Horse Tamers ' on the Monte Cavallo in Rome. As
he had been abroad on service so much, the figure of the
Duke of Wellington was not as yet universally recognized in London.

Twenty-one years had passed since War with France
had been announced by Mr. Pitt in the House of Commons on a wet February night. The House was now lit
by gas, and Members had ceased to feel the pipes
cautiously, convinced that they must be filled with fire.
Advertisements of Patent Warm-Air Stoves were
common on the front pages of newspapers, and each
burner of the new Hydropneumatic Lamp was said to
diffuse a radiance equal to that of six candles. Five
steamboats were plying for hire on the Thames.

During the years of their struggle against Napoleon
Bonaparte, the appearance and manners of the people
of England had undergone such a change as to suggest
that the Pre-War period already belonged to history.
Mr. Wilberforce said that when first he had known the
House, only one honourable Member was openly
religious, and Mr. Hill, of Shropshire, had been regarded as an eccentric. Now, dozens of Members were
regular church-goers, and in the households of forty,
family prayers took place every morning.

The troops returning from France looked very unlike the Expeditionary Force sped on its way, with
Royal attention, from Greenwich in 1793. The Army
had discarded pigtails in 1808. In the Peninsula the
Duke had not been particular as to uniform, provided
that his officers brought their men into the field with

sixty rounds of ammunition apiece. The result was that
hardly two officers dressed alike. General Sir Thomas
Picton habitually wore a tall grey beaver hat, which
would not have looked out of place in St. James's. In
the ranks, tight-fitting coatees with short tails, tight
trousers of blue, black or grey, and short boots, had
deposed the old loose coat, long gaiters and breeches.

Mr. Farington, watching from Richmond Bridge on
a hot Sunday, the gala spectacle of boats coming up the
river with the tide, was gratified to see so many decent
and well-dressed people enjoying the fresh air in blameless gaiety. Many of them had brought their dinners,
and sat upon the grass in parties. Almost all the men
were dressed in black or dark blue, and boots had become an essential article of Sunday finery, even amongst
the lower order of tradesmen and mechanics. The same
sort of thing was noticeable in the newly-created
Regency Park, and other pleasure resorts of the en-
larging capital. Outside small taverns in the vicinity of
the new bridge, at present called ' Strand ' Bridge, but
to be opened next year as 'Waterloo', many a returned
warrior sat telling his tale, and quietly enjoying his pint
and pipe, surrounded by admiring relations. A great
improvement in the standard of comfort was manifest.
Many cottages now had their clock and plated tea-
service. Mr. Farington felt quite optimistic as to the
future of England at peace.

Hard drinking was becoming unfashionable. At
midday, pastrycooks' shops were filled by persons of all
kinds, taking a light repast of buns, tarts and a glass of
whey, priced at sixpence or eightpence. In wealthy
circles dinner was getting later and later, and the

'He's Falling! He's Falling!'

'Rout' had given place to a new horror, called the 'At Home', at which there were no seats, no cards, and any music was drowned by a babble which would not in 1793 have been recognized as conversation. The introduction of an extra meal did not mean that those already in existence were depleted. Dinners still consisted of two courses, but the first course, in a household of moderate means, might include soup, fish, a joint and vegetables; and the second, ragout, game, sweetmeats and fruits. The number of hot dishes composed of several ingredients was increasing.

The children who ran by the sides of muslin-clad Mamas in 'Regent' bonnets and short-waisted spencers, wore ankle-length white washing trousers under their frocks. With the re-opening of communications with France, a change in female dress was inevitable, but so far people who had visited Paris said that the present rage for frills and lappets round the neck and shoulders made all French ladies look like Friesland hens, while *Parisiennes*, seeing for the first time the very décolleté gowns adopted in England during the war years, decried them as shocking. Hair brown and olive were the shades most in favour in London for outdoor wear, and for young ladies the ball dress was almost a uniform. Everyone wore a white satin slip with a transparent over-gown of Celestial blue, Pomona green, or Blush pink. Costumes *à la militaire* were quite outmoded in both capitals. A few Paris bonnets of *tulle*, with crowns of roses, hyacinths, Persian lilac and violets had reached London, and were liked, but for carriage dress and even evening full dress, France was indulging her eternal passion for plaid.

'He's Falling! He's Falling!'

In neither France nor England did ladies foresee that within a few seasons, the costumes known as 'Empire' and 'Regency' were to merge into a style recognized by future generations as 'Early Victorian'. In 1814 the christening of a princess by that name was yet five years distant, but the dressing of hair in Madonna bands, bonnet and shawl, side whiskers, top hats and pantaloons, had already arrived to stay.

An engraver called Landseer was proudly showing Academicians the sketches of animals done by his son, a boy of less than twelve years. Miss Elizabeth Barrett was writing a poem in the garden, and Mrs. Felicia Hemans had delighted her country with *Domestic Affections*. In a dark upper-chamber of Edinburgh Old Town, Mr. Walter Scott found an old acquaintance busy tearing up the novels of her girlhood. She had not opened them for thirty years, and on doing so had been so disgusted by their tone, that she was committing them to the flames. She said that they could do no young person any good, and might do some moral harm. Two novels published anonymously this season were certainly blameless in this respect. *Pride and Prejudice*, which had long sought a publisher, pleased a small, discerning public. *Waverley* lay on every table. In 1814, many people still existed who had worn, in their prime, powder, patch and hoop, but astonishing links with the next century already existed, and Arthur, Duke of Wellington was in the fullness of time to be depicted dandling on his knee a royal infant, his namesake, eldest surviving member of the ruling house of Great Britain in 1941. It was the good fortune of the future Queen-Empress to embody and translate rather

than invent the change in manners and morals dignified
by her name.

Two top-hatted gentlemen, both lame, were observed walking together down Albemarle Street. Mr.
Scott and Lord Byron had met at Mr. Murray's and
liked one another. His lordship, who had been rather
wild, was now about to make a most suitable marriage.
The conduct of a woman of birth, Lady Caroline Lamb,
was universally condemned as extraordinary. Although
married and a mother, she had allowed her passion for
the rising poet to lead her into unbecoming extrava-
gances. Young Lord Byron, her idol, mocked at her
public attempt to take her life, as a result of his coldness.
Since the lady was unfashionably meagre, he unkindly
said that he was haunted by a spectre. The sombre boy
who had sat with his widowed mother in obscure Scottish lodgings watching the people of Aberdeen mourn
Louis XVI, had become the most sought-after guest in
literary London, and his heroines, like those of Mr.
Scott, who genially said that the new poet had driven
him out of the field, were all principally distinguished
by maidenly modesty.

The young Duke of Devonshire, whose lovely but
feckless mother had never in man's memory been out
of debt, showed promise of being a model peer of the
new type. On the death of his father, he had decreed
that all the old tradesmen accustomed to serve his
family should continue to be employed, and hearing
that the funeral order had been given out to strangers,
cancelled such instructions. In the countryside, wives
of benevolent landowners were visiting cottages for
other purposes than inspecting the child out at nurse.

They were decidedly conscious of an industrial revolution, which had produced an underworld of toilers always on the borders of starvation, and a wealthy middle class of a virility unknown in England since the days of Elizabeth Tudor. The poverty of the first order was no longer regarded as synonymous with crime, and sons and daughters of the second were flooding the public and finishing schools. The fact was that the habits and manners known as ' Regency ' had achieved their heyday during the long years before the Prince Regent attained that title, and by 1814 were already threatened.

In Paris, a fragile ghost of Imperial splendours had passed into eternity. The Empress Joséphine had died at 'La Malmaison', of a pneumonia, contracted, according to unfriendly accounts, by arising from a sick-bed on a cold spring day to array herself in muslin to entertain the Tsar. The *Moniteur*, which under Louis XVIII had changed its coat but not its spots, announced on May 14th—' The death of Madame de Beauharnais excites widespread sympathy. This woman was unfailingly gentle, and possessed much charm and attractiveness in manner and in mind. Extremely unhappy during her husband's reign, she sought refuge from his roughness and neglect in the study of Botany.'

In September, delegates of all nations began to arrive in Vienna, and the Balance of Power in Europe occupied many columns of print and hours of conversation. By February, 1815, it appeared that Prussia wanted Saxony, and Russia Poland. The Tsar was being impossibly grasping and dictatorial. The Allies were talking and dancing and quarrelling interminably. In London,

'He's Falling! He's Falling!'

a rowdy mob, in revolt against the Corn Laws, was nightly breaking the windows of the idle rich. Every morning the newspapers detailed, with apparent indifference, what districts had been most affected by the mob last night. 'You can tell Bonaparte,' wrote an English correspondent to an officer about to re-visit Elba, 'that he is quite forgotten in Europe: no one thinks of him now.'

Unfortunately for the Peace-Makers, newspapers of Friday, March 10th, were obliged to issue special editions announcing—'MOST IMPORTANT NEWS. LANDING OF BONAPARTE IN FRANCE,' and ten days later, 'WIDESPREAD DESERTION OF TROOPS TO BONAPARTE,' followed on March 23rd by 'DEPARTURE OF LOUIS XVIII FROM PARIS. ARRIVAL OF BONAPARTE.'

Chapter 11

'Great and Glorious Victory'

Miss Magdalene Hall, second daughter of Sir James Hall, Bart., of Dunglass, Haddingtonshire, was married in March, 1815, to Colonel Sir William Howe De Lancey, K.C.B. The match, which was one of affection, was the result of a friendship struck up on board H.M.S. *Endymion* in January, 1809, between Lieutenant Basil Hall, R.N., and an officer evacuated from Corunna. At the time of Colonel De Lancey's first introduction to the Hall family, his future wife was still a child of the nursery. A considerable disparity of age was noticeable between the happy couple. Miss Hall, as an Englehart miniature attested, was, at the date of her marriage, a startled fawn just emerged from the schoolroom. Sir William, at the age of thirty-six, had decided to settle. He was no longer recognizable as the sparkish, eighteen-year-old dragoon in a powdered wig, who alone of the guests at Mr. Hickey's dinner to Colonel Wellesley at the Garden House, Chinsurah, in 1797, had survived without a headache. In 1815, as a senior officer with a staff appointment in North Britain, he wore his own hair combed into a crest, and side-whiskers partially eclipsed by an upstanding collar and stock. His figure was heavy, his manner severe. But Sir James Hall, geologist and man of letters, neighbour and friend of the author of *The Lady of the Lake* and *Marmion*, was satisfied that he was delivering his untried daughter to a kindly lord and master. Sir William, florid, solid, had good husband and father written plain on his broad countenance. He was of a New England family of French Huguenot extraction. Stern Protestant convictions had impelled the first De Lancey in 1686 to cross the ocean and settle in New York, a city in which the family had prospered exceedingly.

The bride's home in early spring was a lovely sight. Sir William had as yet no country seat. The couple spent the first week after their marriage wandering in the woods of the Dunglass ravine, listening to the voice of the Dunglass burn. Nothing could be more modish than to pass the honeymoon in Scotland, recently discovered as the land of romance and chivalry. Sir William and Lady De Lancey were so employed when the Edinburgh coach brought the news of Bonaparte's landing in France.

Lady De Lancey, who scarcely realized herself yet by that title, found herself by Thursday, June 8th, comfortably established with ' my maid Emma ' and 'my husband, Sir William', on the fourth floor of 'Compte de Lannoy's house, Impasse du Parc, Bruxelles'. Her new possessions also included 'my carriage ' and 'my servant', a Dunglass retainer acting as coachman.

'Great and Glorious Victory'

The farewell to her parents and fifteen-year-old brother, the recall of Sir William to active service, the dash south to London, the crossing from Thames-side to Ostend, the peaceful appearance of the strange foreign country, all seemed to the bride part of a thrilling dream. On the news of Bonaparte's reappearance, the Duke of Wellington had insisted on having his old comrade-in-arms appointed his Quartermaster-General. The issue between Bonaparte and the Allies was to be fought out in Belgium.

Sir William told his bride that he believed they might count on remaining quietly in Brussels for a month at least. He gave her his word that he would never fail to let her know of his probable movements as soon as he knew them himself. He allowed her to read all the newspapers, so as to keep her mind easy. He explained that when he had to leave her, on a campaign which might last some weeks, it was his wish that she should retire to Antwerp, a very strongly fortified port, twenty-five miles distant, from which it would be possible, if necessary, for ladies to beat a retreat by sea. Several officers, hearing of Sir William's plans, arranged that their wives should follow Lady De Lancey's example.

Magdalene had never in her life passed so delightful a time as that she spent in Brussels in June, 1815. Every day Sir William brought two or three old friends back to dinner. She refused all invitations to pay calls or attend balls, so that she might never be absent when Sir William came home from his office. He took her out for a long walk nearly every day, and while they walked, told her anecdotes of his former life, in every one of which she traced evidences of his amiable and generous mind. Now and then, a pang assailed her, at the thought of the approaching conflict, but she chased away the thought, resolved not to lose present bliss by dwelling on the chance of future pain.

On June 14th she did not like the tone of the newspapers, but Sir William's return allayed all her foolish fears, and looking back, she remembered the forenoon of the next day as the happiest in her life. Sir William was engaged to dine with the Spanish Ambassador that evening. He was very unwilling to go, but Magdalene kept him to the point, herself fastening his many medals and crosses on his coat; for the occasion was one for full dress. He turned back at the door, and gave her a smile full of happiness and peace. He looked splendid. Nearly an hour later, she was still watching in the window-seat from which she had waved him a gay farewell, when she saw an aide-de-camp arriving at the gate below. She sent down the name of the house where her husband was dining, and was a little disturbed to see the aide-de-camp set off at the gallop.

Sir William's step sounded on the stair at nine p.m. He was too busy to tell his wife much, except that ' it would soon be all over, now'. A great battle between Bonaparte and the Allies was expected to-morrow. It should be decisive—' a conclusion of the whole business'. Magdalene must be ready to start for Antwerp at six a.m. before the roads became crowded. Her husband would probably join her there in a day or two— might even send for her to come back to Brussels tomorrow night. Now he must get to his desk, and demanded only some strong green tea, as the violent exertion of setting the whole army in motion sometimes quite stupefied him.

Magdalene preserved outward tranquillity, and teased him with no questions. She only asked that she might be allowed to stay in the room where he was working, promising not to speak. Between nine and midnight Sir William went out twice to the Duke's lodgings, a few doors distant, and after his first visit told her that he had found the Duke looking over a map with a Prussian General in full dress uniform— the scene a perfect study for a painter. The Duke, who had been dressing for the Ball, had been attired in chemise and slippers. The Duchess of Richmond's Ball, to which the honeymooning De Lanceys had refused an invitation, was to take place, although the *réveille* might sound in the streets at any moment.

Sir William left his wife at three a.m. to the sound of fifes and bugles and bagpipes. The window of their billet overlooked one of the city gates, and Magdalene saw regiment after regiment passing through, and disappearing into the mist of a very refreshing morning. Many officers were still wearing the pumps and silk hose in which they had danced at the Duchess's ball.

At Antwerp, the Quartermaster-General's letter commending his lady to Captain Mitchell of his department, worked wonders. Magdalene got the last room in a very crowded hotel. It was a small back room up many stairs, and so shut in with other buildings, that no street noises were audible, but she thought this a blessing in disguise. Sir William had made her solemnly promise to believe no rumours, and do nothing without his written order, so she stayed quietly indoors, and tried to rest. In the evening, calm, kind Captain Mitchell came in to tell her the good news of a British victory, but the prospect of more fighting. On Sunday, the 18th, she had to shut the window of her room, although the heat was very oppressive. A noise like the sea rolling at a distance sounded intermittently. She told herself that it reminded her of the waves breaking on the coast below her Scottish home.

Poor Emma, urged by curiosity, went out into the streets, now very noisy, and came back completely frightened, with stories of cartloads of men with ghastly wounds, and all the English ladies flying home by sea, because Bonaparte had taken Brussels. 'Well, Emma,' said Magdalene, ' you know that if the French were firing at this house, I would not move till I was ordered. But you have no such duty. Therefore go, if you like. I daresay any of the families will let you join them.' Emma, who was a London acquisition, said indignantly that she would gladly spend five years in a French prison with her ladyship, and thereafter brought in no more stories.

Next morning Captain Mitchell came at nine a.m. to say that he had seen the casualty list, and that Sir William's name was not there. Magdalene felt so happy that she could not sit down. Two hours later, a slight acquaintance, a lady of title, sent up her name, and Magdalene went down to the inn parlour.

' Poor Mr. James,' began the lady, glancing at her escort. ' He has lost a brother, and I a nephew . . . a dreadful battle, so many killed! ' Magdalene tried to banish the joy from her countenance, and explained apologetically that she was one of the lucky ones. The lady asked, had she heard from Sir William himself, and Magdalene explained ' no,' but that Captain Mitchell had seen the casualty list.

Mr. James, who had been straying up and down the room, looking wretched, then quitted it, and the lady began to talk even more confusedly, asking what Magdalene intended to do if this fighting went on, and if she had any friends who could help her to get to England. A death-like suspicion darted into Magdalene's mind, numbing her senses. She heard the lady saying that she had herself arranged that Sir William's name should be omitted from the list, because he had a young wife in the country, who must not be allowed to see the news first in a public print. Sir William's name had been in the casualty list. Sir William was not dead, only desperately wounded. ' Yes,' said Magdalene, staring. ' He must be wounded first. . . .' She began to pace the room, terrifying the lady, who begged her to try to cry. She did not want to cry, she did not want to waste any more time talking to this lady, who had deceived her, though from the kindest motives, and perhaps prevented her from hearing her husband's last words. She wanted to start at once for the battlefield.

Everyone was very kind, but by dusk of the same evening she was back in Antwerp, after a journey she could hardly remember. A few miles short of Malines her Scottish coachman had noticed, amongst the crowd, a Dunglass neighbour. Mr. Hay, of Duns Castle, who had been searching the battlefield without result for a missing brother, aged eighteen, told Sir William's bride that she was too late. ' In the middle of the action at Waterloo, he was struck by the bursting of a cannon ball and instantly fell. The Duke went and leant over him, and he died like a soldier.'

Magdalene agreed to start for England as soon as possible, since now no note could ever come for her from Sir William. She shut herself in her room, so as to be alone with her grief, and was distracted by Emma scratching at the door, and begging to be let in. In the small hours she was conscious of Emma becoming insistent—

' I am desired to tell you cautiously, my lady . . . I have good news for you.'

' How can you be so inhuman? What is good news for me now? '

' But—Sir William is not dead! '

While she waited for Emma to fetch the carriage, Magdalene was maddened by the thought of the time already lost, and the possibility that she might arrive half an hour too late. She walked up and down her little back room, faster and faster, drawing breaths which sounded like screams. Lieutenant-General John Mackenzie, Commander in Antwerp, was very kind but very firm, when he found her sitting crouched alone on the steep dark inn stairs, glaring into dawn light. He said, ' Lady de Lancey, consider. . . . You are exhausting your strength and spirits to no purpose. . . . You know what dreadful scenes you may have to go through when you reach Waterloo. You will probably require all your courage, and must command yourself for his sake.'

Between eight and nine a.m. Magdalene set off on her journey to the battlefield of Waterloo. Waggons were holding the paved crown of the road, and her carriage had to struggle along the heavy and uneven footpath at the side. She drew down the blinds, so as not to see things. Sometimes the carriage was stationary for ten minutes together, as a whirlpool of carts, horses, and civilians running away on foot, laden with belongings, surged towards Antwerp. The sounds were frightening, and suggested that a good many people had lost their heads. She called out again and again to her coachman, not to provoke anyone. At one point he descended, and tried to lead the carriage past a guarded waggon. Magdalene called to him to get up on his box again at once, and an enraged Prussian officer drew his sword and made several ineffective cuts at the man's legs. The dogged and now furious Scot whipped up his horses, and made a last and successful effort to get past the waggon. The Prussian officer pursued the wildly bucketing carriage at the gallop. He was attempting to wound the horses. Magdalene, quite desperate, let up the blind, let down the window, and petitioned with clasped hands, for a free passage, saying that she was the wife of a dying British officer. The Prussian did not reply, but did not pursue the carriage farther.

Near Brussels the smell of gunpowder was very perceptible, and the heat of the growing June day terrific. While they were held up in a traffic block in the heart of the city, Mr. Hay made another of his sudden appearances, but this time to say that Sir William was still holding his own. 'I have horses standing, harnessed, and you will soon be there if the road is passable—though it was not yesterday, for a horse.'

'Great and Glorious Victory'

The fresh horses screamed at the smells of dead horses and dead men, stacked along the road outside Brussels, and the journey of nine miles occupied three and a half hours. When they got near the village of Mont St. Jean, Mr. Hay rode ahead to discover if Lady de Lancey's presence was still necessary. Half an hour passed. Magdalene, waiting in her coach, was glad now that, although she had not very much practical experience, her education had included the care of the sick. She knew that she could apply leeches neatly, and it occurred to her that, although in her mad rush to leave Antwerp she had packed nothing, she was wearing her new flannel petticoat, which would make a capital fomentation. Emma would help her to deal with the servants of the house in which Sir William was established. Emma was now acting up to her London character as a superior person of excellent judgment. She said that she was thankful she had been at Waterloo. It had done her good to see what other people had to endure. She had never before known how lucky she was in London service.

Mr. Hay returned to say, ' All's well; I have seen him. He expects you.'

The officer who opened the carriage door outside a shockingly wretched-looking hut, said, ' Stop one moment! '

Magdalene asked, ' Is he alive? '

The officer said yes, but as he led her in, begged her ladyship to be composed. ' You must be aware that his life hangs on a very slender hold, and therefore any agitation would be injurious.'

Magdalene promised not to let her husband know

that she had believed he was dead, and when she heard a familiar voice say on a strong note, ' Let her come in! ' all her miseries were forgotten. But when she had entered the poor room where he lay, and he held out his hand and said, ' Come, Magdalene, this is a sad business, is it not? ' she could not speak. She could only sit down by the bedside, on the broken chair offered to her, and slip her hand into his.

This was her situation for six days.[1]

II

Major, the Hon. Henry Percy, aide-de-camp to the Duke of Wellington, reached Lord Castlereagh's house in St. James's Square at eleven p.m. on the soft summer night of June 21st, 1815.

Yesterday's newspapers had contained reports of a battle fought near Brussels on the 16th. Paris was claiming a victory, but London papers had announced, ' Auspicious opening of the Campaign. Repulse of Bonaparte'. In both capitals there was mention of heavy casualties. It was obvious that the enervating pause, while the combatants manœuvred for position, was at an end, and the long-expected first meeting of the Emperor Napoleon and the Duke of Wellington was taking place. Considerable tension existed in London, but not sufficient to disturb the Prince Regent's social arrangements.

[1] Magdalene, widow of Sir William De Lancey who died on June 27th, 1815, of wounds received at Waterloo, remarried in 1819 Captain Henry Hervey, Madras Infantry, and died in 1822, leaving issue.

'Great and Glorious Victory'

Major Percy, who was a cheerful character—as any-one who had survived the retreat from Corunna and three years in a French prison had every right to be—had staged a dramatic entry. When ostlers and inn-keepers of the Dover road found a young staff officer in a dashed uniform demanding fresh horses for a car-riage which had two French eagles poking out of its windows, and four French flags draped over its up-holstery, they did not hesitate to speed him on his way, and spread the good news. Thus villages of Kent received tidings of the Duke's total defeat of Bona-parte, before London. Darkness had fallen by the time that the equipage which told its own tale had charged over Westminster Bridge, and by way of Parliament Street and Whitehall, drawn up at Number 18, St. James's Square.

It was something of an anti-climax to learn that Lord Castlereagh was dining out, but the house of Mr. Boehm was only a few yards distant, and amongst Lord Castlereagh's fellow-guests were the Prince Regent and Lord Liverpool. The story that an aide-de-camp from the Duke was in Town, with despatches containing great and glorious news, spread like lightning. While Major Percy was still telling his tale to a member of the royal family, who could, upon great occasions, assume a captivating grand manner, large crowds assembled in St. James's Square to sing 'God Save the King' in chorus. The French eagles and flags were exhibited in Mr. Boehm's windows. Soon the only anxiety of this wealthy and distinguished foreigner was lest the mob, in their loyal enthusiasm, would attempt to storm the house in which he was being privileged to entertain the First Gentleman of Europe on an occasion truly historic. The mob huzzaed, and the Regent bowed from a balcony. In the City, tired compositors began to set up in block type, 'COMPLETE OVERTHROW OF BONAPARTE'S ARMY. OFFICIAL BULLETIN'.

On the first sheet of *The Times* of the following morning, four columns announced, amongst forthcoming events, a meeting of the Asiatic Society (President, W. Wilberforce, Esq., M.P.), a Sermon to be preached at St. Bride's, Fleet Street, for the benefit of Charity Children, and a concert at the Argyll Rooms. A Person at Hoxton was in want of a family's washing, and, since the century was still young, a number of Wet Nurses offered their services in the frankest of terms. Every experienced servant preferred a situation where a footman was kept, and declared herself 'steady', 'sober' and 'genteel', and since the business in hand in Belgium was one for the professional army, and the Invasion scare had long subsided, many young men 'of undeniable character', aged from eighteen to thirty, sought employment as coachmen, grooms, valets, porters or footmen (in or out of livery).

In the centre pages of the double sheet, nine columns of close print claimed attention. Of these, two were occupied by a long despatch, dated 'Waterloo, June 19th', and signed 'Wellington'. People who had relatives engaged, read with burning anxiety the story of the sanguinary struggle around the farmhouse of La Haye Sainte, and the house and garden of Hougoumont.

The scene which was to form the companion picture to 'The Death of Nelson' in every English

home, was for the first time visualized. The casualty
list showed the names of ten Generals and seventeen
Lieutenant Colonels, ' but whosoever fell on that
glorious day cannot have fallen in vain'. To the
official bulletin *The Times* had as yet little to add, but
the official bulletin closed with the announcement that
during the night, the Prussians, under Marshal
Blücher, who had joined in the pursuit of the enemy,
had captured a large part of Bonaparte's baggage, and
The Courier of the following day knew that in Bonaparte's carriage had been found thousands of copies of
an ' anticipatory ' proclamation dated from the Palace
of Laeken.

' The Allied armies continue to pursue the enemy.'
This sounded like a decisive victory, even to people who
pointed out that Bonaparte himself was still at large. He
had returned to a Paris still exultant over his success of
the 16th, and was demanding a new army for a fresh
effort. Eye-witnesses' descriptions of the action began to
reach the press, and readers learnt that the French Imperial Guard had been ' very nearly destroyed ' and
that the Duke, who had been ' everywhere, exposing
himself as usual to imminent danger, with bullets
whizzing around him', had confessed himself 'never
so nearly beaten', and shed tears for his lost friends.

Illuminations in honour of Waterloo were very
showy. The Admiralty had a crowned ' G.R.' and a
' G.P.R.' surmounted by the Prince of Wales's
feathers, a colossal anchor, and over its principal
entrance, 'Unconquered Wellington'. 'Wellington
and Blücher ' was a common form. Lord Castlereagh's
office displayed crossed swords and cannon balls bathed

in golden light, but the Treasury with 'forty lofty palm trees in green lamps' was awarded the prize for artistic invention.

Rejoicing England was not long kept in suspense as to the fate of Bonaparte. An official announcement of his second abdication reached stop-press columns in London on the night of June 26th. After that, for nearly a month, surmise as to the disposal of 'the Disturber of Europe' alternated with accounts of the advance of Wellington and Blücher on Paris, and their triumphant entry, followed by that of Louis XVIII. Evidently France did not intend to have another Revolution.

English papers gave prominent place to entries for Winchester Races, and reports of Kent Assizes. A complimentary visit of British royalty to the Duchess of Angoulême, at Battersea, was described at length. The Duke of Kent was proposing, now that the Continent was open for travel again, to go abroad, with a view to diminishing his expenses. Old Marshal Blücher was stamping through the Louvre. He had provided himself with a catalogue which proudly noted from what foreign gallery every masterpiece of painting had been purloined. 'From the Düsseldorf Gallery. Humph! I remember it perfectly. Have it taken down.'

On July 21st, the news that Bonaparte had surrendered himself to the British Government, delighted many families on holiday. The Emperor had just escaped Marshal Blücher's flying column, sent to 'La Malmaison' to seize him, dead or alive. He had reached the French coast, hoping to sail for America, but found that project hopeless, owing to British vigilance at sea.

'Great and Glorious Victory'

At Rochefort he had received a government order from Paris, telling him to quit the country within twenty-four hours. Captain Maitland, of H.M.S. *Bellerophon*, of seventy-four guns, lying off Rochefort, had taken him safely on board, but engaged himself merely to carry the Emperor to England.

On April 20th the *Bellerophon* met the *Swiftsure*, on her way to reinforce the Rochefort Blockade. Nothing could exceed the surprise of Captain Weobley when Captain Maitland opened conversation with the words, ' Well, I have got him! '

' Got him? Got whom? ' asked the Captain of the *Swiftsure*.

'Why,' replied the Captain of the *Bellerophon*, 'Bonaparte—the man who has been keeping all Europe in a ferment these twenty years.'

' Is it possible? ' exclaimed Captain Weobley, and then, ' Well, you are a lucky fellow! '

Chapter 12

General Bonaparte

~~~

At seven p.m. on July 24th, H.M.S. *Bellerophon*, accompanied by H.M.S. *Myrmidon* and *Slaney*, dropped anchor in Torbay, and the Emperor said in tones of deep feeling, ' *Enfin, voilà ce beau pays!* ' He added that hitherto all he had seen of England was 'the bold rocks of Dover from Boulogne'. Fate had arranged that his first close view of the country he had failed to invade should be particularly tantalizing. The sun-bathed scene on which the Emperor turned his telescope, included a small watering-place of elegant modern villas, an ancient port, filled with picturesque shipping, and, embowered amongst heavy trees, the ruins of a twelfth-century abbey, long incorporated as a decorative feature in the gardens of an English family mansion. The owner of Torre Abbey, whose park sloped to a sandy bathing beach, and whose window seats commanded an unrivalled prospect of red West Country cliffs, dancing blue waters and bright green meadows, sent out to the *Bellerophon*, with compliments, a luscious gift of show wall-fruit in season. Captain Maitland returned thanks, but had to refuse the donor's request to call upon his guest.

The press announced that no visitors were permitted aboard the *Bellerophon*, 'not even Mrs. Maitland'. On his passage from Rochefort, the Emperor had walked up and down very fast, muttering to himself and taking much snuff; but he now appeared quite happy at having escaped alive from France, and had sent to the Prince Regent a flamboyant letter, describing himself as 'Themistocles, come to claim a seat by the hearth of the British people'.

Regardless of the fact that there was no possible chance of the Emperor landing, and no strangers were allowed even alongside the *Bellerophon*, parties from all over the West Country, and even from London, hastened to Torbay, in hopes of a sight of 'the once-tremendous stranger'. They hired row-boats to take them into the bay, approached as near the vessel as they dared, and were not disappointed. An unmistakable figure appeared at the gangways and stern windows, fixed his spy-glass on boats, and whenever he observed any well-dressed women, pulled off his hat and bowed. Many curious people were able to satisfy themselves that 'Boney's' complexion was 'French yellow', that he was short and stout, and that he had small white hands and showed a good leg.

Plymouth, which was reported as the *Bellerophon*'s next port of call, began to fill with visitors, although by the time this rumour was verified, newspapers were printing accounts of St. Helena as his certain destination. He was to be sent to 'an insulated rock', where neither flatterers nor intriguers could reach him. He was not to be allowed the title or the court which he had enjoyed by the Tsar's request in Elba. Henceforward he was to be known simply as 'General Bonaparte'. Persons who thought that he ought to be brought to trial and hanged, read with vicious satisfaction that St. Helena was infested by rats.

The scenes while the *Bellerophon* lay in Plymouth Sound were even more unbridled than those in Torbay. Several collisions occurred, and more than one tragedy. The boat containing the party of a Mr. Harris of Totnes was run down by a cutter. The First Lieutenant of the *Northumberland* boldly plunged overboard, and succeeded in rescuing Mrs. Harris and an infant from a watery grave, but two ringleted young ladies of boarding-school age sank to rise no more. Throughout the hours of daylight, small hired craft rowed round and round the man-of-war, and at intervals the crew of the *Bellerophon* hung out a board, on which was chalked such items as 'At Breakfast', 'In Cabin with Captain Maitland', 'Writing with his officers'. When the board announced 'Coming on deck' or 'Coffee on deck', excitement swelled to fever-pitch, and eventually over ten thousand gaping and giggling British, tossing on salt billows, caught a glimpse of General Bonaparte, dressed in an olive-green uniform coat with a scarlet collar and epaulettes, a large star on the left breast, white waistcoat, breeches and silk stockings, and shoes with gold buckles. He wore a large shabby cocked hat, with a tricolour cockade, walked in his traditional attitude, with his hands behind his back, and occasionally beckoned up an attendant French officer to answer a question.

After he had learnt his fate, he was reported 'violent', and ceased to show himself. ' They style me "General". They may as well call me Archbishop, for I was head of the Church as well as the Army! My only wish was to purchase a small property in England and end my life there in peace and tranquillity. The idea of St. Helena is a perfect horror to me.' On the day of his transhipment to H.M.S. *Northumberland*, great precautions were taken, and a schooner and a cutter kept off all boats which attempted to approach within a cable's length.

Heavy rain fell while the *Northumberland* lay off Berry Head, and journalists were reduced to describing the very fine bed-linen and toilet equipage of the General's cabin. Someone had noticed a superb gold snuff-box, with the design of an eagle flying from France to Elba. The General had much desired to present to the Captain of the *Bellerophon* a snuff-box bearing his portrait in miniature, encircled with diamonds. Captain Maitland had found the Emperor pleasant in his manner, most ingratiating in his remarks about the fine physique and discipline of the British Navy. ' What I admire most in your ship is the extreme silence and orderly conduct of your men. On board a French ship everyone calls and gives orders, they gabble like so many geese. There has been less noise in this ship, where there are six hundred men, during the whole time I have been in her, than there was on board the *Epervier* with only one hundred men, in my passage from the Ile d'Aix to the Basque roads.' He had praised the captain's cabin, ' *Une belle chambre*', and a miniature of Mrs. Maitland, performed, to tell the truth, by a very inexpensive artist. ' *Qui est cette jolie personne? Ah! elle est très jeune et très jolie!* '

Captain Maitland had regretted he spoke very little French, and explained in reply to the direct question that Mrs. Maitland, who was a daughter of Erin, had brought him one child who had not survived. He had regretted also that he could not allow his wife to come aboard, and that he could not stay after dinner to play *vingt-et-un* with the General, as he had numerous duties to perform. He said that he was only a second cousin of Lord Lauderdale, and had no property in Scotland. The General persisted in the opinion that Britain was always victorious at sea because her ships were manned by superior persons, and officered by well-to-do aristocrats. He was something of a nuisance to the Captain, walking round the decks, asking a thousand questions, while the men were scrubbing, but he thoroughly enjoyed the midshipmen's costume concert. It was difficult to make him understand that Captain Maitland would not at all like him to write to the Prince Regent, suggesting that the Emperor Napoleon's host ought to be advanced to the rank of Rear-Admiral, and that there was, in fact, nothing in this world that the Emperor Napoleon could do for a lean and weather-beaten British naval officer, who was well content that the name of H.M.S. *Bellerophon* should pass down to history.

Stray remarks made by General Bonaparte before he took refuge in the silence and seclusion of his cabin, were eagerly repeated. He had said that Louis XVIII was a good sort of man, but too fond of the pleasures of the table and pretty sayings. The Duchess of Angoulême was, according to him, the one Man in her family. He said that the English artillery had learnt much from the French, but that the French and English cavalry were both first class. He seemed to avoid the subject of the Duke of Wellington. An inveterate propagandist to the last, he said that his object in surrendering himself to the Prince Regent had been that in doing so, he surrendered himself to a Nation. If he had surrendered to the ruler of any other country, his person would have been at the mercy of a single capricious individual. Old Admiral Keith was not happy until the *Northumberland* was under weigh. ' D——n the fellow! If he had obtained an interview with H.R.H., in half an hour they would have been the best friends in Europe.'

On August 8th, London newspapers announced ' Bonaparte has sailed,' but West Country watchers saw the *Northumberland* with two troopships in company, still lingering off Berry Head. On Thursday, 10th, although the wind was fair, she did not take her departure. Editors supposed that she was waiting for the *Weymouth*, which was still taking in stores for the voyage. Not until Friday, 11th, did the ship that carried the Disturber of the World disappear westwards, into the haze of a very fine August day. Accounts of the Prince Regent's celebration of his birthday occupied the principal place in Monday's papers. Slowly the *Northumberland*, accompanied by a frigate and several sloops of war, vanished from sight, and from the press. She was seen off the Manicles . . . England's last note on the subject of General Bonaparte's passage to St. Helena declared him ' quite happy at having escaped justice', and comfortably settled for his long journey, having made searching enquiries as to how many officers on board knew 'Whist'.

II

During the six years spent by General Bonaparte on St. Helena, many anecdotes of his daily round reached England. The usual admirers declared that he was being treated with atrocious harshness and incivility by Sir Hudson Lowe, and pointed out that the Duke himself had passed over Lowe, on account of his temper, when choosing his staff for the Waterloo campaign, and insisted on having the lamented De Lancey, who was, by a strange chance, Lowe's brother-in-law. Philosophers reflected that the appointment of the Governor of St. Helena was a thankless one, and that anyone in charge of General Bonaparte might develop a bad temper. There were stories of the deposed hero's bland and simple manners, his love of children, his patience under physical discomfort. For he had grown very stout and bald, and was often unwell. A sketch of him dressed in tropical costume, in a roomy linen suit and huge sun-hat, was an unintentional caricature. From unsympathetic sources, English homes learnt of bursts of boasting, much not very profound talk, and endless undignified quarrels amongst the suite of an unamusable man.

Of course many people longed to know whether he had ever really intended to invade England, and several visitors asked him outright. But the result of such tact-less temerity was disappointing, for the General seemed to take an impish pleasure in saying exactly the reverse of what was expected, even if it entailed contradicting previous statements. If a guest remarked that naturally the great preparations at Boulogne had merely been part of a masterly scheme to keep England on the alert, while France trained a first-class army for use against Austria, General Bonaparte would reply, with a faint smile, ' Your Mr. Pitt did not think so! ' and proceed to enlarge on the attitude he would have adopted on entering London, ' not as a Conqueror, but as a Liber-ator'. If, on the other hand, his interlocutor supposed him to be the victim of gnawing regret at the failure of his greatest scheme, he was quite capable of saying that his Invasion had been planned to synchronize with an English Revolution, and that until that was an accom-plished fact, he had never intended to embark a man.

In London government departments, officials who had seen despatches opening ' England is ours! All are embarked! Appear for twenty-four hours and all is ended,' were quite certain that he had intended to in-vade. They specified at least two occasions in the au-tumn of 1803, one in the summer of 1804, and others possibly in the spring, as well as the summer of 1805.

The Coronation of George IV was obsessing English editors, when they found themselves obliged to give up space to a paragraph headed 'BONAPARTE IS NO MORE'. After forty days of lingering illness, the General had expired painlessly, in his fifty-second year, of the same disease which had carried off his father in even earlier middle age. The news had travelled with reasonable speed. He had died on Saturday, May 5th, 1821, and the brief paragraph describing his passing appeared in London papers of July 4th.

In London, the question of the hour was whether the King would adhere to his resolution of refusing the Queen admittance to Westminster Abbey, and if so, whether Coronation Day would be marred by dangerous rioting. George IV, as the hour for which he had longed all his life grew near, was even more unpopular than the Prince Regent had been in 1815. After disgraceful efforts, he had failed to divorce his preposterous consort. An unkind tale told that when a messenger had announced the decease of Bonaparte to His Majesty in stage-struck fashion—' Sire! I have to tell you that your greatest enemy is dead!' His Majesty had responded quickly, in tones of boundless relief, ' No! by Ged! Is she? '

His only child, the luckless Charlotte, had died with a still-born son, four years past, and since that date his portly brothers had rushed breakneck into matrimony, determined, whatever the cost, to supply England with an heir.

Kensington, cut off from London by market gardens and country lanes, was an ideal spot in which to rear a precious fatherless child, and in the month of July was looking its best. The widowed lady, of a naturally cheerful and homely countenance, who sat nodding under a fringed parasol in a secluded corner of the palace garden, backed by flowering shrubs and the corner of an old red brick building, which appeared on such a day to be cut out of pasteboard, was scarcely listening to the efforts of an elderly companion to translate items of interest from the English newspaper. She was wondering whether, on his forthcoming visit, her one invaluable adviser would bring her a very handsome present, or merely a very necessary one. The relict of the Duke of Kent was largely dependent on her brother's charity.

Presently her attention was further distracted. The rosy blonde child, attired in a plain cotton frock and frilled pantaloons, who had been set to play on a yellow rug at the feet of her mother and *gouvernante*, had arisen and was intent upon a staggering voyage of exploration. As she opened her arms, to call to her maternal bosom the Princess Alexandrina-Victoria, godchild of the Tsar who had burnt Moscow, the Duchess of Kent heard nothing of the death of General Bonaparte.

Index

Index

Index

Index

Index

359

Index

Index

Index

Index

Index

Index

365

Index

Index

Index

Index

Index

Semaphore Telegraphs, 75, 76; 81; 106

Seringapatam, fall of, 154

Seward, Anna, 'Swan of Lichfield', 17

Shelley, Percy Bysshe, 212

Sheridan, Richard Brinsley, 22; 121; 122; 227; 229

Shockerwick House, visit of Pitt to, 247, 248; 253

Siddons, Mrs Sarah, 205; 223; 275

Slave Trade, Abolition of, 263

Sligo Bay, French fleet in, 90

Smith, James, Irish agent, 71

Smith, Sir Sidney, Admiral, 97; 245

Smolensk, 304

Smugglers and Smuggling, 22, 23; 264; 273; 290

Somerset, Lord Edward, 61

Sophia, Princess, daughter of George III, 171; 289

Sophia Dorothea of Würtemberg, Empress of Russia, wife of Paul I, 116; 283

Soult, Nicholas Jean de Dieu, Marshal Duke of Dalmatia, 180; 278; 287; 310; 313

Southey, Robert, 211; 275

Spain (see also Peninsula), deserts alliance with England, 35; declares war against England, 232; invaded by Napoleon, 268; Joseph Bonaparte, King of, 270; general insurrection, 270

Speaker of the House of Commons, see Addington

Spies, see Agents

Spithead, 39; mutiny at, 64; Victory's return to, 249

Steam Power, first mooted, 187; in operation, 245, 246; 321

Steventon Rectory, residence of Jane Austen, 41

Stewart, Charles William, Baron Stewart, 3rd Marquis London-

derry, Adjutant-General, 296, 297; Ambassador to Vienna, 320

Stewart, Robert, Viscount Castlereagh, 73; as Secretary of State for War, 242; 244; 245; 254, 255; 256; 274; 279; 285; 296; 338, 339

Stuart, Lieutenant-General Sir John, 262

Stuart, Charles, 147

Suez, plan for cutting canal at, 85; 95, 96

'Swan of Lichfield', see Seward

Switzerland, French attack on, 96

Syria, invasion of, 97

T

Talleyrand-Périgord, Charles Meurice de, Minister for Foreign Affairs, 95; 145; 261

Talma, François Joseph, actor, 143

Tate, Colonel, 58; 61

Tataranoff, Colonel, 111

Theatres, general, 55; 57; specified, Covent Garden, 13; 42; 57; 87, 88; 224 et seq; Drury Lane, 226, 227; French, 46; 133

The Rivals, amateur performance of, at The Priory, Stanmore, 255

Thompson, Horatia Nelson, 240, 241, and note

Tierney, George, 83 et seq

Tilsit, Peace of, 257 et seq

Tipú Sahib, Sultan of Mysore, 154

Tone, Theobald Wolfe, 58; 71; 90; 91

Torbay, 37; 344, 345

Torres Vedras, Lines of, 296 et seq

Toulon, siege of, 36; evacuation of, 37; troops embarked at, 85; Napoleon sails from, 96

Toulon Fleet, 231

Toulouse, Wellington advances on, 311; battle of, 312; Wellington enters, 313, 314

Tsarkoye Selo, description of, 51, 52

370

Index

Index

*The author desires to record her most
grateful thanks to the maker of the
Index—Georgette Heyer.*